CW01011287

PETER LUNN: CHILDREN'S PUBLISHER

PETER LUNN: CHILDREN'S PUBLISHER

The books, authors and illustrators

Peter Main

Stirling: Lomax Press, 2010
First edition, 2010
ISBN: 978-0-9560288-1-5

Copies of this book may be obtained from the publisher
(lomaxorders@btinternet.com) or from the author
(plmain@gmail.com).

To Morven

Contents

Acknowledgements   I would like to thank the following people who have helped me greatly in this research by providing information or commenting on parts of the text: Geoff Henley, Hugo Kerr, Sandi Lacey, Robert Lacey, Robin Kinross, Jenny McLachlan, Judith Moss, Pat Schleger and Christopher Todd. I would like to thank staff at the British Library, the National Archives and the National Library of Scotland for their help and unfailing courtesy. I wish also to pay tribute to the work done by the late Alan Smith in compiling a checklist of Peter Lunn books – I was often aware during my bibliographic research that I was treading in his earlier footsteps.

I am particularly grateful to the following: Terry Sole who shares my interest in these books and has provided me with useful information and access to some difficult to find dustjackets; Becky Green for designing the book cover; Forbes Gibb for advice and encouragement and for steering my early steps in the art of descriptive bibliography; my wife Morven for her patience, encouragement, and some great ideas at crucial moments.

A note on monetary references   In parts of this book (particularly in Section 1) I have quoted monetary figures relating to the business dealings of Peter Lunn. In some cases one may wish to know roughly what these amounts equate to in today's terms (i.e. in 2010), and where I feel that this is of particular interest I have translated the amount in brackets afterwards e.g. '£10,000 (£300,000 today)'. For readers wishing to convert other figures they should multiply by a factor of 30 to obtain an approximate equivalent in 2010.

Typographic conventions and abbreviations   Within the text, book titles appear in italic font. Titles of books which were published by Peter Lunn appear in bold italics. The names of authors and illustrators which have their own entries in Section 3 are in standard bold font.

The following abbreviations have been used:

aka	also known as
BL	British Library
n.d.	no date
NLS	National Library of Scotland
ps	pseudonym
rn	real name
Smith	see Main sources consulted
WFL	World Favourite Library for Boys and Girls
Whitaker	see Main sources consulted

INTRODUCTION

I have been a collector of children's books for many years. It is a vast field, and so one has to specialise in particular areas. Early on, I developed an interest in the slim wartime volumes published by the London firm of Peter Lunn, and I became adept at spotting their spines (surprisingly often with dustjackets still in place) buried among others on the shelves of second-hand bookdealers. I was attracted by the 'strangeness' of many of the stories and of the high quality and originality of the illustrations. The urge to collect these books grew over the years into a desire to find out more about the firm which published them and about the individuals who wrote and illustrated them. This book is the outcome my researches.

In **Section 1**, I present a summary of what I have been able to discover about the firm of Peter Lunn and its founder David Gottlieb. Peter Lunn and its sister firm John Westhouse were born and died within a short period during and just after World War II, and have left almost no trace in the publishing record other than the books themselves. One looks largely in vain (and in some frustration) for 'Peter Lunn', 'John Westhouse' or 'David Gottlieb' in the indexes of works on publishing history. Even in the book trade journals of the period the launch and demise of these firms goes unremarked upon. No archives of these firms' records seem now to exist, although some information relating to the winding-up of the companies survives in the National Archives. As will become apparent, I am therefore able to say rather more about the demise of Peter Lunn than about its gestation.

Section 2 contains a descriptive bibliography of all the books published. The books themselves are not abundant in the second-hand market, and some are truly scarce. The stringencies of war-time book publishing dictated modest print-runs, and poor quality materials meant that many books did not survive young hands. However, neither are these books avidly collected, so that one can find copies of many of them without too much difficulty. Almost none of the books (apart from new editions of children's classics) were ever republished after the firm folded. Although Peter Lunn seems to have passed under the radar of many publishing historians, a few of the more perceptive have noted that the firm did make a distinctive and innovative contribution to children's publishing at the time[1]. The bibliography is somewhat unusual in describing dustjackets (at least, where I have been able to see one). There has been a debate for years over whether dustjackets are an integral part of the book, or 'ephemeral'. In books of this period, they were obviously intended to be more than simply protective wrappings and often contain information of bibliographical interest. In some cases they are adorned with an illustration which does not appear inside the book (a good example being Tom Eckersley's wonderful dustjacket for *Cat O' Nine Lives*). Where I have been obliged with the rarer books to describe a copy from the British Library (BL) or the National Library of Scotland (NLS), I am always subject to mixed feelings. On the one hand I am happy that they have preserved a copy of the book at all, but on the other hand I am frustrated by their policy (still maintained) of discarding all dustjackets, so that it is impossible for me to describe them. However practically convenient this practice may be for our deposit libraries, I regard it as indefensible from an archival standpoint.

Section 3 provides short biographical entries for most of the authors and illustrators. Since this book is primarily a work of bibliography rather than biography, the entries lay more emphasis on other published works than might be usual in literary biographies. For the same reason I have usually made no attempt to go back to primary sources in constructing the entries, although in a few cases I have been greatly helped by family members who have given me information which would otherwise have been impossible to obtain.

---

[1] See e.g. Sole, Terry. 'Peter Lunn.' *Book Trade History Group Newsletter*, 1999, 35(3), pp. 6-7 and Crouch, Marcus. *The Nesbit Tradition: The Children's Novel in England 1945-1970*. London: Ernest Benn, 1972, p. 26.

Finally, in **Section 4**, I have been able to gather together a list of at least some of the books which were planned for publication when the company went into liquidation but which never appeared.

One of the most rewarding outcomes for a bibliographer is the discovery of the true names of writers who used pseudonyms, and I have been able to throw light on some of these. For example, we now know who Patrick de Heriz and Peter Lethbridge really were. We know which professor of international standing coyly disguised his only attempt to write a children's book under a pseudonym. There are some unsolved mysteries too. What book did the children's author Modwena Sedgwick write for Peter Lunn? (She made a claim against the company for unpaid royalties.) And there have been other frustrations – I now have to live with the knowledge that I will almost certainly never be able to read about Arbuthnot the Goldfish and his dealings with the Nibworthy family.

Peter Main, Crystal Palace, 2010.

1

HISTORY OF THE PUBLISHER

BACKGROUND   The children's book publisher Peter Lunn (Publishers) Ltd. began trading on 8th April 1943, and went into liquidation on 18th October 1948. During its short life it published 117 books, and at least a further 30 books were part way through the publishing process when it folded. It and its sister company John Westhouse (set up in 1944 to publish adult literature) were launched and run by a German émigré David Gottlieb. In many respects these two companies were run as one; they shared the same offices, many of the same staff, and were in effect two sides of the same coin. Although the focus of this book is the firm of Peter Lunn, it is not always easy to discuss its history in separation from that of John Westhouse[1].

Both firms were primarily commissioners of new work, and particularly of illustration. All Peter Lunn books were illustrated (although by no means all John Westhouse books were) and many of them represent the first ventures into book illustration by artists who went on to enjoy distinguished careers. The climate was right for new book illustration, and Gottlieb astutely exploited the fact. Pre-war immigration of talented graphic designers and artists to Britain from Europe led to a pool of London-based individuals who were prepared to try their hands at book illustration, as the market for work in commercial advertising largely dried up at the start of the war. Although a significant proportion of Peter Lunn's output was republication of children's classics, or of recently published children's favourites from America, new illustrations and dustjacket designs were always commissioned. There was scope for new writing too, although the quality was more variable than the artwork; the worst examples might be said to be barely readable, while the best deserve to be regarded as minor classics. (In the latter category two personal choices would be *The Angry Planet* and *The Avion my Uncle Flew*.)

THE FOUNDER   About David Gottlieb himself, I have been able to discover very little. He was born in Germany on 25th January 1916, and emigrated to Britain at some time during the 1930s, along with (at least) his father Leo, mother Lotte and sister Selma. It is likely that he was Jewish, although I have no direct evidence for this. By nature, he seems to have been an entrepreneur; a few second-hand memories have survived of his more or less workable schemes for making money before he launched Peter Lunn in 1943. Book publishing seems to have been to him just another financial venture, and by 1954 he was already describing himself as an 'industrial designer'. We can guess that he came from a well-off family, since at one stage his mother was able personally to make a sizeable unsecured loan to the company. A humorous caricature of 'Peter Lunn, the Publisher' drawn by John Parsons appears in *Jack Robinson*. Whether this is modelled in any way on Gottlieb I do not know – it certainly shows a man older than Gottlieb was at that time. If we choose to believe that there are elements of Gottlieb here, then he probably wore smart clothes, sported a fur-lined collar and smoked cigars. However, it is more difficult to believe that he also walked around with a cane and a top hat.

When he launched Peter Lunn in 1943, he was a young man of only 27. What do we know of his approach to business? Fragments of evidence point to him as a man prepared to fight his corner. In 1944, Gottlieb commissioned Dylan Thomas to provide accompanying text for a book (to be published by John Westhouse) of images of little-known streets of London. On signing the contract, Thomas was paid a £50 advance, but in the event he never came up with more than a short synopsis, and he admitted to having been unwisely seduced by Gottlieb's 'ready cheque book'[2]. Gottlieb served a writ on Thomas and eventually recovered his money. He was later prepared to fight in court over

---

[1] I hope to publish a bibliography of the Westhouse books as a supplementary volume to this book.

[2] Ferris, Paul (ed). *The Collected Letters of Dylan Thomas*. London: J.M. Dent, 1985, p. 533.

a post-liquidation claim by one of the ex-directors of Lunn/Westhouse, a case which he eventually won on appeal. Hans Schleger (the distinguished émigré graphic designer 'Zéro') worked for a period for John Westhouse, and his widow Pat Schleger recalls that Hans found Gottlieb a tough man to do business with. Whether tough business is good business is another matter, and it is clear from reading the accounts of the official Receiver that he regarded Gottlieb as being the architect of his own misfortunes.

THE OFFICES   The Lunn and Westhouse offices were at 49 Chancery Lane, London WC2 throughout the lives of both companies. The original building has now been demolished, but the contemporary fire insurance plan for this area published by Charles Goad Ltd. shows No. 49 (a few doors down Chancery Lane from its junction with Southampton Buildings) marked as being occupied by the Eagle Star Insurance Company. This company let office space to Gottlieb, as well as to a few patent agents, advertising agents and the like. The Lunn/Westhouse offices were on the first and third floors and were rented for £1,200 per annum. The fact that this included a share of the basement bomb shelter reminds us of the circumstances under which the companies had to operate.

THE COMPANY   When Gottlieb launched Peter Lunn in 1943, the stated aims of the company in the Articles of Association were those of a very general publisher, and made no mention of children's books specifically. However, the five books published in 1943 were all children's books, and the entry for Peter Lunn in the *Writers' and Artists' Yearbook* for 1944 stated that the company was 'prepared to consider MSS. and drawings for children's books'. Entries in later issues read (for Lunn): 'Children's books. Free-lance artists' and designers' work used.', and (for Westhouse): 'Books for adults: fiction, technical, educational.'. Gottlieb himself was never a director of Peter Lunn, except for a short period from July 1948 until it was liquidated. His explanation to the Receiver for this was that he was concerned about being called up for military service, and that if this happened there could be 'internal dislocation' of the company. However, from September 1943 until July 1948 Gottlieb was appointed as a (salaried) company secretary and editor, and he did accept that he had had overall responsibility for the running of the company throughout its life. Peter Lunn's director was initially (Mrs) Cecily Joyce Kaye, but she was soon replaced by a nominal director Bernard William Knott, who was in fact an employee of the company's auditors. Following her resignation as director, Cecily Kaye became the salaried general manager until 1946, at which point she seems to have withdrawn from practical involvement. This did not sever her financial involvement, however. She had supplied an overdraft guarantee upon the launching of the company, and later made other loans to it. Since I have been unable to find out anything about Cecily Kaye, I am not able to throw any light on why she undertook this level of financial commitment to support someone else's venture. She was ultimately the loser; an attempt in 1950 to recover, from Gottlieb personally, money still owed to her failed on appeal. In January 1948, by which time the company's problems were clear to everyone, John Keir Cross (author of a number of Lunn books) joined Bernard Knott as an unpaid director, until both resigned in July, and Gottlieb himself became the director.

THE COMPANY NAME   Why did Gottlieb choose the name 'Peter Lunn' for his company? I have found no evidence that anyone called Peter Lunn (or John Westhouse for that matter) was ever involved with the running of either company. It may be that Gottlieb felt it would be unwise from a business perspective to use his own name, given the prevalence of anti-German sentiment at the time, although it should be said that a number of other émigré publishers did set up companies in their own name. In choosing the name he did, he may have been paying a form of homage to the Olympic skier (and later spymaster) Peter Lunn, who had gained some public approbation for supposedly snubbing the Nazis at the 1936 Winter Olympics, by failing to attend the march-past, despite being the leader of the British ski team. Indeed there is some indirect evidence that Peter Lunn was the inspiration for Gottlieb's choice. In 1948, Peter's father, Arnold Lunn (the famous skier and mountaineer, to be knighted four years later), felt obliged to specifically dissociate his son's name from the firm in his autobiographical work *Mountains of Memory* (Hollis and Carter, 1948):

> '...Peter has no connection with the publishing firm of Peter Lunn Ltd., which was founded by a Mr Gottlieb, who came to England before the war, and who founded Peter Lunn Ltd., at a time when Peter Lunn (who was not consulted) was serving as a Gunnery Officer in the besieged garrison at Malta. Peter Lunn has no legal redress against the use of his name.' (footnote to p. 219)

Why would Lunn have felt it necessary to make such a statement unless Gottlieb had in some way asserted a link between his firm's name and the skier?

THE BOOKS   As one would expect, Peter Lunn's output of books was slow to begin with, as the firm found its feet, and rose steadily over its life. It scored an early success with the publication of Rolf Brandt's *The Fisherman's Son*, which was selected by the Publishers' Association as an 'ambassador book' - one of a selection of the best of new British books, to be sent to America as part of a reciprocal arrangement set up in 1941. However, by the time Peter Lunn hit financial problems in late 1947, according to the Receiver's report Gottlieb had expanded the business 'to an excessive extent' and 'committed the company to a policy of overtrading', although it had traded at profit until then.

It is interesting to see in Fig. 1 below how the output rose over the years, and how the emphasis on the type of book also changed. Most noticeable is the relatively large number of picture books for very young children at the start, which gradually fell away altogether in favour of adventure stories aimed at older children. We can also see a rather sudden rise towards the end in the number of books with an educational emphasis. This culminated in the last two books Lunn published: *Alice's Adventures in Wonderland* and *The Rose and the Ring* (subtitled 'The Lunn Readers' numbers 1 and 2 respectively) which were poor quality productions using recycled materials, and seem to represent a fruitless and rather desperate last-ditch attempt to break into the primary school readers market.

Period	Total books	Classic	Fairy	Adventure	Nature	Educational	Picture	Net profit
launch-mid 1944	10	4	4	3	0	0	4	£ 810
mid 1944-mid 1945	12	0	1	4	0	1	8	£ 1,593
mid 1945-mid 1946	14	1	1	5	2	0	6	£ 2,622
mid 1946-mid 1947	37	4	8	21	6	2	0	£ 2,799
mid 1947 onwards	44	9	9	18	8	14	0	?

Fig. 1   Categorised book output by financial year together with company profits. Book categories, which are not mutually exclusive, are defined on page 29.

A few of the claims made against the company by printers do mention print-runs, and a reasonably consistent figure of around 5,000 copies emerges. This was probably greater for some books expected to sell well, particularly 'pony stories' (subsumed under the category 'Nature' in Fig. 1), judging by their relative abundance on the second-hand market. In a few instances books went into a second impression, but this was quite unusual.

Post-liquidation claims against the company by authors and illustrators tell us that a typical payment for a full-length manuscript was about £100 (£3,000 today). Where royalty deals were negotiated, this might be for from 7% to 10% of sales. The fees paid to illustrators were more variable, but were typically from £7 to £10 for a full-page drawing (£210 to £300 today).

Peter Lunn had to operate under conditions of paper rationing throughout its life. The rules imposed by the Paper Control were that publishers could apply for an allowance of between 25% and 37.5% of their pre-war paper consumption, with a somewhat improved amount if they signed up to the War Book Production Economy Standard agreement. Neither option was available to publishers, like Gottlieb, who began business during the war since there were no pre-war consumption figures on which to base an allowance. They were obliged to forage around as best they could for old paper stock held by paper manufacturers or printers. The consequences are all too obvious in the Lunn books, which typically have thin, poor quality paper and boards. Two exceptions stand out. *The Picture Frame* is a sturdy book with full-colour art reproductions and good quality cartridge paper for the text, and one is tempted to suggest that the author (a well-off Belgian diplomat and art critic) might have underwritten some of the cost of the book's production. The first printing of *Flame* is something of an oddity; it uses what appears to be hand-made art paper and has a note at the end describing (and promoting) its use of Eric Gill's Perpetua typeface. It has something of the feel of a private press production, and was evidently one of Lunn's more popular books, going into a second impression the following year (albeit in a smaller format and using standard paper).

THE LOGOS   Peter Lunn did use several company logos, but they were only ever employed intermittently on some of the earlier books and on advertising material. The four logos I have encountered appear below in Fig. 2.

A   B   C   D

Fig. 2 Four Peter Lunn logos.

Quite early on in the life of the company, their use was dropped entirely, although many of the dustjackets on the later crown octavo format books share an identifiable house style which it is probably easier to appreciate by viewing the jackets than by attempting to describe (typical examples would be the covers for PL40, PL42 and PL76). Why the use of a logo was abandoned I have been unable to discover, although a possible explanation might be a conflict with the publisher Nicholson and Watson, whose 'Poetry London' imprint used a 'PL' logo very similar to that used on the spine of some early Lunn titles. Later Lunn book spines always displayed 'Peter Lunn' in full.

PUBLICATION AND DISTRIBUTION   Books were often published well after the date which appears on the imprint page (in a few cases there were delays of a year or more). All deposit libraries are missing some Lunn titles from their collections, and a few are still not available in any of them. Such problems were not peculiar to Peter Lunn, and can be attributed to the vagaries of war-time book production and distribution; book trade journals of the period often contained notices apologising for late publication. Gottlieb, like many other publishers, entered into an agreement with one of the largest book wholesalers and distributors, Simpkin Marshall Ltd., to buy his publications. As part of this agreement Simpkin Marshall lent £6,000 (£180,000 today) to Peter Lunn to finance the production of books. It was the collapse of this agreement which was to play a significant part in the demise of Peter Lunn.

FINANCIAL PROBLEMS   The earliest signs of the difficulties which were stacking up for Gottlieb seem to have been in the latter months of 1947, when his production of books was at its highest since the company was launched. At this time, for whatever reason (but presumably related to outstanding debts), Simpkin Marshall refused to purchase some Lunn/Westhouse titles. This culminated in the collapse of the purchasing agreement in January 1948 (it was to have remained in force until July), leading to subsequent litigation in which judgement was made against Lunn/Westhouse for £2,500. Simpkin Marshall remained as a creditor for this amount when the companies were liquidated. The failure of the agreement with Simpkin Marshall left Gottlieb with a serious practical problem beyond the financial one. He now had no way of distributing his books – some of which were ready to be distributed and others part of the way down the publishing pipeline. By this time word would have got around, and it is probable that none of the other wholesale distributors wanted to do business with him. Gottlieb's solution was to set up his own (short-lived) distribution company, Ainsworth and Justin Ltd., of which John Keir Cross and A. L. Rendall[3] (a clerk employed by Lunn/Westhouse) were directors. Of course, the expenses associated with setting up such a new sales organisation were in themselves considerable, and by now Gottlieb's head was beginning to slip below the water. In January 1948, his family tried to help. His mother Lotte made a sizeable loan of £6,000 (£180,000 today) to the company, and his sister Selma lent £900 (£27,000 today). Given the preferential claims of the Inland Revenue and other creditors, it is unlikely that they recovered much, if any, of this money.

LIQUIDATION   By the middle of 1948, the patience of Gottlieb's creditors began to run out. In May 1948 one of the firms to whom Peter Lunn owed money, the bookbinder G. A. Cramp and Sons Ltd., obtained judgement against the company for unpaid debts totalling £2,300. By August, some £1,900 remained unpaid, and on 11th August Cramp petitioned for Peter Lunn to be wound up. An order to compulsorily wind up both Lunn and Westhouse was granted at a hearing on 18th October, and a Liquidator was appointed. He in turn appointed a Receiver, Granville White, whose job it was to manage the winding-up of Lunn and Westhouse, if possible to sell the companies for whatever they would fetch, and to attend as far as possible to the outstanding claims from creditors. At the point of liquidation, the company's assets were valued by Gottlieb at £46,000 (£1.4 million today), a figure the Receiver later considered to be an over-estimate. It had liabilities of £49,600.

---

[3] Some of the winding-up papers refer to 'Randall'.

THE SALE TO HUTCHINSON   From the point at which White took over responsibility for Lunn and Westhouse, he handled them for practical purposes as if they were one company. For accounting purposes, money was apportioned in the same ratio as the original valuation of their assets, i.e. roughly 60 : 40, Lunn : Westhouse. We are fortunate from a historical perspective that when White finally presented his bill for his services, a scrutiny committee objected to them as being unacceptably high. This prompted a spirited and outraged response in which White gave a impassioned account of his activities, and the difficulties under which he had laboured – information which would no doubt otherwise have gone unrecorded.

He had found it extremely difficult to find a buyer for the companies, and he came close to giving up the attempt and selling the assets for whatever they would fetch. He blamed the difficulty on Gottlieb and his fellow directors who, he said, had themselves already 'hawked round' the businesses trying to find a buyer. However, White was personally acquainted with Walter Hutchinson (head of the huge Hutchinson publishing empire), and succeeded in obtaining from him a verbal offer to buy Lunn/Westhouse for £10,000 (£300,000 today), together with a deposit of £1,000. This was only achieved after many letters and telephone calls, and the supply of a large amount of data relating to the financial position of the companies. It took a further five fraught months to persuade Hutchinson to complete, during which White stated that Hutchinson '[used] the most violent language about me, my forebears, my firm; in fact anything that came into his mind.'.[4] Eventually, White did manage to obtain completion of the contract in January 1950, at which point Peter Lunn was sold for £6,034 (£180,000 today) to E. J. Burrow Ltd, a company of the Hutchinson Group. This company had no involvement with publishing children's books; rather it published guides, maps and other topographical books. The choice of Burrow as a buyer for Lunn/Westhouse seems illogical, but it was probably no more than an accountancy ploy by Hutchinson to spread his assets. It also strongly suggests that Hutchinson never had any intention of continuing with the Lunn or Westhouse imprints as going concerns, and indeed from the point the companies were sold to Hutchinson, no more books ever appeared under these names.

AFTER THE SALE   From early in 1950, residual stocks of Peter Lunn books appeared on the market in two different ways. Hutchinson remaindered a number of the books during 1950, normally at about half the original cover price. A more imaginative marketing approach was taken by Simpkin Marshall who evidently owned a significant stock of unsold Lunn titles. Whether this was stock previously bought from Peter Lunn under their purchasing agreement, or was stock allocated to them subsequently by the Receiver as settlement for outstanding debts, is unknown; it may have been a combination of both. What Simpkin Marshall did was to assemble a set of 38 titles, all of which were of a reasonably uniform crown octavo size, discard their dustjackets, and to commission the artist Jennetta Vise (who illustrated a number of *Robin* annuals) to design a new uniform dustjacket for the

---

[4] White was later to discover that Hutchinson had been seriously ill during the negotiations, and in fact he died later in 1950. The Coroner's verdict was 'suicide while the balance of mind was disturbed' (obituary of Walter Hutchinson in *Publishers' Circular* for 1950, p. 525).

whole series, where only the title and author changed from book to book. They were then marketed at a uniform price of 3/6d as the 'World Favourite Library for Boys and Girls', a clever move designed to appeal to children's collecting instincts. The second-hand market is now peppered with these issues, and they are a constant trap for the unwary collector, since they are often advertised (and priced) as if they were books in their original state. Most often the books themselves are indeed first editions, but of course their dustjackets are not. The Vise dustjacket does not state when these books were put on the market, but it was most probably in the very early 1950s, and certainly before Simpkin Marshall itself went into liquidation in 1955.

REASONS FOR FAILURE   Granville White took an uncompromising view of Gottlieb's business approach, and considered that the failure of Peter Lunn was due to 'gross mismanagement on the part of David Gottlieb'. Specific reasons he cited were that Gottlieb was trying to expand the business at a time (1947-48) when books sales generally were declining, and that he had set up a large and expensive selling organisation (Ainsworth and Justin) which the company could not afford. Gottlieb's own explanation for failure was essentially the same, although he might not have agreed with the phrase 'gross mismanagement'. He felt that he had no choice but to set up his own system for book distribution, since he needed to sell his books, and he could find no one else to do it. With the advantage of a historical perspective, White's comments do seem rather harsh. Many small publishers went under at around this time, and for very similar reasons.

David Gottlieb died in London the day after his 72nd birthday, and was described on his death certificate as a 'retired company director'. However, I have seen no evidence that he was ever involved again in book publishing. Nevertheless, for a short time he and a core group of talented young writers and illustrators (notable among them were Joseph Avrach, John Keir Cross, Robin Jacques and Rolf Brandt) made an unusual and significant contribution to children's literature during very difficult times. When one reviews the further books in Section 4 which just failed to made it to publication, it is sad to reflect that this contribution could easily have been even larger.

2

DESCRIPTIVE BIBLIOGRAPHY
OF PUBLISHED BOOKS

FORMAT OF THE ENTRIES   In the recording of text, I have distinguished only capitalisation and italicisation. I have not attempted to reflect serif vs. non-serif fonts nor font weight. As is normal, I have recorded line breaks with a vertical bar ($|$), but unlike some bibliographers I have not used $||$ to record a larger than normal break between lines. However, where a particular block of text (or illustration) was evidently intended to begin at a particular point on the page I have indicated this in square brackets (e.g. "[at bottom left]") at that point. In cases where text appears to have been drawn rather than typeset, as often happens when incorporated as part of an illustration, I have recorded this as "[in script]". Unless otherwise stated, text is in black, and illustrations in black and white. Any qualification otherwise (e.g. "[in red]") should be taken as applying only up to the next line break.

The list of entries is ordered by the actual date of publication as given in the entry heading, and within that by author surname. The month of publication is usually available, although occasionally only a year. The entry heading contains the following information:

- **PL number** A unique number used to cross-refer to the entry from elsewhere. Each new edition of the same book is given a new number and its own entry. New impressions are not, but are noted under **Later releases**.

- **Edition number** (if relevant).

- **Name of author** (or editor, etc.) as it appears in the book.

- **Name of illustrator**.

- **Stated date of publication** This is the date as it appears on the imprint page, or if absent, the date on the title page.

- **Actual date of publication** If present, this appears in square brackets. Typically, this is not the date which appears on the book's imprint page, because this date was usually more aspirational than accurate. The date given here reflects my best estimate of actual publication date based on other evidence. The best evidence for the actual month of publication usually comes from the cumulative lists published by Whitaker, and this was typically a few months later than the date on the book. Where no information is available from Whitaker (for some reason a number of books from 1947 do not appear) a date is sometimes available from the *English Catalogue of Books*, or other book trade journals such as *Books of the Month*. In some rare cases, the date from these sources is contradicted by the accession date on the BL or NLS copy.

- **Price** Where possible, this is taken from the price on the dustjacket of the copy described, or, failing that, from the entry in Whitaker or the English Catalogue. In a few cases I have had to rely on the price announced in advertisements, and in this case I have enclosed the price in square brackets, with an explanation in **Notes**.

The body of each entry comprises a transcription of the title page, followed by some or all of the following sections:

Collation I have recorded page dimensions (height x width) to the nearest millimetre. It seemed pointless to record traditional book formats (e.g. 'Crown octavo') since with books of this period it is rarely possible to be certain of original uncut page size, and the use of formats becomes redundant when actual page dimensions have been recorded. In recording the assembly of sections, I have avoided the highly codified representations popular with early books, and opted for clarity over conciseness.

Contents A description of the book's prelims and how the main text is distributed through the pages.

Illustrations   I have recorded page numbers only for full-page and double-page illustrations, but noted when there are others present. I have only attempted to describe the contents of illustrations where they appear on the binding, endpapers or dustjacket. Although I could no doubt have identified the technique of illustration in some cases, I am not an expert in this area and so have avoided doing so altogether.

Paper   A broad description of paper type(s) used. All Peter Lunn books were trimmed along all edges.

Binding   Binding dimensions (height x width x thickness) are recorded to the nearest millimetre. Width is measured from the edge of the spine (at its widest point) to the right-hand cover edge. Thickness is measured from top to bottom cover surfaces. All Peter Lunn books are hardbacks and have sewn bindings. Many of their books were bound in several colours of book-cloth. Where I am aware of variant colours for a book, I have recorded this in **Notes**. However, it seems likely that during a period of paper shortage, binders used whatever cloth came to hand, and it would be unwise to regard any particular cloth colour as diagnostic of a particular issue.

Dustjacket   Dustjacket dimensions (height x width) are recorded to the nearest millimetre. Width is measured with the dustjacket fully opened out. Of course, designers had far more freedom of expression in relation to dustjackets than with the book itself, and this makes them more difficult to describe in a consistent way. I have simply done my best, following the order: front, spine, back, front flap and back flap. Many dustjackets contain advertisements for other books, and most contain a synopsis of some sort. To avoid making the bibliographic entries over-long, I have simply recorded the presence of these rather than transcribing the text. However, the titles of any advertised books are recorded in **Notes**. Reproductions of dustjackets are at 30% actual size.

Copy consulted   Where this entry is absent, the book has been described from a copy in my own collection. I have been able to describe all books (with the exception of *Alice's Adventures in Wonderland*) by consulting either my own copy, or one in the British Library (BL) or the National Library of Scotland (NLS). It is worth recording that, for whatever reason, copies of certain Peter Lunn books are not to be found in any of the deposit libraries.

Later releases   This records any later Lunn editions and impressions I am aware of, and where books were put back on the market at a reduced price. Whitaker records some books being released at lower price during 1950 (after Peter Lunn ceased trading), and this was presumably old stock remaindered by Hutchinson, who acquired the residual stock. If these were issued in their original dustjackets, they were presumably price-clipped, or had their original price overlaid with a new sticker. (However, surprisingly few of the books in my collection show evidence of price alteration.)

The code 'WFL' in this section indicates that the book was released by Simpkin Marshall Ltd as part of the 'World's Favourite Library for Boys and Girls' series, at a uniform price of 3/6d and in a uniform style of dustjacket (see illustration on page 22). A list of the 38 books involved appears on the back of each WFL dustjacket. Where I have recorded '[WFL]', this indicates that the book appears on this list, but I have not seen hard evidence that it was actually released in this form.

Notes   This section begins with a categorisation of the book type, and of its relative scarcity. In relation to book type, I have allocated each book to one or more of the following categories:

- **Classic** Reissue of a classic book by a famous author.
- **Fairy** Fairy stories. Usually a collection of short stories.
- **Adventure** A broad category covering 'exciting happenings', whether set in the past or present.
- **Nature** Books where the main interest is in animals, wildlife or countryside.
- **Educational** Books where the emphasis is on instruction rather than entertainment.
- **Picture** Books for very young children, with only a small amount of simple text and a lot of coloured pictures.

The assessment of scarcity is based both on my own experience of having collected these books for many years, and a survey of their availability in on-line catalogues. The scale I have used ranges from 1 (copies are common, and easily sourced) to 5 (genuinely scarce, and extremely so in dustjacket).

Other comments in this section may include print-run, binding variations, other books advertised, and publishing history. Where a book contains short stories, their titles are listed here.

PL1 Fairy Tales first edition, by Hans Christian Andersen, illustrated by W. Schlosser, 1943, [September 1943], 8/6d.

FAIRY TALES | BY | HANS CHRISTIAN ANDERSEN | *With Pictures by W. Schlosser* | PETER LUNN (PUBLISHERS) LIMITED | FORTY-NINE CHANCERY LANE, LONDON, W.C.2 | 1943

Collation (253 x 197 mm): [1-6], 7-48 in 3 x 16pp sections; [i-iv] 4pp section for double-page illustration; 49-128 in 5 x 16pp sections. All sections uncoded.

Contents [1] half-title: '[at top right] [decorated capital F]airy. | Tales | by | HANS ANDERSEN'; [2] contents; [3] list of illustrations; [4] frontis; [5] title; [6] imprint: 'COPYRIGHT | PRINTED IN GREAT BRITAIN | BY | KENNERLEY PRESS LIMITED LONDON'; 7-128 text.

Illustrations Full-page illustration on p. [4]. Double-page illustration on pp [ii-iii] (pp [i] and [iv] blank). Various other illustrations.

Paper White wove text paper and endpapers.

Binding (260 x 200 x 9 mm): orange cloth. Front cover lettered and stamped in black: 'FAIRY TALES | BY | HANS CHRISTIAN ANDERSEN | [illustration of the Emperor of China with a nightingale]'. Spine and back cover blank.

Copy consulted BL.

Later releases There was a second edition in 1947, with different illustrations and in a different format (see PL56). See also PL105.

Notes Category: Classic/Fairy. **Scarcity:** 4.

Contains the following stories: The Tinder Box; Little Claus and Big Claus; The Travelling Companion; The Princess on the Pea; The Emperor's New Clothes; The Nightingale; The Steadfast Tin Soldier; The Swineherd; The Little Mermaid; The Ugly Duckling; The Wild Swans; The Snow Queen.

PL2 **The Ginger Gang** first edition, written and illustrated by Joseph Avrach, October 1943, 6/-.

THE GINGER GANG | *A Detective Story for Children* | BY | JOSEPH AVRACH | *Illustrated by the Author* | PETER LUNN (PUBLISHERS) LIMITED | FORTY-NINE CHANCERY LANE LONDON W.C.2 | 1943

Collation (216 x 135 mm): [1-7], 8 8pp section; 9-40 in 2 x 16pp sections; 41-48 8 pp section; 49-80 in 2 x 16pp sections; 81-86, [87-88] 8pp section. All sections uncoded.

Contents [1] half-title: 'The | Ginger | Gang | by | Joseph Avrach'; [2] frontis; [3] title; [4] imprint: 'COPYRIGHT | *(First Edition October, 1943)* | PRINTED IN GREAT BRITAIN | BY | KENNERLEY PRESS LIMITED'; [5] list of illustrations; [6] blank; [7], 8-86 text (see illustration list for unnumbered pages); [87-88] blank.

Illustrations Full-page illustrations on pp [2], 14, [18], [31] and [77]. Double-page illustration on pp [44-45]. Various other illustrations.

Paper White wove text paper and endpapers.

Binding (222 x 142 x 8mm): red cloth. Front cover: 'THE | GINGER GANG | [illustration of four boys under a tree being addressed by a fifth] | A Detective Story for Children | BY | JOSEPH AVRACH'; Spine lettered vertically from top: 'THE GINGER GANG [publisher's PL device at bottom]'. Back cover blank.

Dustjacket (223 x 381 mm): white wove paper. Front, spine, back and flaps printed on a uniform orange background. Front: '[in script] The Ginger Gang | [illustration of five boys, four seated and one standing, next to a tree] | *A Detective Story for Children* | By JOSEPH AVRACH | PETER LUNN (PUBLISHERS) LIMITED LONDON W.C.2'. Spine lettered vertically from top: 'THE GINGER GANG [publisher's PL device at bottom]'. The back has an illustration of a street, with a street-lamp and tree in the foreground. Front flap: '[at bottom] SIX SHILLINGS'. The back flap has an advertisement for a book between double rules.

Later releases There was a second edition in 1946 with different illustrations (see PL34).

Notes Category: Adventure. **Scarcity:** 3.

The back flap of the dustjacket advertises *Ferry to Adventure*.

PL3 **The Magic Zoo** by Sylvia Norton, illustrated by Joseph Avrach, 1943, [October 1943], 6/-.

The Magic Zoo | by | Sylvia Norton | With Pictures by Joseph Avrach | [illustration] | Peter Lunn (Publishers) Limited | Forty-Nine Chancery Lane London | 1943

Collation (264 x 212 mm): [1-24] in 3 x 8pp uncoded sections.

Contents [1] title; [2-24] text; verso of front free endpaper has imprint at bottom: 'Printed in London by | Claridge, Lewis & Jordan Ltd. | Wardour Street | W.1.'; Front pastedown has in pale blue, below a diagonal rule in bottom left-hand corner: '6/- | net.'.

Illustrations Various black and white and coloured illustrations integrated with text. The front pastedown and recto of front free endpaper have illustrations in pale blue of a woman looking at an elephant through a window and a woman walking down stairs. The verso of the back free endpaper and back pastedown have illustrations in pale blue of two women, one seated writing at a desk, and a giraffe with a knotted neck.

Paper White wove surfaced text paper. White wove endpapers.

Binding (269 x 216 x 4 mm): red cloth on spine. Boards covered with yellow illustrated paper to within 10 mm of spine. Front: '[illustration of a woman reading a book by candlelight at top right, in red, green and black] | The Magic Zoo | by | Sylvia Norton | [in red] A Peter Lunn Book'. Spine blank. Back has in the centre an illustration in green, blue and black of a woman in silhouette against a landscape.

Copy consulted BL.

Notes Category: Picture. Scarcity: 5.

PL4 **Peter the Sailor** written and illustrated by Joseph Avrach, 1943, [November 1943], 6/-.

PETER THE SAILOR | STORY AND PICTURES | by | JOSEPH AVRACH | FIRST ADVENTURE | [illustration] | PETER LUNN (PUBLISHERS) LTD. | FORTY-NINE CHANCERY LANE, LONDON | 1943

Collation (250 x 176 mm): [1-24] 24pp uncoded section.

Contents [1] title; [2-23] text; [24] imprint: '[illustration] | COPYRIGHT | DUGDALE PRINTING LTD. | 122 Wardour Street, London, W.1'.

Illustrations Illustrations integrated with text throughout. Openings are alternately in full colour and blue monochrome.

Paper White wove text and endpapers.

Binding (257 x 181 x 4 mm): red cloth on spine. Boards covered with glazed illustrated paper, to within 7 mm of spine. The front cover has a coloured illustration, within a red border, of a clothed penguin with a pipe in its beak, a parrot and a suitcase, all in front of a sailing ship. Front cover: '[in red] Peter | [in red] the | [in blue] Sailor | Story and Pictures | [in brown] by | JOSEPH AVRACH | [in blue] * | [in brown] FIRST | [in brown] ADVENTURE [at bottom, in red] A PETER LUNN BOOK'. Spine blank. The back cover has a coloured illustration, within a red border, of a clothed penguin with a pipe, and a parrot on its shoulder, surrounded by other animals. Back cover: '[in red] Peter | [in red] the | [in blue] Sailor | [at bottom] A PETER LUNN BOOK'.

Copy consulted BL.

Notes Category: Picture. Scarcity: 4.

PL5 Robinson Crusoe by Daniel Defoe, illustrated by W. Schlosser, 1943, [December 1943], 8/6d.

ROBINSON CRUSOE | BY | DANIEL DEFOE | A NEW EDITION | WITH PICTURES | BY | W. SCHLOSSER | PETER LUNN (PUBLISHERS) LTD. | FORTY-NINE CHANCERY LANE, LONDON | 1943

Collation (279 x 209 mm): [1-4], 5-112 in 7 x 16pp sections coded: uncoded, B-G; 113-115, [i-ii], 116-130 20pp section coded H; 131-148 20pp section coded I on p. 133 (the last leaf of the section forms the rear pastedown – there is no rear free endpaper). Pages 115, [i-ii] and 116 form a four-page section on thicker paper tipped in to p. 117, for a double-page coloured illustration.

Contents frontispiece, reproducing p. 28, printed on the verso of the front free endpaper; [1] title; [2] '[author details] | UNABRIDGED | COPYRIGHT | PRINTED IN GREAT BRITAIN BY W. S. COWELL, LTD., LONDON AND IPSWICH'; [3] contents; [4] list of illustrations; 5-148 text.

Illustrations Full-page illustrations on pp. 28, 31 and 99. Double-page coloured illustration between pp. 115 and 116. Various other illustrations.

Paper Thin white wove text paper and endpapers. Thicker white wove paper for double-page illustration.

Binding (285 x 215 x 9 mm): yellow cloth on spine. Boards covered with red paper to within 19 mm of spine. Front cover lettered and illustrated in yellow: 'ROBINSON | CRUSOE | by | DANIEL DEFOE | [circular illustration of a sailing ship] | A new unabridged Edition | PETER LUNN (PUBLISHERS) LIMITED | [thick rule] | FORTY-NINE CHANCERY LANE LONDON'. Spine lettered vertically from bottom in red: 'ROBINSON CRUSOE DEFOE'. Back cover blank.

<table>
<tr><td>Dustjacket</td><td>(285 x 566 mm): white wove paper. Front and back, spine and flaps all printed on a uniform red background. All lettering and illustration is in yellow. Front cover reproduces front cover of binding. Spine lettered vertically from bottom: 'ROBINSON CRUSOE DEFOE'. Back cover blank. Front flap: '[at bottom] 8/6 | net'. Back flap blank.</td></tr>
<tr><td>Notes</td><td>Category: Classic/Adventure. Scarcity: 4.</td></tr>
</table>

PL6 Fairy Tales by the Brothers Grimm illustrated by R. A. Brandt, March 1944, [February 1944], 8/6d.

FAIRY TALES | BY | THE BROTHERS GRIMM | A New Edition | *With Pictures by* *R. A. Brandt* | PETER LUNN (PUBLISHERS) LIMITED | FORTY-NINE CHANCERY LANE LONDON | 1944

<table>
<tr><td>Collation</td><td>(235 x 179 mm): [1-6], 7-16 16pp section; 17-48 in 2 x 16pp sections; [i-iv] 4pp section for double-page illustration; 49-96 in 3 x 16pp sections; 97, [98-100] 4pp section. All sections uncoded.</td></tr>
<tr><td>Contents</td><td>[1] half-title: '[decorated capital F]airy Tales | by | THE BROTHERS GRIMM'; [2] frontis., reproducing illustration on p. [87]; [3] title; [4] contents; [5] list of illustrations; [6] imprint: '*First Edition November 1943* | *Second Edition March 1944* | COPYRIGHT | PRINTED IN GREAT BRITAIN | BY | WILLIAMS-COOK LIMITED LONDON'; 7-97 text (pp. 35 and 87 unnumbered); [98-100] blank.</td></tr>
<tr><td>Illustrations</td><td>Full-page illustrations on pp. [2], [35] and [87]. Double-page coloured illustration, on pp. [ii-iii] (pp. [i] and [iv] blank). Various other illustrations.</td></tr>
<tr><td>Paper</td><td>White wove text paper and endpapers. White surfaced wove paper for 4pp insert.</td></tr>
<tr><td>Binding</td><td>(242 x 185 x 7 mm): beige cloth. Front cover stamped in red: '[illustration of dragon] | GRIMM'S FAIRY TALES'. Spine lettered vertically from top in red, and centred on spine: 'GRIMM'S FAIRY TALES'. Back cover blank.</td></tr>
<tr><td>Copies consulted</td><td>BL and NLS.</td></tr>
<tr><td>Notes</td><td>Category: Classic/Fairy. Scarcity: 5.</td></tr>
</table>

The first entry for this book in Whitaker was in February 1944, at 8/6d, and the only copies in both the BL and NLS were accessioned in September 1944 and have '*Second Edition*' on the imprint page. It seems possible, therefore, that the first edition was never issued. The book contains the following stories: The Golden Bird; The Four Clever Brothers; Faithful John; The Three Children of Fortune; The Goose Girl; Rumpelstiltskin; The Young Giant and the Tailor; The Lady and the Lion; Hansel and Grettel; The Giant with the Three Golden Hairs; The Frog Bride; The Blue Light; The King of the Golden Mountain.

PL7 Treasure Island by Robert Louis Stevenson, illustrated by Joseph Avrach, 1943, [March 1944], 8/6d.

TREASURE ISLAND | By | ROBERT LOUIS STEVENSON | A NEW UNABRIDGED EDITION | *WITH PICTURES BY JOSEPH AVRACH* | PETER LUNN (PUBLISHERS) LIMITED | FORTY-NINE CHANCERY LANE LONDON | 1943

Collation   (252 x 193 mm): [1-8], 9-64 in 4 x 16pp sections; 65-72, [i-iv], 73-80 20pp section with 4pp inserted for double-page illustration; 81-112 in 2 x 16pp sections; 113-132 20pp section. All sections uncoded.

Contents   [1] dedication and imprint: 'TO | LLOYD OSBOURNE | AN AMERICAN GENTLEMAN | IN ACCORDANCE WITH WHOSE CLASSIC TASTE | THE FOLLOWING NARRATIVE HAS BEEN DESIGNED | IT IS NOW, IN RETURN FOR NUMEROUS DELIGHTFUL HOURS | AND WITH THE KINDEST WISHES, DEDICATED | BY HIS AFFECTIONATE FRIEND | THE AUTHOR | COPYRIGHT | *Printed by* | *Claridge, Lewis & Jordan Ltd.* | *London, W.1*'; [2] frontis; [3] title; [4] contents; [5] list of illustrations; [6] full-page illustration of map; [7], 8-132 text (see illustration list for unnumbered pages).
The following pages are also unnumbered: 7, 12, 16, 19, 22, 25, 28, 31, 35, 38, 42, 45, 48, 54, 58, 61, 64, 67, 70, 74, 79, 83, 87, 91, 95, 100, 103, 109, 113, 118, 123, 126 and 130;

Illustrations   Full-page illustrations on pp. [2], [6], [8], [34], [41], [75], [78], [85], [88], [92], [99], [104], [116], [119] and [128]. Double-page coloured illustration on pp. [ii-iii] of 4pp insert between 72 and 73 (pp. [i] and [iv] blank).

Paper   White wove text paper and endpapers. White wove surfaced paper for double-page illustration.

Binding   (259 x 199 x 9 mm): blue cloth. Front cover stamped and lettered in black: 'TREASURE ISLAND | by | ROBERT LOUIS STEVENSON | [illustration of sailing ship]'. Spine lettered vertically from bottom: '[publisher's PL device] TREASURE ISLAND'. Back cover blank.

Copies consulted   NLS and my own copy.

Later releases   A second impression appeared in February 1945, with the year 1943 at the bottom of the title page replaced by '[*Reprint February 1945*]'. The binding of the reprint differs: the cloth is red and stamped in gilt, and the orientation of the spine text is reversed, to read vertically from the top. Smith makes an intriguing reference to a reprint 'with a nubile dustjacket'.

Notes   Category: Classic/Adventure. **Scarcity:** 4.

PL8   The Three Princesses of Whiteland and other fairy tales   illustrated by Joseph Avrach, November 1943, [April 1944], 7/6d.

THE THREE PRINCESSES | OF WHITELAND | AND OTHER FAIRY TALES | *A new Collection of Fairy Stories* | *With Pictures by Joseph Avrach* | PETER LUNN (PUBLISHERS) LIMITED | FORTY-NINE CHANCERY LANE LONDON | 1943

Collation   (215 x 135 mm): [1-4], 5-80 in 5 x 16pp sections coded: uncoded, B-E; 81-87, [i-ii], 88-94 16pp section coded F (with 2pp for double-page illustration); 95-125, [126] in 2 x 16pp sections coded G-H.

Contents   [1] title; [2] imprint: '*First Edition November 1943* | COPYRIGHT | PRINTED IN GREAT BRITAIN | BY W.S. COWELL, LIMITED, LONDON AND IPSWICH'; [3] contents; [4] list of illustrations; 5-125, [126] text.

Illustrations   Full-page illustrations on pp. 9, 11, 25, 31, 44, 48, 69, 75, 91, 95, 100, 107, 110 and 125. Double-page coloured illustration between pp 87 and 88. Various other illustrations.

Paper   White wove surfaced text paper. White wove endpapers.

Binding (221 x 143 x 10 mm): red cloth. Front cover: 'THE THREE PRINCESSES | OF WHITELAND | AND OTHER FAIRY TALES | [illustration of old man leaning on stick, reproducing illustration on p. 84]'. Spine lettered vertically from bottom: '[publisher's PL device] THE THREE PRINCESSES OF WHITELAND'. Back cover blank.

Copy consulted BL.

Notes Category: Fairy. Scarcity: 4.

Contains the following stories: The Dwarf with the Long Nose; The Magic Knapsacks; The Boy with the Three Dogs; The Ill-tempered Princess; The Blue Bird; The Three Princesses of Whiteland; Alibea; The Adventures of the Caliph Haroun Alraschid; The Master and his Pupil. See also notes to PL82.

PL9 The Giant Without a Heart illustrated by D. M. Batty, May 1944, [April 1944], 6/-.

THE GIANT WITHOUT A HEART | AN OLD NORSE FAIRY TALE | [illustration] | WITH PICTURES BY D.M.BATTY | PETER LUNN (PUBLISHERS) LIMITED | FORTY-NINE CHANCERY LANE LONDON | 1944

Collation (243 x 182 mm): [1-2], 3-27, [28], 32pp section sewn into binding, with the first and last leaf forming the free endpapers.

Contents [1] title; [2] imprint: 'First Edition May, 1944 | COPYRIGHT | printed in Great Britain by | DUGDALE PRINTING LTD. | 122, Wardour Street, London, | W.1.'; 3-27, [28] text. Pages 14-15 are unnumbered.

Illustrations Full-page coloured illustrations on pp. 17 and 20. Double-page coloured illustration on pp. [14-15]. Various other coloured and black and white illustrations.

Paper White surfaced wove text paper. White wove endpapers.

Binding (249 x 186 x 5 mm): grey cloth, Front cover lettered and stamped in red: 'THE GIANT WITHOUT A HEART | AN OLD NORSE FAIRY TALE | [silhouette illustration of flying giant] | A PETER LUNN BOOK'. Spine and back cover blank.

Dustjacket (249 x 584 mm): white surfaced wove paper. Front, spine and back are printed with a background double-page coloured illustration of a prince, princess and double bed on the left and an approaching giant on the right, reproducing the illustration on pp. [14-15]. Front: '[at top right] *A PETER LUNN BOOK* | [at bottom left] THE GIANT | WITHOUT A HEART'. Front flap: '[at centre] MISS BATTY'S delightful illustrations | provide a charming setting for this old | Fairy Story. This fine Artist has created an | outstanding new book for smaller children. | [at bottom left] *6s. net.*'. Back flap blank.

Notes Category: Picture. Scarcity: 4.

PL10 The Fisherman's Son illustrated by R. A. Brandt, March 1944, [April 1944], 7/6d.

THE FISHERMAN'S | SON | AN OLD CAUCASIAN FAIRY TALE | WITH PICTURES | by | R. A. BRANDT | [illustration] | PETER LUNN (PUBLISHERS) LIMITED | FORTY-NINE CHANCERY LANE LONDON | 1944

Collation (245 x 185 mm): [1-28] 28pp uncoded section. The section is sewn into the binding and there are no free endpapers.

Contents [1-2] blank; [3] title; [4-25] text; [26] full-page illustration; [27] blank; [28] imprint: '[at bottom] COPYRIGHT | *First Edition March 1944* | *Printed in Great Britain* | *by* | KENNERLEY PRESS LIMITED, LONDON'.

Illustrations Full-page coloured illustration on p. [26]. Double-page coloured illustration on pp. [14-15]. Other coloured illustrations integrated with text.

Paper White surfaced wove text paper. White wove endpapers.

Binding (250 x 189 x 4 mm): green cloth. Front cover stamped and lettered in dark green: '[illustration of girl and boy wearing crowns sitting on bench] | THE FISHERMAN'S | SON'. Spine and back cover blank.

Dustjacket (251 x 583 mm): white surfaced wove paper. Front, spine and back are printed with a wrap-around coloured illustration reproducing the double-page illustration on pp. [14-15]. The front has in the foreground a boy with a hat talking to a girl with a crown against a background of various people and animals, which continues on to the back of the dustjacket. Front: 'THE FISHERMAN'S | SON'. There is no lettering on the spine or back. Front flap: '[synopsis] | [at bottom centre] 7s. 6d. net.'. Back flap blank.

Notes Category: Picture/Fairy. **Scarcity**: 4.

The synopsis says that Brandt was inspired by 'an unknown Caucasian fairy tale'. An advertisement in *Books of the Month* stated that The Publishers' Association chose it as an 'ambassador book' which was sent to the United States as being representative of the best British children's books.

PL11 Lucy Maroon by Stephen Macfarlane, illustrated by Bruce Angrave, July 1944, [June 1944], 6/-.

LUCY MAROON | [in script] *the car that loved a policeman* | [in script] *story by* | STEPHEN MACFARLANE | * | [in script] *Pictures by* | BRUCE ANGRAVE | PETER LUNN (PUBLISHERS) LIMITED | FORTY-NINE . CHANCERY LANE . LONDON | 1944

Collation (241 x 183 mm): [1-24] 24pp uncoded section.

Contents [1] title; [2-24] text. Imprint on recto of front free endpaper 'SIX SHILLINGS NET | FIRST PUBLISHED IN JULY 1944 | BY PETER LUNN (PUBLISHERS) LIMITED | FORTY-NINE CHANCERY LANE LONDON | PRINTED IN GREAT BRITAIN BY | KENNERLEY PRESS LIMITED | 1-4 BRITANNIA WALK LONDON N.1 | ALL RIGHTS RESERVED'.

Illustrations Full-page colour illustrations on pp. [7], [20] and [21]. Double-page coloured illustration on pp. [12-13]. Various other coloured and black and white illustrations. Text on title page is incorporated in an illustration of policemen chasing cars.

Paper White wove surfaced text paper, White wove endpapers.

Binding (245 x 187 x 4 mm): red cloth on spine. Boards covered with illustrated paper to within 15mm of spine. Front cover lettered on a coloured illustration of houses, car and policeman: 'LUCY MAROON | the car that loved a policeman | [in script] STORY BY STEPHEN MACFARLANE | [in script] PICTURES BY BRUCE ANGRAVE'. Spine blank. Back cover has a coloured illustration of buildings, church and café.

Copy consulted BL.

Notes Category: Picture. **Scarcity**: 5.

PL12 Detectives in Greasepaint first edition, by Stephen Macfarlane, illustrated by Joseph Avrach, May 1944, [June 1944], 6/-.

PETER LUNN (PUBLISHERS) LTD. | present | DETECTIVES | IN GREASEPAINT | A Story of | THE CHILDREN OF STUDIO J | ON TOUR | [rule] | Written by | STEPHEN MACFARLANE | and pictured by | JOSEPH AVRACH | [rule] | CAST | THE CHILDREN OF STUDIO J, with ERIC JEROME [dotted line] An Actor | ROMNEY TALBOT [dotted line] A Producer | BELLA COURTNEY [dotted line] An Actress | CHESTER WOLFE [dotted line] Another Actor | GEORGE FEDDEN [dotted line] A Pianist | and | JOHN ALLEN [dotted line] A Mystery Man | Actors, Policemen etc. | The action takes place in and near the village of Applegate in Dorset | [rule] | A PETER LUNN PRODUCTION

Collation (244 x 153 mm): [1-7], 8-48 in 3 x 16pp sections; 49-52 4pp section; 53-84 in 2 x 16pp sections. All sections uncoded.

Contents [1] half-title: '[at right] DETECTIVES | IN | GREASEPAINT | BY | STEPHEN MACFARLANE'; [2] frontis; [3] title; [4] contents; [5] list of illustrations; [6] imprint: 'FIRST EDITION MAY 1944 | Copyright | Printed in Great Britain | by CLARIDGE, LEWIS & JORDAN LTD. | LONDON, W.1'; [7], 8-84 text (see illustration list for unnumbered pages).

Illustrations Full-page illustrations on pp. [2], [21], [30], [35], [54], [62], 72 and [77]. Double-page illustration on pp. [50-51]. Various other illustrations.

Paper White wove text paper and endpapers.

Binding (249 x 160 x 6 mm): blue cloth. Front cover stamped in dark blue with illustration of two masks. Spine lettered vertically from top in dark blue: 'DETECTIVES IN GREASEPAINT [publisher's PL device at bottom]'. Back cover blank.

Later releases There was a second edition in 1946, under the author's real name, in a different format and with different illustrations (see PL40).

Notes Category: Adventure. Scarcity: 4.

The book features the same group of children as in *Studio J Investigates* and *Mr Bosanko*.

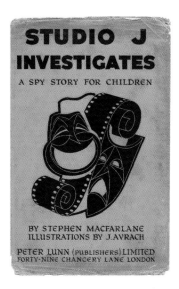

PL13 **Studio J Investigates** first edition, by Stephen Macfarlane, illustrated by Joseph Avrach, April 1944, [June 1944], 6/-.

STUDIO J | INVESTIGATES | *A Spy Story for Children* | BY | STEPHEN MACFARLANE | *With Pictures by* JOSEPH AVRACH | PETER LUNN (PUBLISHERS) LIMITED | FORTY-NINE CHANCERY LANE LONDON | 1944

Collation (215 x 139 mm): [1-7], 8 8pp section; 9-40 in 2 x 16pp sections; 41-48 8pp section; 49-80 in 2 x 16pp sections; 81-92 12 pp section. All sections uncoded.

Contents [1] half-title: '[at right] Studio J | Investigates | *by* | Stephen Macfarlane'; [2] frontis; [3] title; [4] contents; [5] list of illustrations; [6] imprint: 'COPYRIGHT | *(First Edition April, 1944)* | FOR | JENNYANYDOTS | OR | ADAM | PRINTED IN GREAT BRITAIN | BY | COOPER, SCANNELL & CO. LTD., LONDON'; [7], 8-91 text (see illustration list for unnumbered pages); [92] blank.

Illustrations Full-page illustrations on pp. [2], [11], 12, 56 and 73. Double-page illustration on pp. [44-45]. Various other illustrations.

Paper White wove text paper and endpapers.

Binding (221 x 147 x 6 mm): blue cloth. Front cover lettered and stamped in dark blue: 'STUDIO J | INVESTIGATES | [silhouette illustration of boy with camera on tripod] | A Spy Story for Children | BY | STEPHEN MACFARLANE'. Spine lettered vertically from top in dark blue: 'STUDIO J INVESTIGATES [at bottom, publisher's PL device]'. Back cover blank.

Dustjacket (222 x 457 mm): white surfaced wove paper. Front, back, spine and flaps printed in black on a uniform dark yellow background. Front: 'STUDIO J | INVESTIGATES | A SPY STORY FOR CHILDREN | [stylised illustration of a roll of film and two masks] | BY STEPHEN MACFARLANE | ILLUSTRATIONS BY J.AVRACH | PETER LUNN (PUBLISHERS) LIMITED | FORTY-NINE CHANCERY LANE LONDON'. Spine lettered vertically from top: 'STUDIO J INVESTIGATES [at bottom, publisher's PL device]'. Back has publisher's device (Fig. 2D) in the centre. Front flap: '[synopsis, in italic lettering] | [at right] 6/- *net*'. Back flap blank.

Later releases There was a second edition in 1946, under the author's real name, in a different format and with different illustrations (see PL46).

Notes Category: Adventure. **Scarcity**: 4.

This book features the same group of children as *Detectives in Greasepaint* and *Mr Bosanko*.

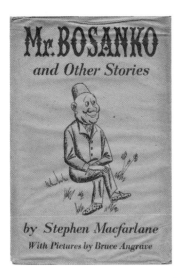

PL14 Mr. Bosanko and other stories   by Stephen Macfarlane, illustrated by Bruce Angrave, August 1944, 6/-.

[in script] Mr. | [in script] BOSANKO | *and Other Stories* | [illustration] | *by Stephen Macfarlane* | *With Pictures by Bruce Angrave* | [publisher's device (Fig. 2C)] | *Peter Lunn (Publishers) Ltd.* | *Forty-Nine Chancery Lane London* | 1944

Collation   (215 x 139 mm): [1-6], 7-8 8pp section; 9-88 in 5 x 16pp sections. All sections uncoded.

Contents   [1] half-title: '[in script] Mr. BOSANKO'; [2] frontis; [3] title, surrounded by a border of swirling lines; [4] contents; [5] list of illustrations; [6] imprint at bottom: '[publisher's device (Fig. 2C)] | FIRST PUBLISHED IN AUGUST 1944 | BY PETER LUNN (PUBLISHERS) LIMITED | FORTY-NINE CHANCERY LANE LONDON | PRINTED IN GREAT BRITAIN BY | COOPER SCANNELL AND COMPANY LIMITED | 6 ELDON STREET LONDON E.C.2 | ALL RIGHTS RESERVED'; 7-71, [72-73], 74-88 text (p. [72] is blank). See illustration list for other unnumbered pages.

Illustrations   Full-page illustrations on pp. [2], [59] and [63]. Various other illustrations.

Paper   White wove text paper and endpapers.

Binding   (220 x 145 x 6 mm): blue cloth. Front cover stamped in centre in red with illustration of seated man wearing fez. Spine lettered vertically from top in red: 'Mr. BOSANKO *and Other Stories* [at bottom] P.L.'. Back cover blank.

Dustjacket   (219 x 505 mm): pink wove paper. All lettering and illustrations on the dustjacket are printed in blue. Front: '[in script] Mr.BOSANKO | *and Other Stories* | [illustration of seated man wearing fez] | *by Stephen Macfarlane* | *With Pictures by Bruce Angrave*'. Spine lettered vertically from top: 'Mr. BOSANKO *and Other Stories* [publisher's PL device at bottom]'. Back has publisher's device (Fig 2C) in centre. Front flap: '[in script] Mr.BOSANKO | and Other Stories | [synopsis] | [at bottom right] 6s. net.'. Back flap: '*Press Reviews of* | "STUDIO J" Books | [reviews of two books]'.

Notes   Category: Adventure. Scarcity: 4.

The back flap has press reviews of *Studio J Investigates* and *Detectives in Greasepaint*, which are the other books featuring the same group of children.

PL15 The Lion and the Vulture by Paul Tabori, illustrated by Joseph Avrach, June 1944, [August 1944], 6/-.

[all in grey] THE LION | AND | THE VULTURE | by | PAUL TABORI | with Pictures by Joseph Avrach | PETER LUNN (PUBLISHERS) LIMITED | [thick rule] | FORTY-NINE CHANCERY LANE LONDON | 1944

Collation (250 x 204 mm): [1-30] 30pp uncoded section, with pp [3-4] as a single leaf tipped in to p. [29]. The section is sewn into the binding without free endpapers.

Contents [1-2] blank; [3] title; [4] imprint: '[all in grey] COPYRIGHT | First Edition June 1944 | Printed in Great Britain | by | W. S. COWELL LIMITED | London and Ipswich'; [5] full-page colour illustration; [6-27] text; [28] full-page colour illustration; [29-30] blank.

Illustrations The full-page colour illustrations on pp. [5] and [28] are reproduced on the front and back of the dustjacket, with additional titling on the front cover. Blue and black illustrations alternate with coloured illustrations on each opening. All are integrated with the text.

Paper White wove text paper and endpapers.

Binding (255 x 207 x 5 mm): green cloth. Front cover is stamped and lettered: '[illustration of lion wearing British army helmet at top left] | THE LION | AND | THE VULTURE | by | PAUL TABORI | [illustration of vulture wearing German army helmet at bottom right] | A PETER LUNN BOOK'. Spine and back cover blank.

Dustjacket (256 x 577 mm): white surfaced wove paper. Front has a coloured illustration of a variety of animals against a landscape with rocks and a signpost in the foreground, and a steam train and hills in the background. Some animals wear British army helmets and hold rifles. Front: '[at top right, in blue] THE LION | [in blue] AND | [in blue] THE VULTURE | [in red] BY PAUL TABORI | [in red] Pictures by Joseph Avrach | [in blue] A PETER LUNN BOOK'. Spine blank. Back has a coloured illustration of various animals standing on grass next to a river looking away from us into a hilly landscape. Front flap is lettered in blue: '[synopsis] | [at bottom] 6/- | net'. Back flap blank.

Notes Category: Picture. Scarcity: 4.

PL16 **The Strange Tale of Sally and Arnold**   by Stephen Macfarlane, illustrated by Arnrid Johnston, August 1944, [September 1944], 4/6d.

> THE *STRANGE TALE OF* | [in red] *SALLY AND ARNOLD* | *By* | *STEPHEN MACFARLANE* | *WITH PICTURES BY* | *ARNRID JOHNSTON* | [illustration] | *PETER LUNN (PUBLISHERS) LTD* | *FORTY NINE CHANCERY LANE* | *LONDON 1944*

Collation   (166 x 219 mm): [1-28] 28pp uncoded section. The section is sewn into the binding and there are no free endpapers. All pages unnumbered.

Contents   [1] imprint: 'FIRST PUBLISHED IN AUGUST 1944 | BY PETER LUNN (PUBLISHERS) LIMITED | FORTY-NINE CHANCERY LANE LONDON | PRINTED IN GREAT BRITAIN BY | DUGDALE PRINTING LIMITED | 122 WARDOUR STREET | LONDON W.1 | ALL RIGHTS RESERVED'; [2] blank; [3] title; [4-26] text; [27-28] blank.

Illustrations   Various coloured illustrations integrated with text throughout.

Paper   White wove text paper and endpapers.

Binding   (170 x 224 x 4 mm): paper-covered illustrated boards, on a green background lightly shaded with black. Front cover: 'The Strange Tale of | SALLY AND ARNOLD | [coloured illustration of pony and truck] | by Stephen Macfarlane | With Drawings by Arnrid Johnston | [at bottom right, in red, within the outline of a book] A | Peter | Lunn | Book'. Spine blank. Back cover has coloured illustration of a girl on a milking stool at centre, and four farm animals in the four corners.

Copy consulted   BL.

Later releases   A reprint was advertised as being available during September 1945, although I have not seen a copy.

Notes   Category: Picture. **Scarcity**: 4.

The book contains further adventures of Mos' Merrily, so can be seen as a sequel to *Lucy Maroon*. The text contains reported conversations with 'Mr Peter Lunn'.

PL17 **Timbu the Monkey**   by Joseph Avrach, illustrated by Arnrid Johnston, October 1944, [November 1944], 4/6d.

> [decorated capital T in red with monkey holding the letter, and the curve of its tail enclosing text in black: 'a PETER LUNN BOOK'][in black]I[in red]M[in black]B[in red] U | [in red] *by* [in black] Joseph Avrach | [in red] *with drawings by* [in black] Arnrid Johnston

Collation   (163 x 243 mm): [1-28] 28pp uncoded section. The section is sewn into the binding and there are no free endpapers. All pages unnumbered.

Contents   [1] title; [2] imprint: '*All Rights Reserved* | *First Edition October 1944* | *Published by Peter Lunn (Publishers) Ltd* | *Forty-nine Chancery Lane London* | *Printed in Great Britain by* | *Dugdale Printing Limited* | *122 Wardour Street London* | *Four Shillings and Sixpence Net*'; [3-26] text; [27-28] blank.

Illustrations   Coloured illustrations on all pages, integrated with text.

Paper   White wove text paper and endpapers.

Binding	(167 x 247 x 3 mm): Boards covered with light blue paper. Front cover: '[all within a wavy red band] TIMBU the Monkey | by Joseph Avrach. Drawings by Arnrid Johnston | [coloured illustration of a monkey peering into the distance and holding a basket of fruit, between two leafy branches] | [at bottom right in red, within the outline of a book] A | Peter | Lunn | Book'. Spine blank. Back cover has a coloured illustration of a monkey, within a wavy red band.
Dustjacket	Although I have not seen an example of the jacket, it is reproduced in monochrome on the front cover of the December 1944 issue of *Books of the Month*, and evidently reproduced the design of the paper binding.
Copy consulted	NLS.
Notes	Category: Picture. Scarcity: 5.

PL18 Lord Dragline the Dragon written and illustrated by Bruce Angrave, 1944, [December 1944], 8/6d.

	LORD DRAGLINE | THE DRAGON | *The story of a Real Dragon who actually lives today!* | [illustration] | *Story and Pictures by* | BRUCE ANGRAVE [all of the preceding enclosed in turreted wall decoration] | *1944* | *Peter Lunn (Publishers) Limited* | *Forty-nine Chancery Lane London*
Collation	(215 x 278 mm): [1-24] 24pp uncoded section.
Contents	[1] title; [2-24] text.
Illustrations	Various full-page, double-page and smaller illustrations integrated with the text. All are in combinations of black, blue, pink and green. Front pastedown and recto of front free endpaper is printed as a double-page spread with part of a spoof newspaper showing reports of Lord Dragline. Similar but different reports on rear endpapers.
Paper	White wove surfaced text paper. White wove endpapers,
Binding	(221 x 283 x 4 mm): red cloth decorated in gilt. Front cover has an illustration of a mechanical digger stamped in gilt in centre. Spine and back cover blank.
Copy consulted	BL.
Notes	Category: Picture. Scarcity: 4.

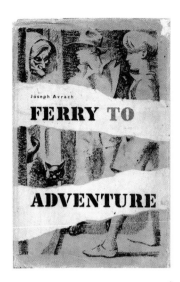

PL19 **Ferry to Adventure** by Joseph Avrach, illustrated by R. A. Bartlett, September 1944, [December 1944], 7/6d.

Joseph Avrach | Ferry to Adventure | *Illustrated by R.A.Bartlett* | [publisher's device (Fig. 2C)] Peter Lunn *(Publishers)* Limited | 49 Chancery Lane . London 1944

Collation (216 x 139 mm): [1-6], 7-95, [96] in 6 x 16pp uncoded sections.

Contents [1] half-title: '*Joseph Avrach* | Ferry to Adventure'; [2] frontis; [3] title; [4] imprint: '*First Edition September 1944* | *All rights reserved* | Printed in Great Britain by Claridge, Lewis & Jordan, 68-70 Wardour Street London W.1'; [5] list of illustrations; [6] blank; 7-95,[96] text (see illustration list for unnumbered pages).

Illustrations Full-page illustrations in reddish-brown on pp. [2], [8], [14], [16], [24], [27], [31], [37], [39], [41], [59], [62], [65] and [93]. Double-page illustration in reddish-brown on pp. [56-57].

Paper White wove text paper and endpapers.

Binding (222 x 144 x 10 mm): red cloth lettered in gilt. Front cover has illustration stamped in gilt of a boat next to a quay. Spine lettered vertically from top: 'Ferry to Adventure [at bottom] peter lunn'. Back cover blank.

Dustjacket (221 x 458 mm): white surfaced wove paper. Front: 'Joseph Avrach | FERRY TO | ADVENTURE'. The wording is on two white diagonal panels overlying an illustration, on a salmon-pink background, of two boys speaking to an old woman with a cat. Spine lettered vertically from top 'Ferry to Adventure [at bottom] peter lunn'; Back blank. Front flap is lettered on a white and salmon-pink background '[synopsis] | 7/6 *net*'. Back flap blank.

Later releases There was a second impression with book and dustjacket identical to the first, except for the date on the imprint page, which reads '*Second Edition September 1945*'.

Notes Category: Adventure. **Scarcity:** 4.

The book was published in French under the title *Message pour le Moyen-Orient* (Tissot, 1946). Advance advertising for the book stated that: '...R. Bartlett's unusual drawings for this book are produced in Botticelli-red.'.

PL20 **The Blue Egg** by Stephen Macfarlane, illustrated by Enrique Garrán, December 1944, 6/-.

> THE BLUE EGG | by | STEPHEN MACFARLANE | [in script] with Pictures by Enrique Garrán | A Peter Lunn Book

Collation (267 x 208 mm): [1-24] 24pp uncoded section. The section is sewn into the binding and there are no free endpapers. All pages unnumbered.

Contents [1] imprint. At bottom left: '*All rights reserved* | First edition December 1944 | Published in Great Britain | by Peter Lunn (Publishers) Limited | 49 Chancery Lane London'. At bottom right: 'Printed by Dugdale Printing Ltd | 122 Wardour Street London W1'; [2] blank; [3] title, plus start of text; [4-22] remainder of text; [23-24] blank.

Illustrations Full-page coloured illustrations on pp. [11] and [14]. Double-page coloured illustration on pp. [12-13]. Various other illustrations in red and black, integrated with text.

Paper White wove text paper and endpapers.

Binding (271 x 214 x 4 mm): lemon cloth. Front cover lettered in dark blue: 'The | blue | Egg'. Spine and back cover blank.

Copy consulted NLS.

Notes Category: Picture. Scarcity: 4.

PL21 **The Sampler Story** by Audrey Blair, illustrated by Menena J. Schwabe, March 1945, [April 1945], 6/-.

> [all in red, incorporated within a coloured illustration] THE SAMPLER STORY | WRITTEN BY | AUDREY BLAIR | AND PICTURED BY | MENENA J. SCHWABE | PETER LUNN (PUBLISHERS) LIMITED | FORTY NINE CHANCERY LANE, LONDON | 1945

Collation (165 x 219 mm): [1-28] 28pp page uncoded section sewn into binding. There are no free endpapers.

Contents [1] imprint: '[at bottom] FIRST PUBLISHED IN MARCH 1945 | BY PETER LUNN (PUBLISHERS) LIMITED | FORTY-NINE CHANCERY LANE LONDON | PRINTED IN GREAT BRITAIN BY | DUGDALE PRINTING LIMITED | 122 WARDOUR STREET | LONDON, W.1 | ALL RIGHTS RESERVED'; [2] blank; [3] title; [4] illustration, incorporating at bottom: 'PRINTED BY DUGDALE PRINTING LIMITED LONDON W.1'; [5-26] text; [27-28] blank.

Illustrations Full-page coloured illustrations on pp. [4], [25] and [26]. Double-page coloured illustrations on pp. [14-15] and [20-21]. Many other coloured illustrations incorporated with the text. All illustrations imitate cross-stitch embroidery.

Paper White wove text paper and endpapers, all printed with a buff criss-cross pattern in imitation of an embroidery canvas.

Binding (171 x 222 x 5 mm): yellow cloth. Front cover: '[stamped in red, in imitation of cross-stitch] THE SAMPLER STORY | [illustration of house in octagonal frame]'. Spine and back cover blank.

Dustjacket (170 x 513 mm): white wove paper, printed on the front with a buff criss-cross pattern in imitation of an embroidery canvas. The edge of the front has a blue border, surrounding: '[all in red] THE SAMPLER STORY | WRITTEN BY | AUDREY BLAIR | AND PICTURED BY | MENENA J. SCHWABE | [coloured illustration of boy in cap, rocking-horse and girl] | [all in red] PETER LUNN (PUBLISHERS) LIMITED | FORTY NINE, CHANCERY LANE, LONDON | 1945'. Spine blank. Back has a coloured illustration of various objects in a circular formation, surrounded by a blue border. Front flap: '[at bottom] 6s.net.'. Back flap blank.

Notes Category: Picture/Educational. **Scarcity:** 4.

PL22 Mukrah the Dwarf [by Wilhelm Hauff], illustrated by Acanthus, December 1944, [May 1945], 7/6d.

[all in script] Mukrah the Dwarf | An Old Fairy Tale | with Pictures by Acanthus | [illustration] | Peter Lunn (Publishers) Limited | Forty-Nine Chancery Lane London | 1944

Collation (248 x 184 mm): [1-36] 36pp uncoded section sewn into binding. There are no free endpapers.

Contents [1-2] blank; [3] title; [4] imprint, with four coloured illustrations in the corners: 'First published in December 1944 | by Peter Lunn (Publishers) Limited | Forty-nine Chancery Lane London | Printed in Great Britain by | Dugdale Printing Limited | One Hundred and Twenty-two Wardour Street | London. W.I. | All rights reserved'; [5-34] text; [35-36] blank.

Illustrations Full-page coloured illustrations on pp. [7], [16-17] and [25]. Double-page coloured illustration on pp. [18-19]. Various other coloured illustrations.

Paper White wove text paper and endpapers.

Binding (254 x 190 x 6 mm): orange cloth. Front cover stamped at centre in gilt script lettering: 'Mukrah | the Dwarf'. Spine and back cover blank.

Dustjacket (255 x 570 mm): white surfaced wove paper. Front, spine and back are printed with a double-page coloured illustration two figures in turbans running from left to right in front of cheering spectators, reproducing the illustration on pp. [18-19]. Front: '[in script] Mukrah the Dwarf | *an old Fairy tale* | *with pictures by* [in script] Acanthus'. Front flap: '[synopsis] [at bottom right] 7s. 6d. net'. Back flap blank.

Notes Category: Picture/Fairy. Scarcity: 4.

This is an adaptation of one of Hauff's fairy tales 'The Story of Little Mook' (see PL101).

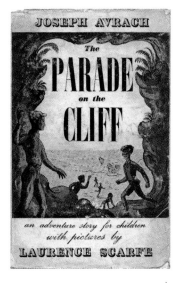

PL23 The Parade on the Cliff by Joseph Avrach, illustrated by Laurence Scarfe, April 1945, [August 1945], 7/6d.

Joseph Avrach | The Parade on the Cliff | *illustrated by Laurence Scarfe* | [at right] PETER LUNN . LONDON 1945

Collation (215 x 140 mm): [1-8], 9-64 in 4 x 16pp sections; 65-70, [71-72] 8pp section. All sections uncoded.

Contents [1] half-title: '[at right] The Parade on the Cliff'; [2] frontis; [3] title; [4] imprint: '[at bottom] first published in April 1945 | by Peter Lunn (Publishers) Limited | 49 Chancery Lane . London | *all rights reserved*'; [5] list of illustrations; [6] '[at bottom] Printed in Great Britain by Claridge Lewis & Jordan | 68-70 Wardour Street W1'; [7] 'books by the same author | *The Ginger Gang* | *Peter the Sailor* | *Timbu the Monkey* | *Ferry to Adventure*'; [8] blank; 9-70, [71] text (see illustration list for unnumbered pages); [72] [illustration].

Illustrations Full-page illustrations on various single-colour backgrounds on pp. [2], [22], [38], [56], [66] and [69]. Various other illustrations on single-colour backgrounds.

Paper White wove text paper and endpapers.

Binding (220 x 145 x 7 mm): pale purple-brown cloth. Front cover stamped at centre in gilt with a seashell motif within a broken oval frame. Spine lettered vertically from top in gilt: 'JOSEPH AVRACH [at centre] *The Parade on the Cliff* [at bottom] PETER LUNN'. Back cover blank.

Dustjacket (221 x 459 mm): white surfaced wove paper. Front cover: '[in coloured outline lettering] JOSEPH AVRACH | [within a coloured illustration of children playing on a beach] The | PARADE | on the | CLIFF | [below illustration] *an adventure story for children* | *with pictures by* | [in coloured outline lettering] LAURENCE SCARFE'. Spine lettered vertically from top: 'JOSEPH AVRACH [at centre] *The Parade on the Cliff* [at bottom] PETER LUNN'. Back cover blank. Front flap: '[synopsis] | [at bottom right] 7/6 net'. Back flap blank.

Notes Category: Adventure. **Scarcity:** 3.

PL24 The Mechanical Emperor written and illustrated by Bruce Angrave, May 1945, [September 1945], 6/-.

The | [in coloured capital letters imitating articulated metal components] MECHANICAL | [in similar lettering] EMPEROR | *a very moral tale* | *by* | Bruce Angrave | PETER LUNN (PUBLISHERS) LIMITED . FORTY NINE CHANCERY LANE | LONDON 1945

Collation (276 x 211 mm): [1-24] 24pp uncoded section. All pages unnumbered.

Contents [1] title; [2-24] text. The front pastedown and free endpaper have a double-page illustration of interlocking gear-wheels in blue. Three of the wheels contain text in orange. First wheel has imprint: 'THE | MECHANICAL | EMPEROR | *First Edition May 1945* | *All rights reserved* | * | *Printed in Great Britain by Dugdale* | *Printing Ltd 122 Wardour Street* | *London W1 for Peter Lunn (Publish-* | *ers) Ltd 49 Chancery Lane WC2* | SIX SHILLINGS | NET'. Second wheel has a synopsis. Third wheel has a list of characters in the story. The back free endpaper and pastedown have a double-page map in blue of 'Mechanalia'.

Illustrations Full-page illustrations in orange, blue, purple and black on pp. [2], [4], [7], [9], [11], [14], [16], [18] and [23]. Various other coloured and black and white illustrations integrated with text.

Paper White wove text paper and endpapers.

Binding (281 x 215 x 7 mm): orange cloth. Front cover is stamped in gilt with a stylised illustration of a robot sitting on grass. Spine and back cover blank.

Copy consulted NLS.

Notes Category: Picture. **Scarcity:** 4.

Author listed as 'Bruce Angwin' in Whitaker.

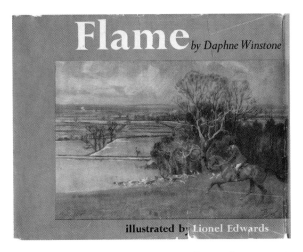

PL25 Flame by Daphne Winstone, illustrated by Lionel Edwards, September 1945, [November 1945], 8/6d.

Daphne Winstone | Flame | *illustrated by Lionel Edwards* | Peter Lunn . London . 1945

Collation (196 x 248 mm): [1-9], 10-79, [80] in 5 x 16pp uncoded sections.

Contents [1] half-title: '[at right] Daphne Winstone Flame'; [2-3] author details; [4] illustrator details; [5] imprint: 'first published in September 1945 | by Peter Lunn (Publishers) Limited | 49 Chancery Lane London | *all rights reserved* | printed in Great Britain by Kennerley Press Limited 1-4 Britannia Walk London N I'; [6] blank; [7] title; [8-9] synopsis; 10-79 text, in double columns; [89] typeface details. Pages 11, 23, 31 and 68 are unnumbered. See illustration list for other unnumbered pages.

Illustrations Full-page illustrations on pp. [16], [19], [33], [36], [39], [48], [54] and [59]. Double-page illustration on pp. [26-27]. Various other illustrations.

Paper White textured laid paper for text pages. White wove endpapers.

Binding (202 x 254 x 10 mm): buff cloth. Front cover lettered in red at bottom right: 'Flame'. Spine lettered vertically from top in red: '*Daphne Winstone* [in centre] Flame [at bottom] *Peter Lunn*'. Back cover blank.

Dustjacket (203 x 693 mm): white surfaced wove paper. All of the dustjacket is printed against a uniform light brown background. Front: '[in white] Flame [in black] by *Daphne Winstone* | [coloured illustration of a mounted huntsman blowing a horn and following a pack of hounds in a landscape of fields] | illustrated by [in white] Lionel Edwards'. Spine lettered vertically from top: '*Daphne Winstone* [in centre, in white] Flame [at bottom, in black] *Peter Lunn*'. Back blank. Front flap: '[author details] | *The book is illustrated* | [at right] *by* LIONEL EDWARDS | [at bottom right] *8/6 net*'. Back flap blank.

Later releases Reprinted in February 1946 in a slightly smaller format, but using the same printing blocks for the main text. The imprint page has a line inserted between the first and second lines of the original: 'reprinted February 1946'. The binding has dimensions 190 x 252 x 9 mm, is orange-brown cloth (with variants in blue and yellow), and is lettered in gilt. Page dimensions are 185 x 247 mm, and all paper is white wove. Dustjacket dimensions are 191 x 692 mm, and the back flap has a review reprinted from *The Sunday Times*.

Notes Category: Nature. **Scarcity**: 1.

The use of what appears to be hand-made art paper for the first issue is unique among Peter Lunn's output. A smaller format was chosen for the second issue, which had the effect of bringing it into uniformity with the four later 'horse' books published by Lunn.

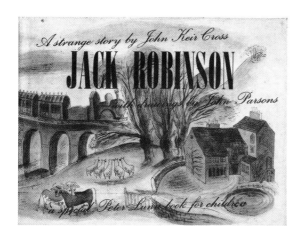

PL26 Jack Robinson by John Keir Cross, illustrated by John R. Parsons, December 1945, 5/-.

JOHN KEIR CROSS: | JACK ROBINSON | [in script] *with pictures by* [in lettering] JOHN R. PARSONS | [tapered rule] | [in script] *a* [in lettering] PETER LUNN [in script] *book*

Collation (182 x 239 mm): [1-28] 28pp uncoded section. Section is sewn into binding, and there are no free endpapers.

Contents [1-2] blank; [3] title; [4-26] text; [27] blank; [28] imprint: '[at bottom] FIRST PUBLISHED IN DECEMBER 1945 | BY PETER LUNN (PUBLISHERS) LIMITED | FORTY-NINE CHANCERY LANE LONDON | PRINTED IN GREAT BRITAIN BY | DUGDALE PRINTING LIMITED | 122 WARDOUR STREET | LONDON W.1 | *ALL RIGHTS RESERVED*'.

Illustrations Coloured illustrations integrated with the text throughout.

Paper White wove text paper and endpapers.

Binding (186 x 244 x 4 mm): orange cloth lettered and stamped in black. Front cover has text enclosed in oval frame supported at left by man with spindly arms and legs, long hair and moustache; at top right by a cow; and at bottom right by a young girl: '[in script] *by John Keir Cross* | JACK ROBINSON | [in script] *with drawings by* | [in script] *John Parsons*'. Spine and back cover blank.

Dustjacket (186 x 660 mm): white wove paper. The front, spine and back have a single double-page coloured illustration of a castle at left with two children on a bridge over a river waving handkerchiefs at a train in the centre passing over an aqueduct. On the right is a field with cows, sheep, trees and some buildings and a pond enclosed by a wall. Front: '[in script] *A strange story by John Keir Cross* | JACK ROBINSON | [in script] *with drawings by John Parsons* | [at bottom in script] *a special Peter Lunn book for children*'. Spine blank. Back: [lettered at left, vertically from bottom] JACK ROBINSON | [in script] *a Peter Lunn book*'. Front flap: '[synopsis] | [at right] 6s net'. Back flap blank.

Notes Category: Picture. Scarcity: 3.

On the copy examined, the '6s' of the price on the front flap has been overlaid with a printed label for '5s', presumably by the publisher before it was issued. Whitaker lists the book as published at 5/–. Like *The Strange Tale of Sally and Arnold*, the story features 'Mr Peter Lunn' as a character.

PL27 The Island Sanctuary by Sam Campbell, [illustrated by Will Forrest], December 1945, [January 1946], 8/6d.

THE ISLAND | SANCTUARY | BY SAM CAMPBELL | [illustration] | PETER LUNN | LONDON | 1945

Collation (184 x 118 mm): [1-6], 7-160 in 10 x 16pp sections; 161-168 8pp section; 169-182, [183-184] 16pp section. All sections uncoded.

Contents [1] half-title: '[at right] The Island Sanctuary'; [2] frontis; [3] title; [4] imprint: '*First published in December 1945 by* | PETER LUNN (PUBLISHERS) LTD. | *49 Chancery Lane London* | *All rights reserved* | *Printed in Great Britain by* | W. S. CAINES LTD. | *Andover House Plaistow London E.13*'; [5] contents; [6] 'To | GINY AND CAROL'; 7-182 text; [183-184] blank.

Illustrations Full-page illustration on p. [2]. Various other illustrations.

Paper White wove text paper and endpapers.

Binding (190 x 123 x 14 mm): blue cloth. Front cover blank. Spine lettered vertically from top in gilt: 'SAM CAMPBELL: ISLAND SANCTUARY PETER LUNN'. Back cover blank.

Dustjacket (189 x 454 mm): white wove paper. Front printed on a uniform green background: 'SAM CAMPBELL | THE ISLAND | SANCTUARY | [illustration within a white oval panel of birds flying] | A story of rich adventure & | strange, lively friendships on | a beautiful island. You should meet | Salt and Pepper, the two porcupines, | Bunny Hunch & Big Boy, the bear cubs. [device of hand pointing to right]'. Spine lettered vertically from top: 'THE ISLAND SANCTUARY SAM CAMPBELL [lettered horizontally] PETER | LUNN'. Back: 'Other | Peter Lunn | books | for children | [advertisements for three books] | PETER LUNN | *49 Chancery Lane London*'. Front flap has a synopsis, continuing the text from the front cover, and price at bottom right (clipped on the copy described). Back flap blank.

Later releases [WFL].

Notes Category: Nature. Scarcity: 3.

The back cover of the dustjacket has advertisements for *The Angry Planet, The Spanish Galleon* and *Ferry to Adventure*. The book was first published in America as *Too Much Salt and Pepper* (Bobbs-Merrill, 1944).

PL28   The Angry Planet   first edition, by John Keir Cross, illustrated by Robin Jacques, October 1945, [January 1946], 8/6d.

THE ANGRY PLANET | [double rule] | An authentic first-hand account of a journey to Mars in | the space-ship *Albatross*, compiled from notes and records | by various members of the expedition, and now assembled | (together with illustrations) and edited for publication by | JOHN KEIR CROSS | *from manuscripts made available by* | STEPHEN MACFARLANE | [double rule] *The illustrations are by* | ROBIN JACQUES | [double rule] | PETER LUNN LONDON | 1945

Collation   (185 x 121 mm): [1-8], 9-192 in 12 x 16pp sections coded AA-EE, GG-HH, uncoded, KK-MM, OO; 193-200 8pp section coded PP.

Contents   [1] half-title: '[at right] THE ANGRY PLANET'; [2] frontis; [3] title; [4] imprint: '*First published in October 1945* | *by Peter Lunn (Publishers) Limited* | *49 Chancery Lane London* | *All rights reserved* | *Printed in Great Britain* | *by* | METROPOLITAN PRESS | 4/5 DENMARK STREET | LONDON WC2'; [5] 'THE STORY | [contents]'; [6] 'TO AUDREY'; [7] 'IMPORTANT | EDITOR'S NOTE ON THE | ILLUSTRATIONS | [note] | [at right] J.K.C. | [start of illustration list] | [at right] *Continued overleaf*'; [8] 'ILLUSTRATIONS (Continued) | [rest of illustration list]'; 9-200 text (see illustration list for unnumbered pages).

Illustrations   Full-page illustrations on pp. [2], [54], [66], [113], [148], [156], [162] and [172]. Various other illustrations.

Paper   White wove text paper and endpapers.

Binding   (191 x 128 x 10 mm): orange-red cloth. Front cover blank. Spine lettered vertically from top in gilt: '*THE ANGRY PLANET . KEIR CROSS* [lettered horizontally at bottom] PETER | LUNN'. Back cover blank.

Dustjacket   (191 x 432 mm): white wove paper. Front and spine are printed on a uniform pale yellow background. Front: '[at left, lettered vertically from bottom] *THE ANGRY PLANET* | One of the most fantastic and | [illustration of two boys climbing over palisade, looking at space-ship] | thrilling children's adventure | [illustration of space-ship travelling near planets] | stories ever written; with drawings | [illustration of tent in landscape with aliens] | as unusual & strange as the story | [at right, lettered vertically from top] BY JOHN KEIR CROSS'. Spine lettering alternates between horizontal and vertical (from top) modes: '[horizontal] JOHN [vertical] *THE* [horizontal] KEIR [vertical] *ANGRY* [horizontal] CROSS | [vertical] *PLANET* [horizontal] PETER | LUNN'.

Back: 'If you liked | THE ANGRY | PLANET | you will also certainly like | THE SPANISH | GALLEON | written by Tudur Watkins | with drawings by Jack Matthews | [illustration of four men, three seated at table] | Boys versus smugglers | in a packed story of adventures of over a hundred years ago. Thrills and adventures. | Published by | PETER LUNN 49 CHANCERY LANE LONDON'. Front flap '[synopsis] | [at right] 8/6 net'. Back flap blank.

Later releases There was a second edition (see PL38). This was newly typeset, and had some extra illustrations by Robin Jacques which were not included in the first edition. Also [WFL], although probably the second edition was used for this.

Notes Category: Adventure. **Scarcity:** 3.

There is a misprint ('same' for 'some' in line 18 of p. 47) which is corrected in the second edition. The back of the dustjacket has an advertisement for *The Spanish Galleon*. The book was published in America by Coward-McCann in 1945, and a sequel, *SOS from Mars*, was published by in Britain by Hutchinson (n.d. circa 1954), and in America as *The Red Journey Back* (Coward-McCann, 1954). Although the Hutchinson edition was unillustrated, the American one was illustrated by Robin Jacques, with six full-page illustrations and small vignettes for chapter headings.

PL29 The Spanish Galleon   by Tudur Watkins, illustrated by Jack Matthews, November 1945, [January 1946], 8/6d.

THE | SPANISH | GALLEON | AN ADVENTURE STORY BY | TUDUR WATKINS | WITH DRAWINGS BY | JACK MATTHEWS | PETER LUNN | 1945

Collation (214 x 135 mm): [1-6], 7-16 16pp section coded A; 17-24 8pp section coded B; 25-117, [118-120] in 6 x 16pp sections coded C, uncoded, uncoded, F, G, uncoded.

Contents [1] half-title: '[at right] THE SPANISH GALLEON | by Tudur Watkins'; [2] illustration; [3] title; [4] frontis; [5] '[illustration] | THE STORY | [contents] | AND DRAWINGS | throughout the book'; [6] imprint: 'First published in | November 1945 by | PETER LUNN (PUBLISHERS) LIMITED | 49 Chancery Lane | London | All rights reserved | Printed in Great Britain by | H. O. LOESCHER, LTD.'; 7-117 text (see illustration list for unnumbered pages); [118-120] blank.

Illustrations Full-page illustrations on various single-colour backgrounds on pp. [4], [20], [31], [40], [48], [57], [62], [69], [80] and [96]. Various other illustrations.

Paper   White wove text paper and endpapers.

Binding   (219 x 142 x 9 mm): deep yellow cloth. Front cover blank. Spine lettered vertically from top in gilt: '*THE SPANISH GALLEON . TUDUR WATKINS . PETER* | *LUNN*'. Back cover blank.

Dustjacket   (216 x 469 mm): white surfaced wove paper. Front has illustration at top right on a brown background of a lamp and treasure chest, and at bottom left on a brown background of two armed men looking through a door. The remainder of the front has text on a grey stippled background: '*A new Peter* | *Lunn book* | *THE* | *SPANISH* | *GALLEON* | *An unusual* | *adventure story* | *set in the early* | *19th century* | *and packed* | *with thrills.* | *By Tudur* | *Watkins* | *with drawings* | *by Jack* | *Matthews*'. Spine lettered vertically from top: '*THE SPANISH GALLEON . TUDUR WATKINS . PETER* | *LUNN*'. Back: '*If you liked this book* | *you will like* | [advertisement for a book] | PETER LUNN | 49 CHANCERY LANE LONDON'. Front flap: '[synopsis] | [at bottom right] 8/6 net'. Back flap blank.

Later releases   Reissued in August 1950 at 3/6d.

Notes   Category: Adventure. **Scarcity**: 1.

There is a variant binding in red cloth. The back of the dustjacket has an advertisement for *The Angry Planet*. The book's synopsis states that it is the story of a BBC serial play broadcast on Children's Hour. A Dutch edition was published in Antwerp as *Het Spaans Galjoen*, and the story was also serialised in 1948 in the French magazine *Spirou* as 'Le Galion Espagnol'.

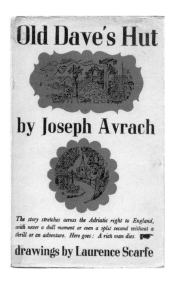

PL30   Old Dave's Hut   by Joseph Avrach, illustrated by Laurence Scarfe, December 1945, [February 1946], 8/6d.

OLD DAVE'S | HUT | AN ADVENTURE STORY | FOR CHILDREN | BY JOSEPH AVRACH | DRAWINGS BY LAURENCE SCARFE | PETER LUNN LONDON 1945

Collation   (212 x 135 mm): [1-6], 7-112 in 7 x 16pp sections coded: uncoded, B-G; 113-140 28pp section coded H.

Contents   [1] half-title: '[at right] OLD DAVE'S HUT'; [2] frontis; [3] title; [4] 'By the same author: | *The Ginger Gang* | *Peter the Sailor* | *The Parade on the Cliff* | *Ferry to Adventure* | *Timbu the Monkey*'; [5] contents; [6] imprint: 'First Edition: December 1945 | Published by Peter Lunn (Publishers) Limited | 49 Chancery Lane London | All rights reserved | Printed in Great Britain | by Dugdale Printing Limited | 122 Wardour Street | London W.1'; 7-140 text (see illustration list for unnumbered pages).

Illustrations	Full-page illustrations on various single-colour backgrounds on pp. [2], [22], [35], [43], [53], [73], [77], [94], [118] and [139]. Various other illustrations on single-colour backgrounds.
Paper	White wove text paper and endpapers.
Binding	(218 x 140 x 9 mm): red cloth. Front cover blank. Spine lettered vertically from top in gilt: 'JOSEPH AVRACH: OLD DAVE'S HUT [at bottom] PETER LUNN'. Back cover blank.
Dustjacket	(219 x 507 mm): thick white wove paper. Front: 'Old Dave's Hut	[illustration on a red scallop-edged background of buildings by the sea]	by Joseph Avrach	[illustration on a red scallop-edged background of town with memorial and church]	*The story stretches across the Adriatic right to England,*	*with never a dull moment or even a split second without a*	*thrill or an adventure. Here goes: A rich man dies.* [device of hand pointing to right]	drawings by Laurence Scarfe'. Spine lettered vertically from top: 'JOSEPH AVRACH . OLD DAVE'S HUT . PETER LUNN'. Back: 'Other children's books	published by	PETER LUNN	include:	[advertisements for five books]	PETER LUNN	49 CHANCERY LANE LONDON'. Front flap has a synopsis, continuing the text on the front cover, with price at bottom right (clipped on the copy described). Back flap blank.
Notes	Category: Adventure. **Scarcity:** 3.
	The back of the dustjacket had advertisements for *The Ginger Gang, Ferry to Adventure, The Parade on the Cliff, The Spanish Galleon* and *The Angry Planet*.

PL31 Lilybelle written and illustrated by William and Brenda Stobbs, n.d., [March 1946], 7/6d.

	LILYBELLE	*The Story of Captain Grimm*	*and the gay, game s.s. Lilybelle*	[illustration]	by	William and Brenda Stobbs	[tapered rule]	PETER LUNN
Collation	(258 x 203 mm): [1-4] 4pp section; [5-20] in 2 x 8pp sections; [21-44] 24pp section. All sections uncoded.
Contents	[1] half-title: 'LILYBELLE	[illustration]'; [2] imprint: '[at bottom] *Published by Peter Lunn (Publishers) Ltd*	*49 Chancery Lane London*	*All rights reserved*	*Printed by Keliner Hudson & Kearns Ltd*	*Hatfields Stamford Street SE 1*'; [3] title; [4-43] text; [44] illustration.
Illustrations	Full-page coloured illustrations on pp. [5], [9], [13], [15], [19], [39], and [41]. Full-page black and white illustrations on pp. [21], [27], [28], [33], [35], [36], [40] and [44].
Paper	White wove surfaced text paper, White wove endpapers.
Binding	(264 x 205 x 6 mm): beige cloth. Front cover has illustration of two ships at bottom right. Spine and back cover blank.
Copy consulted	BL.
Notes	Category: Picture. **Scarcity:** 5.
	It is not stated how William and Brenda Stobbs collaborated on this book, although the illustrations are clearly in William's style.

PL32 The Man with the Red Umbrella written and illustrated by R. A. Brandt, March 1946, [April 1946], 8/6d.

The Man | with the Red Umbrella | *A mysterious story written and illustrated by* | R.A.BRANDT | PETER LUNN | *London 1946*

Collation   (197 x 156 mm): [1-6], 7-96 in 6 x 16pp uncoded sections.

Contents   [1] half-title: 'THE MAN WITH THE RED UMBRELLA'; [2] frontis., reproducing illustration on p.[75]; [3] title; [4] imprint: 'First published in March 1946 by │ BY PETER LUNN (PUBLISHERS) LIMITED │ 49 Chancery Lane London WC2 │ *All rights reserved* │ Printed by │ H.O.LOESCHER LTD. │ 175 Regent Street London W1'; [5] contents; [6] illustration; 7-96 text (see illustration list for unnumbered pages).

Illustrations   Full-page illustrations on pp. [2], [6], [9], [13], [17], [27], [35], [41], [49], [61], [75] and [91].

Paper   White wove text paper and endpapers.

Binding   (201 x 161 x 9 mm): pale blue cloth. Front cover has an illustration at bottom right of a man (stamped in black), holding an umbrella (stamped in red). Spine lettered vertically from top in gilt: 'THE MAN WITH THE RED UMBRELLA R.A.BRANDT [at bottom] PETER LUNN'. Back cover blank.

Copy consulted   BL.

Notes   Category: Picture. **Scarcity:** 4.

PL33   The Story of Titania and Oberon   by Jo Manton, illustrated by Phyllis Bray, September 1945, [April 1946], 4/6d.

[all in script] The Story of │ Titania │ and │ Oberon │ [all in type] *from A Mid-summer Night's Dream by Shakespeare* │ [at left] pictures by │ [in script] Phyllis Bray [at right, in type] *told by* │ [in script] Jo Manton

Collation   (167 x 220 mm): [1-28] 28 pp uncoded section.

Contents   [1] title; [2-28] text; verso of front free endpaper has imprint in blue: '[illustration] │ A PETER LUNN BOOK │ All Rights Reserved │ First Edition September 1945 │ Published by Peter Lunn (Publishers) Ltd │ Forty-nine Chancery Lane London │ Printed in Great Britain by │ Dugdale Printing Limited 122 Wardour Street London'.

Illustrations   Full-page coloured illustrations on all pages, some integrated with text panels. The front pastedown and the recto of the front free endpaper has a double-page coloured illustration with a man seated on a rock overlooking the sea at left and a mermaid astride a sea-creature at right. The recto of the back free endpaper has an illustration in blue and blue-green. The verso of the back free endpaper and back pastedown has a double-page coloured illustration of a flying fairy carrying a naked child against a landscape of trees, flowers, river and mountains.

Paper   White wove text paper and endpapers. Page edges and cover boards trimmed flush.

Binding   (167 x 220 x 4 mm): boards and textile strip for spine all covered with illustrated paper. Front cover is lettered in white on a red background: 'Titania and Oberon │ [coloured illustration in oval panel of a winged fairy and a man with a donkey's head, under a canopy of flowers] │ [at bottom left] a Peter Lunn book'. Spine blank. Back cover has a pattern of flowers and insects in white on a red background, signed 'Phyllis Bray', overlaid within a white rectangular panel by: '[synopsis] │ 4s. 6d. net'.

Copy consulted   BL.

Notes   Category: Classic/Picture. **Scarcity:** 4.

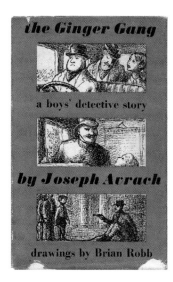

PL34 The Ginger Gang second edition, by Joseph Avrach, illustrated by Brian Robb, May 1946, 6/-.

THE GINGER GANG | A DETECTIVE STORY | FOR CHILDREN | JOSEPH AVRACH | [illustration] | ILLUSTRATED BY | BRIAN ROBB | PETER LUNN | 1946

Collation (216 x 139 mm): [1-6], 7-127, [128] in 8 x 16pp uncoded sections.

Contents [1] half-title: '[at right] THE GINGER GANG'; [2] frontis; [3] title; [4] imprint: 'First published in October 1943 | Second edition May 1946 | by Peter Lunn (Publishers) Ltd | 49 Chancery Lane London W C 2 | All rights reserved | Printed in Great Britain | by Kennerley Press Ltd | 1-4 Britannia Walk City Road London'; [5] contents; [6] blank; 7-127 text; [128] blank.

Illustrations Full-page illustration on p. [2]. Various other illustrations.

Paper White wove text paper and endpapers.

Binding (221 x 143 x 8 mm): orange-red cloth. Front cover stamped at bottom with illustration of a boy striding along a street. Spine lettered vertically from top in black: 'THE GINGER GANG BY JOSEPH AVRACH [at bottom] PETER LUNN'. Back cover blank.

Dustjacket (222 x 471 mm): white wove paper. Front and spine are printed on a uniform brown background. Front: 'The Ginger Gang | [illustration on white panel of two men and girl in a car] | a boys' detective story | [illustration in white panel of policeman and child] | by Joseph Avrach | [illustration in white panel of man pointing a gun at some children] | drawings by Brian Robb'. Spine lettered vertically from top: 'The Ginger Gang by Joseph Avrach PETER LUNN'. Back has an advertisement for a book. Front flap: '[synopsis] | [at bottom right] 6s.'. Back flap. 'Other | Peter Lunn | books | for | children | [advertisements for five books]'.

Notes Category: Adventure. Scarcity: 3.

The back of the dustjacket has an advertisement for *The Angry Planet*. The back flap has advertisements for *Peter the Sailor*, *The Parade on the Cliff*, *Old Dave's Hut*, *Crooked Lane* and *Timbu the Monkey*. This is a new edition of PL2 in a different format and with new illustrations. The book was published in French under the title *La Bande Coquelicot* (literally, 'The Poppy Gang') by Tissot in 1946.

PL35 **The Story of a Tree** by R. A. Brandt and Stephen Macfarlane, April 1946, [May 1946], 6/-.

[in script] *R.A.Brandt and Stephen MacFarlane* | THE STORY OF A TREE | [in script] *Peter Lunn (Publishers) Limited* [all on a full-page green background silhouette illustration]

Collation (196 x 255 mm): [1-28] 28pp uncoded section. The section is sewn into the binding and there are no free endpapers.

Contents [1-2] blank; [3] title; [4-26] text; [27] blank; [28] imprint: 'FIRST PUBLISHED IN APRIL 1946 | BY PETER LUNN (PUBLISHERS) LIMITED | FORTY-NINE CHANCERY LANE LONDON | PRINTED IN GREAT BRITAIN BY | DUGDALE PRINTING LIMITED | 122 WARDOUR STREET | LONDON W.1 | *ALL RIGHTS RESERVED*'.

Illustrations Full-page colour illustrations on pp. [6], [8], [10], [13], [16], [19], [21] and [23]. Dull green silhouette illustrations as background to text on other pages.

Paper White wove text paper and endpapers.

Binding (203 x 260 x 5 mm): yellow cloth. Front cover has a green silhouette illustration of a tree, bird and mouse at right. Spine and back cover blank.

Copy consulted BL.

Later releases Reissued in August 1950 at 2/6d.

Notes Category: Picture. Scarcity: 5.

Brandt was responsible for the illustrations for this book, and they earned him the News Chronicle Award for a New Illustrator.

PL36 **Why The Sea is Salt** and other fairy stories illustrated by R. A. Brandt, March 1946, [May 1946], 10/6d.

A beautiful old Norse folk tale | WHY THE SEA | IS SALT | and other fairy stories | with many drawings | by R.A.Brandt | a Peter Lunn book | 1946

Collation (275 x 216 mm): [1-8] 8pp section; 9-56 in 3 x 16pp sections; 57-64, [i-iv], 65-72 20pp section; 73-104 in 2 x 16pp sections; 105-124 20pp section . All sections uncoded.

Contents [1] half-title: 'Why the Sea is Salt'; [2] frontis., reproducing illustration on p. [33]; [3] title; [4] imprint: '*First published in March 1946* | *by Peter Lunn (Publishers) Ltd* | *49 Chancery Lane London* | *All rights reserved* | *Printed in Great Britain* | *by Kennerley Press Ltd* | *1-4 Britannia Walk City Road London*'; [5] contents; [6] blank; [7] list of illustrations; [8] blank; 9-124 text (see illustration list for unnumbered pages).

Illustrations Full-page illustrations on various single-colour backgrounds on pp. [2], [13], [25], [33], [67], [77] and [109]. Double-page coloured illustration on pp. [ii-iii] (pp. [i] and [iv] blank). Various other illustrations.

Paper White wove text paper. White wove surfaced paper for endpapers and double page illustration.

Binding (275 x 216 x 13 mm): pictorial board covers, with front and back boards reproducing the coloured illustration on pp. [i-iv], of an underwater scene with various varieties of sea-life, and a kettle firing a shower of salt from its spout into a fish's mouth. Front lettered within a white panel over illustration: 'WHY THE SEA IS SALT | AND OTHER FAIRY TALES | A PETER LUNN BOOK'. Spine lettered vertically from top: 'Why the Sea is Salt and other Fairy Stories [at bottom] Peter Lunn'.

Copy consulted BL.

Notes Category: Fairy. **Scarcity**: 5.

There is a variant binding in green cloth with gilt titling on the spine and an illustration stamped in gilt on front cover. Contains: Mother Holle; Not a Pin to Choose between them; King Grisly-Beard; The Nose; Hans in Luck; Marko the Rich; Ashputtel; Snowdrop; The Water of Life; The Three Aunts; Why the Sea is Salt; The Lad who went to the North Wind; Boots and the Troll; The Blue Belt; The Princess on the Glass Hill; The Salad; The Sorcerer's House; The Giant Wizard with the Twelve Heads; The Best Wish.

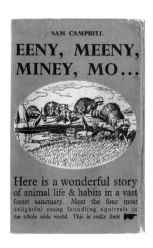

PL37 Eeny, Meeny, Miney Mo by Sam Campbell, [illustrated by Will Forrest], April 1946, [July 1946], 7/6d.

EENY, MEENY, | MINEY MO | BY SAM CAMPBELL | [illustration] | PETER LUNN | LONDON | 1946

Collation (185 x 118 mm): [1-6], 7-160 in 10 x 16pp sections; 161-168 8pp section; 169-183, [184] 16pp section. All sections uncoded.

Contents [1] half-title: '[at right] EENY MEENY MINEY MO'; [2] frontis; [3] title; [4] imprint: 'First published in April 1946 by | PETER LUNN (PUBLISHERS) LIMITED | 49 CHANCERY LANE LONDON | All rights reserved. | MADE IN GREAT BRITAIN | Printed by | W. S. CAINES LTD | Andover House | Plaistow London E.13'; [5] contents; [6] 'To | DUKE'; 7-183 text; [184] blank.

Illustrations full-page illustration on p. [2]. Various other illustrations.

Paper White wove text paper and endpapers.

Binding (189 x 124 x 12 mm): blue cloth. Front cover blank. Spine lettered vertically from top in gilt: 'EENY, MEENY, MINEY, MO: CAMPBELL [at bottom] PETER LUNN'. Back cover blank.

Dustjacket (190 x 463 mm): white wove paper. Front printed on a uniform blue background: 'SAM CAMPBELL | EENY, MEENY, | MINEY, MO... | [illustration within a white oval panel of five racoons crossing water] | Here is a wonderful story | of animal life & habits in a vast | forest sanctuary. Meet the four most | delightful young foundling squirrels in | the whole wide world. This is really their [device of hand pointing to right]'. Spine lettered vertically from top: 'EENY MEENY MINEY MO: SAM CAMPBELL PETER | LUNN'. Back: 'Sam Campbell's | other books | [advertisements for two books] | PETER LUNN | 49 Chancery Lane London'. Front flap: '[synopsis, continuing the text from the front cover] | [at right] 7s. 6d. net.'. Back flap blank.

Notes Category: Nature. **Scarcity:** 4.

The back of the dustjacket has advertisements for *The Island Sanctuary* and 'How's Inky?' (i.e. *How is Inky?*). This book was first published in America as *Eeny, Meeny, Miney, Mo–and Still-Mo* (Bobbs-Merrill, 1945).

PL38 The Angry Planet second edition, by John Keir Cross, illustrated by Robin Jacques, July 1946, 8/6d.

THE ANGRY PLANET | An authentic first-hand account of a journey to Mars | in the space-ship *Albatross*, compiled from notes and | records by various members of the expedition, and now | assembled (together with illustrations) and edited by | JOHN KEIR CROSS | *from manuscripts made available by* | STEPHEN MACFARLANE | *The illustrations are by* | ROBIN JACQUES | PETER LUNN LONDON | 1946

Collation (183 x 121 mm): [1-8], 9-16 16pp section coded AA at left and A at right; 17-192 in 11 x 16pp sections coded B-K, uncoded, M; 193-216 24pp section coded N.

Contents [1] half-title: '[at right] THE ANGRY PLANET'; [2] frontis; [3] title; [4] imprint: '*First published in October 1945* | *by Peter Lunn (Publishers) Limited* | *49 Chancery Lane London* | *New edition July 1946* | *All rights reserved* | *Printed in Great Britain* | *by* | H. O. LOESCHER LTD | *70 Brewer Street WI*'; [5] 'THE STORY | [contents]'; [6] 'TO AUDREY'; [7] 'IMPORTANT | EDITOR'S NOTE ON THE | ILLUSTRATIONS | [note, signed 'J.K.C.' at end] | [start of illustration list] | [at right] *Continued overleaf*'; [8] 'ILLUSTRATIONS (*continued*) | [rest of illustration list]'; 9-216 text (see illustration list for unnumbered pages).

Illustrations Full-page illustrations on pp. [2], [25], [59], [73], [123], [161], [169], [173] and [185]. Various other illustrations.

Paper White wove text paper and endpapers.

Binding (190 x 126 x 14 mm): orange-red cloth. Front cover blank. Spine lettered vertically from top in gilt: 'THE ANGRY PLANET . KEIR CROSS [lettered horizontally at bottom] PETER | LUNN'. Back cover blank.

Dustjacket (192 x 432 mm): the dustjacket is otherwise the same as that of the first edition.

Later releases [?WFL] (see entry for PL28).

Notes Category: Adventure. **Scarcity:** 3.

See Notes for the first edition (PL28).

PL39 The Owl and the Pussycat by John Keir Cross, illustrated by Robin Jacques, May 1946, [July 1946], 7/6d.

[The title is spilt over two pages, inset into two rounded rectangular panels against a double-page illustration]
[on right-hand page] The Owl | and the | Pussycat | by | John | Keir Cross
[on left-hand page] Drawings | by | Robin Jacques | published by | Peter Lunn | London 1946

Collation (185 x 117 mm): [1-8], 9-158, [159-160] in 5 x 32pp sections coded A-E on the first, and A*-E* on the ninth, page of each section.

Contents [1] half-title: 'THE OWL AND THE PUSSYCAT'; [2-3] title; [4] imprint: 'First published in May 1946 by | PETER LUNN (PUBLISHERS) LIMITED | 49 Chancery Lane London | All rights reserved | Made in Great Britain | Printed by | H. O. LOESCHER LIMITED | 70 Brewer Street London W1'; [5] contents; [6] '[illustration] Look once, look twice, | Look round about - | And in a trice | What's In is Out!...'; [7] part I contents; [8] blank; 9-62 part I text; [63] part II contents; [64] blank; 65-120 part II text; [121] part III contents; [122] blank; 123-158 part III text; [159-160] blank. (See illustration list for other unnumbered pages.)

Illustrations Full-page illustrations on pp. [21], [25], [39], [83], [91], [129] and [145]. Various other illustrations.

Paper White wove text paper and endpapers.

Binding (188 x 122 x 10 mm): red cloth. Front cover blank. Spine lettered vertically from top in gilt: 'THE OWL & THE PUSSYCAT * JOHN KEIR CROSS PETER LUNN'. Back cover blank.

Dustjacket (189 x 395 mm): thick pale green wove paper. The front is lettered over an illustration in orange of a man holding a guitar with two girls (a mirror image of the illustration on p. [39]): 'The Owl & the Pussycat | a strange story for children | written by | John | Keir | Cross | with | drawings | by | Robin | Jacques'. Spine lettered vertically from top: 'The Owl and the Pussycat * John Keir Cross [at bottom] Peter Lunn'. Back: 'Other Peter Lunn books | also by John Keir Cross | [advertisements for five books] | PETER LUNN | 49 Chancery Lane London'. Front flap: '[synopsis] | [at bottom right] 7s 6d net'. Back flap blank.

Notes Category: Adventure. Scarcity: 3.

The back of the dustjacket has advertisements for *The Angry Planet*, *Studio J Investigates*, *Detectives in Greasepaint*, *Mr Bosanko* and *The White Magic* (the last of which was published by John Westhouse). This book was published in America by Coward-McCann in 1947 as *The Other Side of Green Hills*.

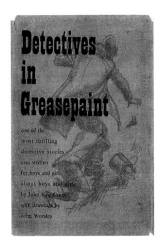

PL40 Detectives In Greasepaint second edition, by John Keir Cross, illustrated by John Worsley, May 1946, [August 1946], 6/-.

[double-page title with text surrounded by illustrations of the heads and names of seven children] DETECTIVES IN GREASEPAINT | by John Keir Cross | drawings by | John Worsley | published by | Peter Lunn | London | 1946

Collation (185 x 123 mm): [1-9], 10-128 in 8 x 16pp sections coded: uncoded, B-H; 129-139, [140] 12pp section coded K.

Contents [1] half-title: '[at right] DETECTIVES IN GREASEPAINT'; [2-3] title; [4] blank; [5] 'THE STORY | [contents] | *Also pictures in the text by* | JOHN WORSLEY'; [6] imprint: 'FIRST PUBLISHED BY | PETER LUNN (PUBLISHERS) LIMITED | IN MAY 1944 | *REVISED EDITION MAY 1946* | *All rights reserved* | Printed in Great Britain by | WEST BROTHERS, MITCHAM'; [7] 'To | *Shirley Sleigh*'; [8] '*Other books by John Keir Cross* | THE ANGRY PLANET | STUDIO J INVESTIGATES | MR. BOSANKO | THE OWL AND THE PUSSY CAT | WHITE MAGIC'; 9-139 text (see illustration list for unnumbered pages); [140] blank.

Illustrations Full-page illustrations on pp. [13], [34], [37], [45], [48], [81], [89], [100], [117] and [126]. Various other illustrations.

Paper White wove text paper and endpapers.

Binding (192 x 130 x 10 mm): blue cloth. Front cover stamped in gilt with illustration of two masks. Spine lettered vertically from top in gilt: 'DETECTIVES IN GREASEPAINT [at bottom, publisher's PL device]'. Back cover blank.

Dustjacket (192 x 420 mm): thick grey-green wove paper. Front is lettered on a background illustration in red of a boy rugby-tackling a man, reproducing illustration on p. [126]: 'Detectives | in | Greasepaint | one of the | most thrilling | detective stories | ever written | for boys and girls | by John Keir Cross | with drawings by | John Worsley'. Spine lettered vertically from top: 'DETECTIVES IN GREASEPAINT * Keir Cross [at bottom] PETER | LUNN'. Back: 'OTHER BOOKS FOR BOYS AND GIRLS | PUBLISHED BY | PETER LUNN | [advertisements for six books] | PETER LUNN | FORTY NINE CHANCERY LANE. LONDON WC2'. Front flap: [synopsis] | [at bottom right] 6s | *net*'. Back flap blank.

Notes Category: Adventure. **Scarcity:** 2.

The back of the dustjacket has advertisements for *Studio J Investigates*, *Mr Bosanko*, *The Angry Planet*, *The Owl and the Pussycat*, *The White Magic* (published by Westhouse) and *The Story of a Tree*. This is a new edition of PL12, under the author's real name, in a different format and with different illustrations. It features the same group of children as in *Studio J Investigates* and *Mr Bosanko*.

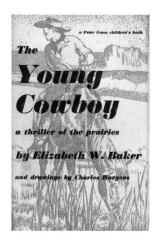

PL41 The Young Cowboy by E. W. Baker, illustrated by Charles Hargens, June 1946, [September 1946], 6/-.

THE YOUNG COWBOY | E. W. BAKER | [illustration] | ILLUSTRATED BY CHARLES HARGENS | PETER LUNN | LONDON | 1946

Collation (181 x 120 mm): [i-ii], 1-30 32pp section; 31-66 36pp section; 67-130 in 2 x 32pp sections; 131-170 40pp section; 171-194, [195-198] 28pp section. All sections uncoded. Pages [197-198] form the back pastedown. The is no back free endpaper.

Contents [i-ii] blank; [1] half-title: '[at right] THE YOUNG COWBOY'; [2] frontis., reproducing illustration on p. [51]; [3] title; [4] imprint: '*First published in June 1946 by* | PETER LUNN (PUBLISHERS) LTD | *49 Chancery Lane London WC2* | *All rights reserved* | *Printed in Great Britain by* | F. R. BRITTON AND COMPANY LIMITED | *Shenton Street London SE15*'; [5] contents; [6] 'TO MY NEPHEWS | Bill and Bobby, Stan, Brookes and Glynn'; 7-194 text (see illustration list for unnumbered pages); [195-198] blank.

Illustrations Full-page illustrations on single-colour backgrounds on pp. [2], [15], [51], [89] and [167]. Various other illustrations.

Paper White wove text paper and endpapers.

Binding (186 x 128 x 11 mm): pale orange-brown cloth. Front cover has illustration stamped in brown at bottom right of a cowboy on a horse, which is cropping grass. Spine lettered vertically from top in brown: '*The Young Cowboy . Baker* [at bottom] *Peter Lunn*'. Back cover blank.

Dustjacket (185 x 407 mm): white wove paper. Front is lettered against a background illustration in red of a cowboy on a horse, which is cropping grass, in a prairie landscape. Front: '[at right] *a Peter Lunn children's book* | The | Young | Cowboy | *a thriller of the prairies* | *by* Elizabeth W. Baker | *and drawings by Charles Hargens*'. Spine lettered vertically from top: '*The Young Cowboy . Baker* [at bottom] *Peter Lunn*'. Back: '*Other Peter Lunn* | *thrillers* | *for children* | [advertisements for five books] | *Peter Lunn* | *49 Chancery Lane London*'. Front flap: '[synopsis] | [at bottom right] 6s'. Back flap blank.

Notes Category: Adventure. Scarcity: 4.

The advertisement for this book on the back flap of *Song of Arizona* prices it at 6/9d. The back of the dustjacket has advertisements for *The Angry Planet, The Spanish Galleon, The Phantom, Old Dave's Hut* and *The Hunting of Zakaroff*. The book was first published in America, as *Stocky, Boy of West Texas* (John C. Winston, 1945).

PL42 Night Cargoes by Nicholas Cavanagh, illustrated by William Stobbs, September 1946, 8/6d.

NIGHT CARGOES | *a smuggling story* | NICHOLAS CAVANAGH | DRAWINGS BY | WILLIAM STOBBS | PETER LUNN | LONDON 1946

Collation (185 x 122 mm): [1-8], 9-224 in 14 x 16pp sections coded: uncoded, B-H, uncoded, K-O.

Contents [1] half-title: '[at right] NIGHT CARGOES'; [2] frontis., reproducing illustration on p. [147]; [3] title; [4] imprint: '*First published in September 1946 by* | PETER LUNN (PUBLISHERS) LTD | 49 CHANCERY LANE | LONDON WC2 | *All rights reserved* | TO | MICHAEL | *Printed in Great Britain by* | SAMUEL SIDDERS & SON LTD | 115 SALUSBURY ROAD | LONDON NW6'; [5-6] illustration followed by contents; [7-8], 9-224 text (page [8] blank). See illustration list for unnumbered pages.

Illustrations Full-page illustrations on single-colour backgrounds on pp. [2], [13], [29], [55], [75], [85], [115], [147], [185] and [221]. Various other illustrations on single-colour backgrounds.

Paper White wove text paper and endpapers.

Binding (190 x 128 x 15 mm): beige cloth. Front cover has illustration of four pistols stamped in gilt; Spine lettered vertically from top in gilt: 'Night Cargoes * Cavanagh [at bottom] A Peter Lunn Book'. Back cover blank.

Dustjacket (188 x 442 mm): white wove paper. Front, spine and back are printed on a uniform beige background. Front cover: 'Night Cargoes | [illustration in red of boy on cliff] | [partly overlying the upper illustration] a thrilling story of smugglers in | Nelson's time: by Nicholas Cavanagh | with drawings by William Stobbs | [illustration in black of boy in sea cutting a mooring-rope]'. Spine lettered vertically from top 'NIGHT CARGOES * CAVANAGH A PETER LUNN BOOK'. Back cover: 'Other titles in Peter Lunn | Adventure | yarns for boys and girls | [advertisements for seven books] | PETER LUNN | 49 Chancery Lane London'. Front flap: '[synopsis] | For children between the ages | of 8 and 16 years. | [at right] 8s 6d'. Back flap blank.

Later releases [WFL].

Notes Category: Adventure. **Scarcity:** 4.

The back of the dustjacket has advertisements for *Studio J Investigates, Mr Bosanko, Detectives in Greasepaint, The Owl and the Pussycat, The Lost Mountain, The Haunted Island* and *Old Dave's Hut. Sister to the Mermaid* is a sequel to this book. In 1952, *Night Cargoes* was republished by Longmans, Green & Co in a 'concise' edition, illustrated by Alma K. Lee.

PL43 The Lost Mountain by John Sylvester, illustrated by Francis Gower, July 1946, [September 1946], 8/6d.

the Lost Mountain | a strange adventure | JOHN SYLVESTER | with drawings by Francis Gower | PETER LUNN | LONDON | 1946

Collation (185 x 123 mm): [1-6], 7-207, [208] in 13 x 16pp sections. All sections uncoded.

Contents [1] half-title: '[at right] THE LOST MOUNTAIN'; [2] frontis; [3] title; [4] imprint: 'First published in July 1946 | BY PETER LUNN (PUBLISHERS) LIMITED | 49 Chancery Lane London | All rights reserved | Printed in Great Britain | BY W. S. CAINES LIMITED | 193 Balaam Street London E13'; [5] '[illustration] | [contents] | and many illustrations | by Francis Gower'; [6] 'FOR | JOHN ANTHONY'; 7-207 text (see illustration list for unnumbered pages); [208] blank.

Illustrations Full-page illustrations on various single-colour backgrounds on pp. [2], [9], [75], [87], [111], [135], [153], [155], [163], [197] (duplicating p. [135] against a different background colour) and [201]. Various other illustrations.

Paper White wove text paper and endpapers.

Binding (190 x 130 x 14 mm): green cloth. Front cover stamped with illustration of man surrounded by armed fighters. Spine lettered vertically from top: 'THE LOST MOUNTAIN JOHN SYLVESTER PETER LUNN'. Back cover blank.

Dustjacket (191 x 481 mm): white wove paper. Front and spine are printed on a uniform grey background. Front: '[illustration at left of man surrounded by armed fighters] [illustration at right of parachutists descending] | the Lost Mountain | [illustration in red of man in bowler hat on a horse approaching armed fighters] | by JOHN SYLVESTER | *a children's adventure story*'. Spine lettered vertically from top: '[in red] THE LOST MOUNTAIN [in black] JOHN SYLVESTER [at bottom, in red] PETER LUNN'. Back: '*Amongst other stories of* | [in red] strange adventures | *published by Peter Lunn* | *are the following titles* | [advertisements for nine books] | [in red] PETER LUNN | 49 Chancery Lane London'. Front flap: '[synopsis] | [at right] 8s. 6d.'. Back flap blank.

Later releases WFL.

Notes Category: Adventure. Scarcity: 4.

The repeated illustration on p. [197] appears to be a mistake. The story-line at that point suggests it should have repeated the frontispiece illustration. The back cover of the dustjacket has advertisements for *The Phantom, The Angry Planet, The Man with the Red Umbrella, Old Dave's Hut, The Parade on the Cliff, Crooked Lane, The Ginger Gang, Night Cargoes* and *The Haunted Island*.

PL44 Crooked Lane by Joseph Avrach, illustrated by Leonard Rosoman, August 1946, [October 1946], 8/6d.

CROOKED | LANE | JOSEPH AVRACH | WITH | DRAWINGS BY | LEONARD ROSOMAN | PETER LUNN | LONDON | 1946

Collation (182 x 117 mm): [1-6], 7-160 in 5 x 32pp sections coded: uncoded, B-E; 161-177, [178-180] 20pp section coded F.

Contents [1] half-title: '[at right] CROOKED LANE'; [2] frontis., reproducing illustration on p. 171; [3] title; [4] imprint: '*First published in August 1946 by* | PETER LUNN (PUBLISHERS) LTD | *49 Chancery Lane London* | *All rights reserved* | *Printed in Great Britain by* | *Samuel Sidders & Son Ltd* | *115 Salusbury Road* | *London N W 6*'; [5] contents; [6] blank; 7-177, [178] text (see illustration list for unnumbered pages); [179-180] blank.

Illustrations Full-page illustrations on pp. [2], 8, 15, 26, 32, [44], [48], 65, 90, 103, 119, [130], 140, 149, 162 and 171.

Paper White wove text paper and endpapers.

Binding (187 x 123 x 13 mm): deep yellow cloth. Front cover stamped in purple at bottom right with illustration of a house in a wood. Spine lettered vertically from top in purple: 'Crooked Lane * Joseph Avrach A Peter Lunn Book'. Back cover blank.

Dustjacket (188 x 442 mm): white wove paper. Front, spine and back are uniformly coloured beige, with the colour overlapping about 9mm on to the front and back flaps. Front has an illustration at top left, in brown, of a man in a bowler hat blowing smoke into a boy's face, and another in brown at bottom right of two men seated at a table. Front: '[at top right] Crooked | Lane | by Joseph | Avrach', '[at bottom left] *a children's* | *thriller :* | *drawings* | *by Leonard* | *Rosoman*'. Spine lettered vertically from top: 'CROOKED LANE * JOSEPH AVRACH [at bottom] PETER LUNN'. Back: '*Amongst other stories of* | strange adventures | *published by Peter Lunn* | *are the following titles:* | [advertisements for eight books] | PETER LUNN | 49 Chancery Lane London'. Front flap: '[synopsis] | [at right] 8s 6d net'. Back flap blank.

Notes **Category**: Adventure. **Scarcity**: 4.

The back of the dustjacket has advertisements for *The Phantom, The Angry Planet, The Man with the Red Umbrella, Old Dave's Hut, The Parade on the Cliff, The Ginger Gang, Night Cargoes* and *The Haunted Island*.

PL45 How is Inky? by Sam Campbell, illustrated by Bob Kuhn, 1946, [October 1946], 6/-.

HOW IS INKY? | SAM CAMPBELL | [illustration] | PETER LUNN | LONDON | 1946

Collation (185 x 119 mm): [1-8], 9-112 in 7 x 16pp sections; 113-132 20pp section. All sections uncoded.

Contents [1] half-title: '[at right] HOW IS INKY?'; [2] frontis; [3] title; [4] imprint: 'FIRST PUBLISHED IN GREAT BRITAIN | BY PETER LUNN (PUBLISHERS) LIMITED | 49 CHANCERY LANE LONDON | *All rights reserved* | MADE IN GREAT BRITAIN | *Printed by* W. S. CAINES LTD. | *Andover House Plaistow London E13*'; [5] '[illustration] | [contents] | *and many drawings by* | Bob Kuhn'; [6] blank; [7] '*other books by* | Sam Campbell | THE ISLAND SANCTUARY | EENY, MEENY, MINEY, MO'; [8] blank; 9-132 text.

Illustrations Full-page illustration on p. [2]. Various other illustrations.

Paper White wove text paper and endpapers.

Binding (190 x 125 x 11 mm): blue cloth. Front cover blank. Spine lettered vertically from top in gilt: 'HOW IS INKY? SAM CAMPBELL [at bottom] PETER LUNN'. Back cover blank.

Dustjacket (191 x 454 mm): white wove paper. Front and spine are lettered against a uniform grey background. Front: 'How Is Inky? | [illustration in red of a porcupine eating a book] | A charming real-life animal story | about Inky the naughty porcupine | by Sam | Campbell | with | drawings | by | Bob Kuhn [illustration at bottom right of porcupine and a pair of boots]'. Spine lettered vertically from top 'HOW IS INKY? SAM CAMPBELL [at bottom] PETER LUNN'. Back: 'Sam Campbell's | other books | [advertisements for two books] | Both Published by | PETER LUNN | 49 Chancery Lane London'. Front flap: '[synopsis] | [at right] 6/- net.'. Back flap blank.

Notes Category: Nature. Scarcity: 2.

The back cover of the dustjacket has advertisements for *The Island Sanctuary* and *Eeny, Meeny, Miney, Mo*. This book was first published in America as *How's Inky?* (Bobbs-Merrill, 1943).

PL46 Studio J Investigates   second edition, by John Keir Cross, illustrated by John Worsley, August 1946, [October 1946], 6/-.

[double-page title with text surrounded by illustrations of the heads and names of seven children] STUDIO 'J' INVESTIGATES | by John Keir Cross | drawings by | John Worsley | *published by* | Peter Lunn | London | 1946

Collation (183 x 120 mm): [1-8], 9-143, [144] in 9 x 16pp uncoded sections.

Contents [1] half-title: '[at right] STUDIO J INVESTIGATES'; [2-3] title; [4] imprint: '*First published in April 1944 by* | PETER LUNN (PUBLISHERS) LIMITED | 49 Chancery Lane London | Second edition August 1946 | All rights reserved | Printed in Great Britain by | SAMUEL SIDDERS & SON LTD | 115 Salusbury Road London NW6'; [5] '[contents] | and many illustrations by | JOHN WORSLEY'; [6] 'For | JENNYANYDOTS | or | ADAM'; [7] 'Other books by | John Keir Cross | Detectives in Greasepaint | Mr. Bosanko | The Angry Planet | The Owl and the Pussycat | The White Magic | The Story of a Tree'; [8] frontis; 9-143 text (see illustration list for unnumbered pages); [144] blank.

Illustrations Full-page illustrations on pp. [8], [15], [19], [39], [59], [71], [87], [97], [121] and [139]. Double-page illustration on pp. [114-115]. Various other illustrations.

Paper   White wove text paper and endpapers.

Binding   (189 x 127 x 11 mm): red cloth. Front cover blank. Spine lettered vertically from top in gilt: 'STUDIO "J" INVESTIGATES by John Keir Cross [at bottom] PETER LUNN'. Back cover blank.

Dustjacket   (188 x 483 mm): thick orange wove paper. Front has text integrated with an illustration at top right of a boy watching a man opening a door in a fence, an illustration at lower left in blue of a shed, and an illustration at bottom right of a boy looking at cinematic equipment. Front: 'A Peter Lunn Book | JOHN | KEIR CROSS | Studio | 'J' | investigates | a thrilling spy | story for boys and | girls by the author of | "Detectives in Greasepaint" | with drawings by | John Worsley'. Spine lettered vertically from top: 'STUDIO "J" INVESTIGATES * KEIR CROSS [at bottom] PETER LUNN'. Back: 'Other books for boys and girls | published only by | [in blue] PETER | [in blue] LUNN | [advertisements for six books] | PETER LUNN | 49 *Chancery Lane London*'. Front flap has synopsis, and price at bottom right (clipped on the copy described). Back flap blank.

Later releases   [WFL].

Notes   Category: Adventure. Scarcity: 3.

The back of the dustjacket has advertisements for *Night Cargoes, Mr Bosanko, Detectives in Greasepaint, The Owl and the Pussycat, The Lost Mountain* and *The Haunted Island*. This is a new edition of PL13, under the author's real name, in a different format and with different illustrations.

PL47 The Haunted Island   by E. H. Visiak, illustrated by Jack Matthews, May 1946, [October 1946], 8/6d.

THE HAUNTED ISLAND | *Being the History of an Adventure to an Island in* | *the Remote South Sea. Of a Wizard there. Of his* | *Pirate Gang; His Treasure; His Combustible; His* | *Skeleton Antic Lad. Of his Wisdom; Of his Poesy;* | *His Barbarous Cruelty; His Mighty Power. Of a* | *Volcano on the Island. And of the Ghostly Terror* | [illustration] | BY E. H. VISIAK | *Illustrated by Jack Matthews* | PETER LUNN | London 1946

Collation   (176 x 121mm): [1-6], 7-128 in 8 x 16pp sections coded: uncoded, A*, uncoded, B*, C, C*, D, D*; 129-136 8pp section coded E; 137-164 28pp section coded F.

Contents [1] half-title: 'THE HAUNTED ISLAND'; [2] frontis.; [3] title; [4] imprint: *'First published in May 1946 by* | PETER LUNN (PUBLISHERS) LIMITED | *49 Chancery Lane London* | *All rights reserved* | *Printed by* | SAMUEL SIDDERS & SON LIMITED | *115 Salusbury Road* | *London NW6';* [5] contents; [6] illustration; 7-164 text (see illustration list for unnumbered pages).

Illustrations Full-page illustrations in black on various single-colour backgrounds on pp. [2], [23], [33], [51], [79], [109], [127] and [141].

Paper White wove surfaced text paper. White wove endpapers.

Binding (180 x 127 x 9 mm): black cloth. Front cover blank. Spine lettered vertically from top in gilt: 'THE HAUNTED ISLAND * VISIAK PETER LUNN'. Back cover blank.

Dustjacket (182 x 418 mm): thick grey wove paper. Front is lettered around an illustration in red at top right of two sailing ships in combat, and an illustration in black at bottom left of two men armed with swords facing up to each other. Front: 'The | Haunted | Island | a strange | story of incredible | adventures in a South Sea island | ruled by a wizard; by E. H. VISIAK | with illustrations by JACK MATTHEWS | a new | Peter | Lunn | book'. Spine lettered vertically from top: 'THE HAUNTED ISLAND * VISIAK [at bottom] PETER LUNN'. Back cover: *'Other books published by Peter Lunn for* | children | include : | [advertisements for eight books] | Peter Lunn | 49 Chancery Lane London'. Front flap: '[synopsis] | *8s 6d'.* Back flap blank.

Later releases [WFL]. There was also a reissue in October 1950 at 3/6d, which may be the WFL issue.

Notes Category: Adventure. **Scarcity**: 3.

The back of the dustjacket advertises *The Ginger Gang, Old Dave's Hut, The Parade on the Cliff, Ferry to Adventure, Crooked Lane, The Spanish Galleon, The Angry Planet* and *The White Magic* (published by Westhouse). *The Haunted Island* was first published by Elkin Matthews in 1910.

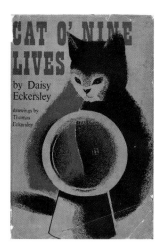

PL48 Cat O' Nine Lives by Daisy Eckersley, illustrated by Tom Eckersley, July 1946, [November 1946], 7/6d.

CAT | O' NINE LIVES | BY DAISY ECKERSLEY | WITH DRAWINGS BY | TOM ECKERSLEY | [illustration] | PETER LUNN | LONDON 1946

Collation (182 x 122 mm): [1-9], 10-96 in 6 x 16pp sections; 97-116 20pp section. All sections uncoded.

Contents [1] half-title: 'CAT O' NINE LIVES'; [2] frontis; [3] title; [4] imprint: '*First published in July 1946 by* | PETER LUNN (PUBLISHERS) LIMITED | 49 CHANCERY LANE | *All rights reserved* | *Printed in Great Britain by* | GALE AND POLDEN LIMITED | IDEAL HOUSE OXFORD CIRCUS | LONDON'; [5] contents; [6] 'TO OUR SONS | ANTHONY AND RICHARD'; [7] '*You will find several* | PICTURES | *of Cat o' Nine Lives* | by Tom Eckersley | *throughout the book*'; [8] illustration; [9], 10-116 text (see illustration list for unnumbered pages).

Illustrations Full-page illustrations in black against various single-colour backgrounds on pp. [2], [8], [13], [26], [33], [42], [55], [63], [75], [87], [95], [99] and [111]. Various other illustrations in black against single-colour backgrounds.

Paper White wove text paper and endpapers.

Binding (189 x 129 x 11 mm): pale blue cloth. Front cover stamped in gilt at bottom right with an illustration of a cat next to a brazier. Spine lettered vertically from top in gilt: 'Cat o' Nine Lives * Eckersley [at bottom] Peter Lunn'. Back cover blank.

Dustjacket (190 x 439 mm): white surfaced wove paper. Front and spine are printed against a uniform green background. Front: '[at top left, in red] CAT O' NINE | [in red] LIVES | by Daisy | Eckersley | drawings by | Thomas | Eckersley'. Front has an illustration in black and red, below and to the right of the lettering, of a cat gazing into a crystal ball. Spine lettered vertically from top: '[in red] CAT O' NINE LIVES [in black] * ECKERSLEY [at bottom, in red] PETER LUNN'. Back: 'Other books for children | published by | [in red] PETER LUNN | [advertisements for four books] | [in red] PETER LUNN | 49 *Chancery Lane London*'. Front flap: '[synopsis] | at bottom right] 7s. 6d. net'. Back flap blank.

Notes Category: Nature. Scarcity: 5.

The print-run was 5042. The back cover has advertisements for *The Man with the Red Umbrella*, *The Story of a Tree*, *The Haunted Island* and *Fairy Tales with a Twist*.

PL49 The Hunting of Zakaroff by W. B. Macmillan, illustrated by Bernard Venables, September 1946, [November 1946], 8/6d.

W. B. MACMILLAN | The Hunting | of Zakaroff | [illustration] | DRAWINGS BY | BERNARD VENABLES | PETER LUNN | LONDON 1946

Collation (183 x 118 mm): [1-6], 7-192 in 6 x 32pp sections coded: uncoded, B-E, uncoded; 193-217, [218-220] 28pp section coded G on p. 193, G* on p. 195, and G** on p. 199.

Contents   [1] half-title: 'THE HUNTING OF ZAKAROFF'; [2] frontis., reproducing illustration on p. [209]; [3] title; [4] imprint: '*First published in September 1946 by* | PETER LUNN (PUBLISHERS) LIMITED | *49 Chancery Lane London* | *All rights reserved* | *Printed in Great Britain by* | H O LOESCHER LIMITED | *70 Brewer Street London*'; [5] contents; [6] 'All *characters in this book are* | *completely imaginary and any* | *coincidence of names is unintentional*'; 7-217 text (see illustration list for unnumbered pages); [218-220] blank.

Illustrations   Full-page illustrations on pp. [2], [67], [113], [161] and [209].

Paper   White surfaced wove text paper. White wove endpapers.

Binding   (189 x 122 x 11 mm): red cloth. Front cover blank. Spine lettered vertically from top in gilt: 'The Hunting of Zakaroff W. B. MACMILLAN [at bottom] PETER LUNN'. Back cover blank.

Dustjacket   (187 x 441 mm): white wove paper. Front, spine and back are printed on a uniform orange background. The front is lettered down the left of the cover, with the words of the title in larger bold font: 'The | a Peter Lunn | Hunting | children's novel | of | of | adventure | Zakaroff | by W. B. Macmillan | with drawings | by Bernard | Venables'. The right of the front has three Illustrations. At top, two boys with a motor-bike in front of a house; in middle, two boys crossing a railway line; at bottom, two boys tying up a third blanket-covered figure. Spine lettered vertically from top: 'The Hunting of Zakaroff W. B. MACMILLAN [at bottom] PETER LUNN'. Back: 'Other books for boys and girls | published only by | PETER | LUNN | [advertisements for six books] | PETER LUNN | *49 Chancery Lane London*'. Front flap: '[synopsis] | [at bottom right] 8s 6d net'. Back flap blank.

Notes   Category: Adventure. Scarcity: 3.

The back of the dustjacket has advertisements for *Night Cargoes*, *Mr Bosanko*, *Detectives in Greasepaint*, *The Owl and the Pussycat*, *The Lost Mountain* and *The Haunted Island*.

PL50   **Black Beauty**   by Anna Sewell, illustrated by Lionel Edwards, August 1946, [November 1946], 9/6d.

Anna Sewell | Black Beauty | *illustrated by Lionel Edwards* | Peter Lunn | London 1946

Collation   (185 x 245 mm): [1-2], 3-95, [96] in 3 x 32pp uncoded sections. A leaf for the frontispiece is tipped in to the verso of the front free endpaper.

Contents	[1] title; [2] imprint: 'this edition first published in August 1946	by Peter Lunn (Publishers) Limited	49 Chancery Lane London	*all rights reserved*	printed in Great Britain by Kennerley Press Limited 1-4 Britannia Walk London N I'; 3-95, [96] text, in double columns. See illustration list for unnumbered pages (pp. 43-44 are also unnumbered).
Illustrations	Coloured frontispiece on verso of leaf tipped in to front free endpaper. Full-page illustrations on pp. [7], [9], [15], [17], [24], [30], [41], [57], [59], [75], [79], [89] and [92]. Double-page illustration on pp. [64-65]. Various other illustrations.
Paper	White wove text paper and endpapers. White surfaced wove paper for frontispiece.
Binding	(190 x 249 x 13 mm): orange-brown cloth. Front cover lettered in gilt at bottom right: 'Black Beauty'. Spine lettered vertically from top in gilt: 'BLACK BEAUTY BY ANNA SEWELL & LIONEL EDWARDS * PETER LUNN'. Back cover blank.
Dustjacket	(193 x 693 mm): white surfaced wove paper. All of dustjacket is printed against a uniform yellow background. Front: '[at left] THE WORLD-FAMOUS HORSE	CLASSIC: BY ANNA SEWELL', '[at right] Black Beauty	[coloured illustration of horse and foal on grass looking at the viewer against a background of buildings]	[at left] PUBLISHED BY PETER LUNN [at right] ILLUSTRATED BY Lionel Edwards'. Spine lettered vertically from top: 'BLACK BEAUTY BY ANNA SEWELL & LIONEL EDWARDS * PETER LUNN'. Back: 'Peter Lunn has also published FLAME: *one of the best*	[coloured illustration of a mounted huntsman blowing a horn and following a pack of hounds in a landscape of fields]	*animal stories ever written – and by a girl aged twelve*	*Illustrated by Lionel Edwards and uniform with this volume*'. Front flap: '[synopsis]	[at right] 9s 6d net'. Back flap has an advertisement for a book.
Later releases	There was a second impression of 8600 copies in 1948. The title page is dated 1948, and the first line of the imprint page is replaced by 'first edition published 1946	second edition - - 1948'. The boards used for the binding are thinner, giving a binding thickness of 10mm. I have not been able to view the second impression dustjacket.
Notes	Category: Nature. Scarcity: 1.
	The back of the dustjacket advertises *Flame*. The back flap has an advertisement for *Horses and Riders*.

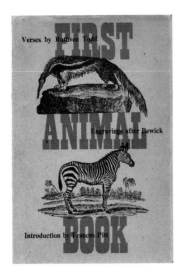

PL51 First Animal Book with verses by Ruthven Todd and engravings after Thomas Bewick, August 1946, [November 1946], 9/6d.

FIRST | ANIMAL BOOK | verses by Ruthven Todd: | and engravings selected | from Bewick's HISTORY OF | QUADRUPEDS, published 1818 | PETER LUNN | London 1946

Collation (218 x 139 mm): [1-9], 10-143, [144] in 9 x 16pp sections coded: uncoded, B-I.

Contents [1] half-title: 'First Animal Book'; [2] frontis; [3] title; [4] imprint: *'First published in August 1946 by* | PETER LUNN (PUBLISHERS) LIMITED. | 49 CHANCERY LANE LONDON, W C 2 | *All rights reserved* | *Printed in Great Britain by* | W. S. COWELL LIMITED | BUTTER MARKET IPSWICH'; [5-8] foreword, signed 'FRANCES PITT'; [9] 'ANIMALS | *by Mr Bewick* | AND | VERSES | *by Mr Todd*'; 10-141 text; 142-143 index; [144] blank.

Illustrations Full-page illustration on p. [2]. Each opening of the text relates to one animal, with text description on the left-hand page and a Bewick engraving on the right, above a four-line stanza by Todd.

Paper White wove text paper and endpapers.

Binding (222 x 145 x 14 mm): beige cloth. Front cover blank. Spine lettered vertically from top: 'FIRST ANIMAL BOOK RUTHVEN TODD PETER LUNN'. Back cover blank.

Dustjacket (221 x 459 mm): thick buff wove paper. Front: '[at top left] Verses by Ruthven Todd | [at middle right] Engravings after Bewick | [at bottom left] Introduction by Frances Pitt'. This text overlies: '[in red] FIRST | [illustration of anteater] | [in red] ANIMAL | [illustration of zebra] | [in red] BOOK'. Spine lettered vertically from top: 'FIRST ANIMAL BOOK * RUTHVEN TODD PETER LUNN'. Back: '[in red] More children's books | from Peter Lunn | [advertisements for six books] | [in red] PETER LUNN | 49 Chancery Lane London'. Front flap: '[synopsis] | [at bottom right] 9s. 6d. net'. Back flap blank.

Notes Category: Nature/Educational. **Scarcity:** 2.

The introduction is by Frances Pitt, an author of many animal books for children. Todd is credited only with the verses which appear on the right-hand pages, and the text on the left-hand pages is unattributed, although this may also be by Todd. It is unrelated to Ralph Beilby's text in the original editions of *A General History of Quadrupeds*. The reference on the title page to the '1818' edition of this book is mysterious, since the sixth edition was published in 1811, and the seventh in 1820. The back of the dustjacket advertises *Detectives in Greasepaint*, *Mr Bosanko*, *Full Fathom Five*, *Here Lies Gold*, *The Story of a Tree* and *English Trees*.

PL52   Danger in Provence   by Oswell Blakeston, illustrated by Frank Baber, December 1946.

OSWELL BLAKESTON | DANGER | IN PROVENCE | WITH DRAWINGS | BY FRANK BABER | [illustration] | PETER LUNN | LONDON 1946

Collation (186 x 121 mm): [1-6], 7-32 32pp section; 33-224 in 6 x 32 sections; 225-236, [237-240] 16pp section. All sections uncoded.

Contents [1] half-title: 'DANGER IN PROVENCE'; [2] frontis., reproducing illustration on p. [91]; [3] title; [4] imprint: 'FIRST PUBLISHED IN DECEMBER 1946 BY | PETER LUNN (PUBLISHERS) LIMITED | 49 CHANCERY LANE LONDON | *All rights reserved* | PRINTED IN GREAT BRITAIN | BY THE GLOUCESTER PRESS BRIGHTON'; [5] contents; [6] 'To Max Chapman | who worked with me on this book'; 7-236, [237] text (see illustration list for unnumbered pages); [238-240] blank.

Illustrations Full-page illustrations on pp. [2], [62], [91], [110], [145], [201] and [219]. Various other illustrations.

Paper White wove text paper and endpapers.

Binding (191 x 128 x 16 mm): ochre cloth. Front cover blank. Spine lettered vertically from bottom in gilt: 'Danger in Provence * Blakeston Peter Lunn'. Back cover blank.

Copy consulted BL.

Notes Category: Adventure. **Scarcity:** 5.

I have seen no reference to the published price of this book.

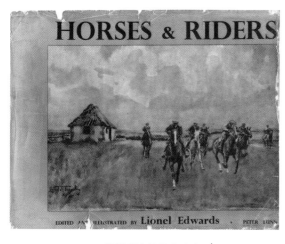

PL53   Horses And Riders   by various authors, edited and illustrated by Lionel Edwards, September 1946, [December 1946], 9/6d.

HORSES AND RIDERS | an anthology for horsemen | (and horsewomen) of all ages | edited and illustrated by | LIONEL EDWARDS | PETER LUNN: LONDON: 1946

Collation (188 x 242 mm): [1-7], 8-12 12pp section, with leaf for frontispiece tipped in to p. [2]; 13-72 in 5 x 12pp sections; 73-79, [80] 8pp section. All sections uncoded.

Contents [1] half-title: '[at right] Horses and Riders'; [2] blank; [3] title; [4] imprint: 'First published in September 1946 by | Peter Lunn (Publishers) Limited | 49 Chancery Lane London | *All rights reserved* | Printed in Great Britain by | H. O. Loescher Limited | 70 Brewer Street London WI'; [5] '[list of contents and authors] | Illustrated by Lionel Edwards'; [6] illustrator details; [7] blank; 8-79 text, in double columns (see illustration list for unnumbered pages); [80] blank.

Illustrations Coloured frontispiece on verso of leaf tipped in to p. [2]. Full-page illustrations on pp. [23], [33], [35], [46], 59, [61], [64], [69], [73] and [77].

Paper White wove text paper and endpapers. White surfaced wove paper for frontispiece.

Binding (192 x 248 x 9 mm): green cloth. Front cover lettered in gilt at bottom right: 'Horses and Riders'. Spine lettered vertically from top in gilt: 'HORSES AND RIDERS * LIONEL EDWARDS * PETER LUNN'. Back cover blank.

Dustjacket (193 x 693 mm): white surfaced wove paper. All of the dustjacket is printed against a uniform salmon-pink background. Front: 'HORSES & RIDERS | [coloured illustration of a horse-race in a field against a cloudy sky, reproducing frontispiece] | EDITED AND ILLUSTRATED BY Lionel Edwards * PETER LUNN'. Spine lettered vertically from top: 'HORSES & RIDERS BY LIONEL EDWARDS [at bottom] PETER LUNN'. Back: '*Peter Lunn have also published FLAME: one of the best* | [coloured illustration of a mounted huntsman blowing a horn and following a pack of hounds in a landscape of fields] | *animal stories ever written – and by a girl aged twelve* | *Illustrated by Lionel Edwards and uniform with this volume*'. Front flap: '[synopsis] | [at right] 9s 6d net'. Back flap has an advertisement for a book.

Notes Category: Nature. **Scarcity**: 2.

There are variant bindings in beige, blue and brown cloth. The book contains the following contributions: 'Sporting Adventures' by 'Syko'; 'The Hunt at Halford Gorse' by 'Punter'; 'A Rare Bad 'Un' by 'Jockey'; 'Between Two Steeples' by A. Chaser; 'A Ride on a Four-Year-Old' by J. Moray Brown. The back of the dustjacket advertises *Flame*. The back flap has an advertisement for *Black Beauty*.

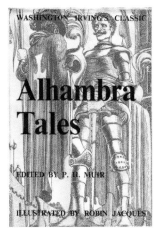

PL54 Alhambra Tales by Washington Irving, selected and edited by P. H. Muir, illustrated by Robin Jacques, November 1946, [January 1947], 8/6d.

WASHINGTON IRVING'S | ALHAMBRA | TALES | EDITED BY P. H. MUIR | AND WITH DRAWINGS | BY ROBIN JACQUES | PETER LUNN | LONDON: 1946

Collation (183 x 122 mm): [1-6], 7-221, [222-224] in 14 x 16pp sections. All sections uncoded.

Contents [1] half-title: '[at right] ALHAMBRA TALES'; [2] frontis., reproducing illustration on p. [105]; [3] title; [4] imprint: '*First published in November 1946 by* | PETER LUNN (PUBLISHERS) LIMITED | *49 Chancery Lane London* | *All rights reserved* | *Printed in Great Britain by* | GALE & POLDEN LTD | *Ideal House* | *London W*'; [5] '[contents] | *and with many drawings by* | ROBIN JACQUES'; [6] blank; 7-221 text (see illustration list for unnumbered pages); [222-224] blank.

Illustrations Full-page illustrations on pp. [2], [47], [77], [87], [105], [111], [151], [173], [197] and [215]. Various other illustrations.

Paper White wove text paper and endpapers.

Binding (188 x 131 x 21 mm): ochre cloth. Front cover stamped at right in gilt with an illustration of a standing man in armour holding a sword in front of him. Spine lettered vertically from top in gilt: 'ALHAMBRA TALES * WASHINGTON IRVING [at bottom] PETER | LUNN'. Back cover blank.

Dustjacket (188 x 444 mm): white surfaced wove paper. Front is lettered over a background illustration in red of two men in armour facing each other, one holding a sword in front of him and the other holding a pennant in one hand and a plumed helmet in the other: 'WASHINGTON IRVING'S CLASSIC | Alhambra | Tales | EDITED BY P. H. MUIR | ILLUSTRATED BY ROBIN JACQUES'. Spine lettered vertically from top: 'ALHAMBRA TALES * WASHINGTON IRVING [at bottom] PETER LUNN'. Back: 'Peter Lunn | [in red] adventure stories | [in red] for children | [advertisements for four books] | [in red] Peter Lunn | 49 Chancery Lane London'. Front flap has synopsis, with price at bottom right (clipped on the copy described). Back flap blank.

Notes Category: Classic/Fairy. Scarcity: 3.

The back of the dustjacket has advertisements for *The Angry Planet*, *The Spanish Galleon*, *The Phantom* and *Old Dave's Hut*.

PL55 Full Fathom Five by N. R. Syme, illustrated by Eric Saunders, November 1946, [January 1947], 8/6d.

N R SYME | FULL FATHOM FIVE | WITH ILLUSTRATIONS FROM DEEP | DIVING BY SIR ROBERT H. DAVIS | REDRAWN BY ERIC SAUNDERS | [illustration] | PETER LUNN | LONDON: 1946

Collation (184 x 123 mm): [1-8], 9-32 32pp section coded A2 on p. 9; 33-224 in 6 x 32pp sections coded B1-G1 on first page and B2-G2 on ninth page of each section; 225-228 4pp section uncoded; 229-243,[244] 16pp section coded J.

Contents [1] half-title: '[at right] FULL FATHOM FIVE'; [2] frontis; [3] title; [4] imprint: 'First published in November 1946 by | Peter Lunn (Publishers) Limited | 49 Chancery Lane London W C 2 | England | All rights reserved | Printed in Great Britain by | Paramount Printing Co Ltd | Carkers Lane Highgate Road | London N W 5'; [5] contents; [6] blank; [7] preface, signed 'N.R.S.' at bottom right; [8] blank; 9-243 text (pp. 69 and 71 unnumbered); [244] blank.

Illustrations Full-page illustrations on pp. [2], 67, [69], [71], 73, 145, 147, 190, 192 and 195. Various other illustrations.

Paper White wove text paper and endpapers.

Binding (190 x 128 x 13 mm): pale blue cloth.. Front cover blank. Spine lettered vertically from top: 'FULL FATHOM FIVE [N.] R. Syme * PETER LUNN' (text partly obscured by BL label). Back cover blank.

Copy consulted BL.

Later releases [WFL].

Notes Category: Educational. **Scarcity**: 5.

The Preface acknowledges: Robert H. Davis, author of 'Deep Diving and Submarine Operations', Commander Edward Ellsberg U.S.N. for 'Men Under the Sea', Mr David Scott for 'Seventy Fathoms Deep' and Mr J. G. Lockhart for other facts.

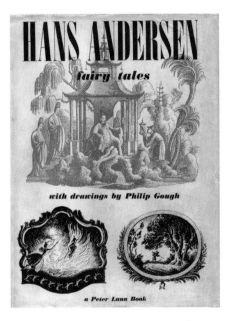

PL56 Hans Andersen's Fairy Tales second edition, illustrated by Philip Gough, January 1947, [February 1947], 10/6d.

Hans Andersen's │ Fairy Tales │ [illustration] │ with drawings by │ Philip Gough │ PETER LUNN │ LONDON 1946 [sic]

Collation (244 x 185 mm): [1-6], 7-128 in 8 x 16pp sections; 129-139, [140] 12pp section. All sections uncoded.

Contents [1] half-title: '[at top right] HANS ANDERSEN'S FAIRY TALES'; [2] frontis., reproducing illustration on p. [121]; [3] title; [4] imprint: 'First published in 1943 by │ PETER LUNN (PUBLISHERS) LIMITED │ 49 Chancery Lane London │ NEW EDITION January 1947 │ All rights reserved │ Printed in Great Britain by │ KENNERLEY PRESS LTD. │ 1/4 Britannia Walk London N.1'; [5] contents; [6] blank; 7-139 text (see illustration list for unnumbered pages); [140] blank.

Illustrations All illustrations are in black on various single-colour backgrounds. Full-page illustrations on pp. [2], [41], [59], [63], [73], [91], [107] and [121]. Various other illustrations.

Paper White wove text paper and endpapers. Endpapers are printed in salmon-pink with a floral design in alternating diamonds.

Binding (250 x 189 x 14 mm): maroon cloth. Front cover has an illustration of a ballerina stamped in gilt at bottom right. Spine lettered in gilt: '[vertically from top] ANDERSEN [horizontally] FAIRY | TALES | * | [at bottom] PETER | LUNN'. Back cover blank.

Dustjacket (249 x 583 mm): white surfaced wove paper. Front: 'HANS ANDERSEN | *fairy tales* | [illustration in red of oriental figures around and inside a pagoda, partly underlying title lettering] | *with drawings by Philip Gough* | [illustration at left of fairy waving wand at a soldier burning on a bonfire] [illustration at right of a traveller walking through a wooded landscape] | *a Peter Lunn Book*'. Spine lettered horizontally: 'HANS | ANDERSEN | FAIRY | TALES | * | [at bottom] PETER | LUNN'. Back has illustration of a princess on top of a bed with many layers of mattress, with courtiers in attendance, reproducing p. [41] on a pale green background. Front flap: '[synopsis] | [at bottom right] 10s 6d net' Back flap: 'Other Peter Lunn | Titles | [advertisements for four books]'.

Copies consulted BL and my own copy.

Later releases See also PL105.

Notes Category: Classic/Fairy. **Scarcity:** 4.

A variant binding exists with orange-red cloth. The text is identical to the Schlosser edition (PL1). The back flap of the dustjacket advertises *Alhambra Tales*, *Arabian Nights*, *The Dark Blanket* and *The Enchanted Glen*.

PL57 **Selected Tales from the Arabian Nights** edited by Hugh Anderson, illustrated by Robin Jacques, November 1946, [February 1947], 8/6d.

SELECTED TALES | FROM THE | ARABIAN NIGHTS | EDITED BY | HUGH ANDERSON | DRAWINGS BY | ROBIN JACQUES | PETER LUNN | LONDON | 1946

Collation (181 x 119 mm): [1-6], 7-16 16pp section uncoded; 17-192 in 11 x 16pp sections coded B-M; 193-212 20pp section coded N on p. 193 and N* on p.195; 213-225, [226-228] 16pp section coded O.

Contents [1] half-title: 'THE ARABIAN NIGHTS'; [2] frontis; [3] title; [4] imprint: '*First published in November 1946 by* | PETER LUNN (PUBLISHERS) LIMITED | 49 Chancery Lane London | *All rights reserved* | *Printed in Great Britain by* | H.O.LOESCHER LIMITED | 70 BREWER STREET | LONDON'; [5] illustration and contents; [6] blank; 7-[226] text (see illustration list for unnumbered pages); [227-228] blank.

Illustrations Full-page illustrations on pp. [2], [35], [57], [85], [103], [131], [159], [175], [183], [191], [203], [208] and [220]. Various other illustrations.

Binding (186 x 126 x 14 mm): orange-red cloth lettered in gilt. Front cover blank. Spine lettered vertically from top: 'Arabian Nights [a] child's entertainment * Peter Lunn' (text partly obscured by BL label). Back cover blank.

Paper White wove text paper. Coarse thin buff wove endpapers.

Copy consulted BL.

Later releases WFL.

Notes Category: Classic/Fairy. **Scarcity:** 3.

Contains the following stories: Introduction, incorporating The Story of Scheherazade and the Sultan, initialled H.A. at the end (although contents page refers to the Introduction as 'including the stories of Scheherazade and the Ox and the Ass'); The Enchanted Horse; The Story of Ali Cogia, a Merchant of Bagdad; The Story of Amgiad and Assad; The Three Sisters; Abou Hassan, the Wag: or The Sleeper Awakened; The Seven Voyages of Sinbad the Sailor.

PL58 Sister to the Mermaid by Nicholas Cavanagh, illustrated by William Stobbs, November 1946, [February 1947], 8/6d.

NICHOLAS CAVANAGH | SISTER | TO THE MERMAID | DRAWINGS BY | WILLIAM STOBBS | [illustration] | PETER LUNN | LONDON 1946

Collation (179 x 120 mm) [1-6], 7-192 in 6 x 32pp sections coded: uncoded, B-C, uncoded, E, uncoded; 193-217, [218-220] 28pp section coded N.

Contents [1] half-title: 'SISTER TO THE MERMAID'; [2] frontis., reproducing p. [83]; [3] title; [4] imprint: 'First published in November 1946 by | PETER LUNN (PUBLISHERS) LTD | 49 CHANCERY LANE | LONDON WC2 | All rights reserved | Printed in Great Britain by | SAMUEL SIDDERS & SON LTD | 115 SALUSBURY ROAD | LONDON NW6'; [5] contents; [6] 'TO OUR PARENTS | "There are many advantages in sea-voyaging, | but security is not one of them." | SAADI.'; 7-217 text (see illustration list for unnumbered pages); [218-220] blank.

Illustrations Full-page illustrations on pp. [2], [10], [16], [49], 61, 78, [83], [117], [145], [161], [180], [198] and 201. Various other illustrations.

Paper White wove text paper and endpapers.

Binding (183 x 130 x 12 mm): black cloth. Front cover blank. Spine lettered vertically from top in gilt: 'SISTER TO THE MERMAID * Cavanagh * PETER LUNN'. Back cover blank.

Dustjacket (183 x 443 mm): white wove paper. Front is lettered on a background illustration in purple and black of a ship's prow and pirates: '[at top left] Sister | to the | Mermaid | [at bottom] a story of pirates and treasure trove for | boys & girls: by Nicholas Cavanagh | and with drawings by William Stobbs'. Spine lettered horizontally 'SISTER | TO THE | MERMAID | * | [in purple] CAVANAGH | [at bottom] PETER | LUNN'. Back: 'Peter Lunn have published these | [in purple] adventure stories | for boys and girls | [advertisements for six books] | PETER LUNN | 49 CHANCERY LANE LONDON'. Front flap: '[synopsis] | [at right] 8s 6d net'. Back flap blank.

Notes   Category: Adventure. **Scarcity:** 3.

The back of the dustjacket advertises *Studio J Investigates*, *Mr Bosanko*, *The Angry Planet*, *The Owl and the Pussycat*, *The White Magic* (published by Westhouse) and *The Lost Mountain*. The book is a sequel to *Night Cargoes*, and it may have had a working title of 'Men of Barbary'.

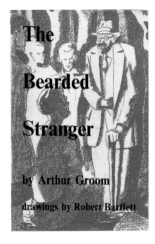

PL59 **The Bearded Stranger** by Arthur Groom, illustrated by Robert Bartlett, March 1947, 8/6d.

ARTHUR GROOM | THE BEARDED | STRANGER | WITH DRAWINGS BY | ROBERT BARTLETT | PETER LUNN | LONDON | 1947

Collation (185 x 121 mm): [1-6], 7-24 24pp section coded A; 25-213, [214-216] in 6 x 32pp sections coded B, C, uncoded, E-G.

Contents [1] half-title: '[at right] *The Bearded Stranger*'; [2] frontis., reproducing illustration on p. [61]; [3] title; [4] imprint: '*First published in March 1947 by* | *Peter Lunn (Publishers) Ltd* | *49 Chancery Lane* | *London W C 2* | *All rights reserved* | *Printed in Great Britain by* | *Kennerley Press Ltd* | *1/4 Britannia Walk* | *London N 1*'; [5] contents; [6] acknowledgement; 7-213, [214] text; [215-216] blank.

Illustrations Full-page illustrations on pp. [2], [61], [105] and [146]. Double-page illustrations on pp. [42-43], [88-89] and [186-187]. Various other illustrations.

Paper White wove text paper and endpapers.

Binding (190 x 125 x 12 mm): grey cloth. Front cover blank. Spine lettered horizontally in gilt: 'The | Bearded | Stranger | * | Groom | [at bottom] Peter | Lunn'. Back cover blank.

Dustjacket (190 x 452 mm): white surfaced wove paper. Front cover is lettered over a background illustration in red of a bearded man in a hat with four boys, reproducing the illustration on p. [61]: 'The | Bearded | Stranger | by Arthur Groom | drawings by Robert Bartlett'. Spine lettered horizontally: 'THE | BEARDED | STRANGER | * | GROOM | [at bottom] Peter | Lunn'. Back is lettered against a red background: 'Peter Lunn publishes other | adventure stories | for boys and girls | [advertisements for six books] | Peter Lunn | 49 Chancery Lane London'. Front flap: '[in red] The Bearded Stranger | [synopsis] | [at right] 8s 6d net | [in red] A Peter Lunn children's book'. Back flap blank.

Later releases [WFL].

Notes Category: Adventure. Scarcity: 4.

There is an acknowledgement to Beresford Webb, editor of 'Camping and Outdoor Life', for details on camping. The back of the dustjacket advertises *Detectives in Greasepaint, Mr Bosanko, Full Fathom Five, Here Lies Gold, The Story of a Tree* and *English Trees*.

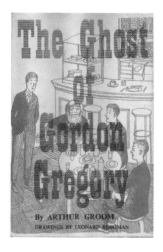

PL60 The Ghost of Gordon Gregory by Arthur Groom, illustrated by Leonard Rosoman, November 1946, [March 1947], 8/6d.

ARTHUR GROOM | THE GHOST OF | GORDON GREGORY | [illustration] | DRAWINGS BY | LEONARD ROSOMAN | PETER LUNN | LONDON | 1946

Collation (186 x 120 mm): [1-6], 7-192 in 12 x 16pp sections coded: uncoded, B, uncoded, D-F, uncoded, H, J-M; 193-204 12pp section coded N on p. 193 and N* on p. 195; 205-236 in 2 x 16pp sections coded O-P.

Contents [1] half-title: 'THE GHOST OF GORDON GREGORY'; [2] frontis., reproducing illustration on p. [45]; [3] title; [4] imprint: 'First published in November 1946 by | Peter Lunn (Publishers) Ltd | 49 Chancery Lane | London WC2 | All rights reserved | Printed in Great Britain by | H O Loescher Ltd | 70 Brewer Street | London'; [5] contents; [6] blank; 7-236 text (see illustration list for unnumbered pages).

Illustrations Full-page illustrations on pp. [2], [13], [33], [45], [61], [71], [79], [97], [130], [154], [163], [179], [201] and [213]. Various other illustrations.

Paper White wove text paper and endpapers.

Binding (192 x 130 x 14 mm): black cloth. Front cover blank. Spine lettered vertically from top in gilt: 'The Ghost of Gordon Gregory * Arthur Groom * Peter Lunn'. Back cover blank.

Dustjacket (190 x 420 mm): white wove paper. Front is lettered against a background illustration in grey of a man and two boys seated at a table in a café, with another boy standing, reproducing the illustration on p. [179]. Front lettered in red 'The Ghost | of | Gordon | Gregory | By ARTHUR GROOM | DRAWINGS BY LEONARD ROSOMAN'. Spine lettered vertically from top in red: 'The Ghost of Gordon Gregory * Arthur Groom [at bottom] PETER | LUNN'. Back: '[in grey] Peter Lunn has published for | [in red] boys and girls | [in grey] these other books: | [advertisements in grey for six books] | [in red] Peter Lunn | [in grey] 49 Chancery Lane London'. Front flap is lettered in grey: '[synopsis] | [at right] 8s 6d net'. Back flap blank.

Later releases Reissued in August 1950 at 5/-. Also WFL.

Notes Category: Adventure. Scarcity: 4.

The back of the dustjacket advertises *Studio J Investigates*, *Mr Bosanko*, *The Angry Planet*, *The Owl and the Pussycat*, *The White Magic* (published by Westhouse) and *The Lost Mountain*.

PL61 The Phantom by John Sylvester, illustrated by Bernard Venables, November 1946, [March 1947], 8/6d.

THE | PHANTOM | JOHN SYLVESTER | [illustration] | with drawings by | BERNARD VENABLES | PETER LUNN | LONDON | 1946

Collation (185 x 122 mm): [1-7], 8-256 in 8 x 32pp sections; 257-266, [267-268] 12pp section. All sections uncoded.

Contents [1] half-title: '[at top right] THE PHANTOM'; [2] frontis., reproducing illustration on p. [225]; [3] title; [4] imprint: 'First published in November 1946 by | PETER LUNN (PUBLISHERS) LIMITED | 49 Chancery Lane London | *All rights reserved* | Printed in Great Britain by | Kennerley Press Limited | 1-4 Britannia Walk | London'; [5] contents; [6] blank; [7], 8-266, [267] text (pp. 7, 16, 27, 37, 41, 49, 62, 71, 83, 96, 110, 121, 123, 135, 146, 158, 170, 185, 199, 214, 225, 229, 243, 255 and 267 unnumbered); [268] blank.

Illustrations Full-page illustrations on pp [2], [41], [121] and [225]. Various other illustrations.

Paper White wove text paper and endpapers.

Binding (191 x 129 x 17 mm): black cloth. Front cover blank. Spine lettered in gilt: '[vertically from top] THE PHANTOM * JOHN SYLVESTER [at bottom] PETER | LUNN'. Back cover blank.

Dustjacket Front, spine and back are printed on a uniform pale blue background. Front: '[illustration of two boys entering a room] | [in red] THE PHANTOM | a children's adventure story | by John Sylvester | with drawings by Bernard Venables | [illustration in red of two boys and a girl looking down at a man emerging from a hole in the ground]'. Spine lettered horizontally: 'THE | PHANTOM | * | JOHN | SYLVESTER | [at bottom] PETER | LUNN'. Back: 'Other books for boys and girls | published only by | [in red] PETER LUNN | [advertisements for six books] | [in red] PETER LUNN | *49 Chancery Lane London*'. Front flap: '[synopsis] | [at bottom right] 8s 6d net'. Back flap blank.

Copies consulted BL and private collection.

Notes Category: Adventure. Scarcity: 4.

There is a variant binding in brown cloth. The back of the dustjacket has advertisements for *Studio J Investigates*, *Mr Bosanko*, *The Angry Planet*, *The Owl and the Pussycat*, *The White Magic* (published by Westhouse) and *The Lost Mountain*.

PL62 International Patrol by Paul Tabori, illustrated by Walter Goetz, March 1947, [8/6d].

PAUL TABORI | INTERNATIONAL | PATROL | WITH DRAWINGS BY | WALTER GOETZ | PETER LUNN . LONDON . 1947

Collation (185 x 120 mm): [1-6], 7-160 in 5 x 32pp sections coded: uncoded, B-E; 161-177, [178-180] 20pp section coded F.

Contents [1] half-title: '[at right] INTERNATIONAL PATROL'; [2] frontis., reproducing illustration on p. [20]; [3] title; [4] imprint: '*First published in March 1947 by* | PETER LUNN (PUBLISHERS) LTD | *49 Chancery Lane London WC2* | *All rights reserved* | *Printed in Great Britain by* | SAMUEL SIDDERS AND SON LTD | *115 Salusbury Road NW6*'; [5] contents; [6] blank; 7-177 text (see illustration list for unnumbered pages); [178-180] blank.

Illustrations Full-page illustrations on pp. [2], [20], [30], [44], [59], [69], [89], [121], [131], [149] and [159]. Various other illustrations.

Paper White wove text paper and endpapers.

Binding (190 x 127 x 14 mm): cream cloth. Front cover blank. Spine lettered vertically from top in gilt: 'International Patrol * Tabori * [at bottom] Peter Lunn'. Back cover blank.

Dustjacket (190 x 456 mm): white wove paper. Front and spine are printed on a uniform red background. Front: 'INTERNATIONAL | PATROL | A MOST ORIGINAL SCOUT STORY | WRITTEN BY PAUL TABORI | DRAWINGS BY WALTER GOETZ | [illustration against a yellow background of a group of boy scouts standing to attention with two scout leaders]'. Spine lettered horizontally: 'Inter- | national | Patrol | * | Tabori | [at bottom] Peter | Lunn'. Back: '[in red] OTHER PETER LUNN BOOKS | [in red] FOR BOYS AND GIRLS | [in red] INCLUDE | [advertisements for five books] | [in red] PETER LUNN | 49 Chancery Lane London'. Front flap: '[in red] International Patrol | [synopsis] | [in red] a Peter Lunn Book | [in red] for boys & girls | [price at bottom right, clipped on the copy described]'. Back flap has an advertisement for a book.

Later releases WFL.

Notes Category: Adventure. **Scarcity:** 4.

The back of the dustjacket has advertisements for *Detectives in Greasepaint, Mr Bosanko, Full Fathom Five, Here Lies Gold* and *The Story of a Tree*. The back flap has an advertisement for *The Phantom*. Advertised at 8/6d in the June 1947 issue of *The Publisher*.

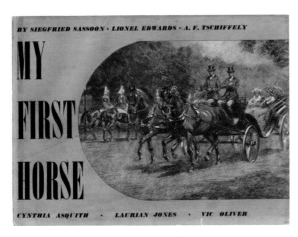

PL63 My First Horse by various authors, illustrated by Lionel Edwards, March 1947, 9/6d.

My First Horse | SIEGFRIED SASSOON A. F. TSCHIFFELY | CYNTHIA ASQUITH LIONEL EDWARDS | LAURIAN JONES VIC OLIVER | PETER LUNN LONDON 1947

Collation (182 x 250 mm): [1-8], 9-16 16pp section, with a leaf for frontispiece tipped in to p. [3]; 17-80 in 4 x 16pp uncoded sections.

Contents [1] half-title: '[at right] My First Horse'; [2] blank; [3] title; [4] imprint: 'First published in March 1947 by | Peter Lunn (Publishers) Limited | 49 Chancery Lane London | *All rights reserved* | Printed in Great Britain by | H. O. Loescher Limited | 70 Brewer Street London WI'; [5] '[list of contents and authors] | Illustrated by Lionel Edwards'; [6] blank; [7-8], 9-80 text, in double columns (see illustration list for unnumbered pages).

Illustrations Coloured frontispiece on verso of leaf tipped in to p. [3]. Full-page illustrations on pp. [10], [12], [18], [20], [23], [29], [33], [37], [39], [40], [46], [51], [64], [72] and [79]. Double-page illustration on pp. [54-55]. Various other illustrations. Both sets of endpapers are printed in brown with the same double-page illustration of a coach and four being driven through a group of armed soldiers, which appears on pp. [54-55].

Paper White wove text paper. White cartridge endpapers. White surfaced paper for frontispiece.

Binding (187 x 255 x 8 mm): yellow cloth. Front cover stamped in gilt at bottom right with an illustration of a huntsman on a horse. Spine lettered vertically from top in gilt: 'MY FIRST HORSE ILLUSTRATED BY LIONEL EDWARDS [at bottom] PETER LUNN'. Back cover blank.

Dustjacket (188 x 705 mm): white surfaced wove paper. Front is printed on a uniform blue background, and is lettered around a coloured illustration of a carriage and riders pulled by two horses against a wooded background: 'BY SIEGFRIED SASSOON * LIONEL EDWARDS * A. F. TSCHIFFELY | MY | FIRST | HORSE | CYNTHIA ASQUITH * LAURIAN JONES * VIC OLIVER'. Spine lettered vertically from top: 'MY FIRST HORSE [at bottom] PETER LUNN'. Back is lettered against a coloured illustration of a horse-race against a cloudy landscape: '[at left] *If you liked* | *My First Horse* | *you will like*', '[at right] HORSES AND RIDERS', '*another book uniform with this volume and also illustrated by Lionel Edwards* | PUBLISHED BY PETER LUNN'. Front flap: '[synopsis] | [at bottom right] 9s 6d net'. Back flap: '*Peter Lunn has* | *also published* | [advertisement for a book]'.

Notes Category: Nature. Scarcity: 1.

There is a variant binding in grey cloth. The book contains the following contributions: 'Thoughts on Horses and Hunting' by Siegfried Sassoon; 'A Gaucho in the Pampa' by A. F. Tschiffely; 'Granny's Story' by Cynthia Asquith; 'An Artist and his Horse' by Lionel Edwards; 'My Welsh Pony' by Laurian Jones; 'I Become a Racehorse Owner' by Vic Oliver. The back of the dustjacket has an advertisement for *Horses and Riders*. The back flap has an advertisement for *Black Beauty*.

PL64 **The Dark Blanket** and other fairy stories   by Ida Burrow, illustrated by John Bainbridge, November 1946, [April 1947], 6/-.

BY IDA BURROW | [in red] THE DARK BLANKET | THE DUSTY MILLER | [in light blue] SOPHONISBA | FAIRY STORIES | DRAWINGS BY | JOHN BAINBRIDGE | PETER LUNN | LONDON 1946

Collation (183 x 121 mm): [1-6], 7-128 in 8 x 16pp sections; 129-137, [138-140] 12pp section. All sections uncoded.

Contents [1] half-title: 'THE DARK BLANKET | AND OTHER FAIRY STORIES'; [2] frontis., reproducing illustration on p.[19]; [3] title; [4] imprint: 'FIRST PUBLISHED IN NOVEMBER 1946 | BY PETER LUNN (PUBLISHERS) LIMITED | 49 CHANCERY LANE LONDON | * | *All rights reserved* | *Printed by* | W.S.CAINES LTD | *Andover House* | *Plaistow London E13*'; [5] illustration, with contents below; [6] 'To | Pamela, Auspin and José'; 7-137 text (see illustration list for unnumbered pages); [138-140] blank.

Illustrations Full-page illustrations on pp. [2], [9], [19], [25], [47], [59], [66], [77], [89], [101], [107], [112] and [114]. Various other illustrations. All illustrations coloured in pale blue and red.

Paper White wove text paper and endpapers.

Binding (189 x 128 x 14 mm): blue cloth. Front cover blank. Spine lettered vertically from top in gilt: 'The Dark Blanket & Other Fairy Stories * Burrow * Peter Lunn'. Back cover blank.

Dustjacket (190 x 483 mm): Front and spine are printed on a uniform red background. Front: 'The Dark Blanket | and other fairy stories | [illustration in red, pale blue and black within a white circular panel of milkmaid milking a cow] | [in script] by Ida Burrow | WITH DRAWINGS BY JOHN BAINBRIDGE'. Spine lettered horizontally: 'The | Dark | Blanket | and | other | Fairy | Stories | by | Ida | Burrow | [at bottom] Peter | Lunn'. Back: '[in red] More Peter Lunn favourites | [in red] for children | [advertisements for six books] | [in pale blue] PETER LUNN | 49 CHANCERY LANE LONDON'. Front flap: '[synopsis] | [at right] 6s. net'. Back flap blank.

Later releases [WFL].

Notes Category: Fairy. Scarcity: 4.

There is a variant binding in maroon cloth. The back of the dustjacket has advertisements for: *Detectives in Greasepaint*, *Mr Bosanko*, *Full Fathom Five*, *Here Lies Gold*, *The Story of a Tree* and *English Trees*.

PL65 The Avion my Uncle Flew by Cyrus Fisher, illustrated by Richard Floethe, December 1946, [April 1947], 8/6d.

CYRUS FISHER | THE AVION | MY UNCLE FLEW | ILLUSTRATED BY | RICHARD FLOETHE | [illustration] | PETER LUNN | LONDON | 1946

Collation (185 x 121 mm): [1-8], 9-253, [254-256] in 8 x 32pp sections coded: uncoded, B-H.

Contents [1] half-title: 'THE AVION MY UNCLE FLEW'; [2] frontis; [3] title; [4] imprint: '*First published in December 1946 by* | *Peter Lunn (Publishers) Ltd* | *49 Chancery Lane* | *London W C 2* | *All rights reserved* | *Printed in Great Britain by* | *Samuel Sidders & Son Ltd* | *115 Salusbury Road* | *London N W 6*'; [5] contents; [6] blank; [7] foreword, signed 'CYRUS FISHER' at bottom right; [8] '*Oddly enough, this book about the unusual adven-* | *tures of young Mr. Littlehorn last summer in France* | *is dedicated with much affection to three young ladies* | *whose great-grandfather came from that very same* | *part of France:* | MARTA JEHANNE, | SARAL DIETER | *and* | JEANNE HILDEGARDE LEORA.'; 9-253 text; [254-256] blank.

Illustrations Full-page illustration on p. [2]. Various other illustrations.

Paper White wove text paper and endpapers.

Binding (190 x 130 x 17 mm): black cloth . Front cover blank, Spine lettered vertically from top in gilt: 'THE AVION MY UNCLE FLEW * Fisher * PETER LUNN'. Back cover blank.

Dustjacket (189 x 455 mm): white wove paper. Front is lettered on a background illustration in red, pale blue, green, black and white of a glider flying over some people and a car: '[in red at top right] The Avion | My Uncle | Flew | [in red script at middle left] by Cyrus Fisher | drawings by | Richard Floethe'. Spine lettered horizontally: 'THE | AVION | MY | UNCLE | FLEW | * | FISHER | [at bottom] PETER LUNN'. Back: 'Peter Lunn has published for | [in red] boys and girls | these other books: | [advertisements for six books] | [in red] Peter Lunn | 49 Chancery Lane London'. Front flap has synopsis, and price at bottom right (clipped on the copy described). Back flap has further synopsis material (with 'Littlejohn' as a misprint for 'Littlehorn').

Notes Category: Adventure. Scarcity: 3.

The back of the dustjacket advertises *Studio J Investigates*, *Mr Bosanko*, *The Angry Planet*, *The Owl and the Pussycat*, *The White Magic* (published by Westhouse) and *The Lost Mountain*. The book was first published in 1946 in America by Appleton-Century. It won a Newbery Honor citation in 1947 and has since been frequently reprinted in America by Scholastic Press.

PL66 Voyage to Chivalry by Edmund Hardy, illustrated by Robin Jacques, April 1947, 8/6d.

EDMUND HARDY | VOYAGE TO CHIVALRY | DRAWINGS BY | ROBIN JACQUES | [illustration] | PETER LUNN | LONDON 1947

Collation (184 x 122 mm): [1-6], 7-256 in 8 x 32pp sections coded: uncoded, B-H; 257-267, [268] 12pp section uncoded.

Contents [1] half-title: '[at right] VOYAGE TO CHIVALRY'; [2] frontis., reproducing illustration on p. [37]; [3] title; [4] imprint: '*First published in April 1947 by* | PETER LUNN (PUBLISHERS) LIMITED | *49 Chancery Lane London* | *All rights reserved* | *Printed in Great Britain by* | H. O. LOESCHER LIMITED | *70 Brewer Street London*'; [5] contents; [6] '*To my Mother*'; 7-267, [268] text (see illustration list for unnumbered pages).

Illustrations Full-page illustrations on pp. [2], [37], [62], [111], [126], [147], [163], [186], [213], [242] (duplicating p. [37]) and [264].

Paper White wove text paper and endpapers.

Binding (189 x 128 x 18 mm): deep pink cloth. Front cover blank. Spine lettered horizontally in gilt: 'Voyage | to | Chivalry | * | Hardy | [at bottom] Peter | Lunn'. Back cover blank.

Dustjacket (190 x 442 mm): white wove paper. Front lettered on a uniform red background: 'a thrilling pageant of the crusades | [solid circle decoration] Voyage to Chivalry | [lettered at left, vertically from bottom] Voyage to Chivalry | [lettered horizontally] by | Edmund | Hardy | with | drawings | by | Robin | Jacques'. Below and to right of lettering is an illustration on a blue background of a man in armour wielding a sword against two men in turban-type headgear. Spine lettered horizontally against a uniform blue background: 'Voyage | to | Chivalry | * | by | Edmund | Hardy | with | drawings | by | Robin | Jacques | [at bottom] Peter | Lunn'. Back: 'Peter Lunn has published other | [in red] adventure stories | for boys and girls | [advertisements for five books] | [in blue] Peter Lunn | 49 Chancery Lane London'. Front flap: '[in red] Voyage to Chivalry | [synopsis] | [at right] 8s 6d net | [in red] A Peter Lunn book for boys and girls'. Back flap blank.

Later releases WFL.

Notes Category: Adventure. Scarcity: 4.

The back of the dustjacket has advertisements for *Studio J Investigates, Mr Bosanko, The Angry Planet, The Owl and the Pussycat* and *The Lost Mountain*.

PL67 African Folk Tales by Yoti Lane, illustrated by Blair Hughes-Stanton, November 1946, [April 1947], 8/6d.

YOTI LANE | AFRICAN | FOLK TALES | [illustration] | WITH DRAWINGS BY | BLAIR HUGHES-STANTON | PETER LUNN | LONDON: 1946

Collation (182 x 123 mm): [1-8], 9-208 in 13 x 16pp sections coded: uncoded, B-N; 209-240 32pp section coded O.

Contents [1] half-title: 'AFRICAN FOLK TALES'; [2] frontis., reproducing illustration on p. [225]; [3] title; [4] imprint: 'First published in November 1946 by | PETER LUNN (PUBLISHERS) LIMITED | 49 Chancery Lane | London W C 2 | All rights reserved | Printed in Great Britain by | SAMUEL SIDDERS & SON LTD | 115 Salusbury Road | London N W 6'; [5-6] illustration followed by contents; [7] foreword signed 'YOTI LANE' at bottom right; [8] 'To Lynn | who loves animals'; 9-240 text (see illustration list for unnumbered pages).

Illustrations Full-page illustrations on various single-colour backgrounds on pp. [2], [11], [47], [70], [96], [115], [142], [171], [184], [213] and [225]. Various other black and white illustrations.

Paper White wove text paper and endpapers.

Binding (188 x 129 x 18 mm): pale olive-green cloth. Front cover blank. Spine lettered vertically from top in gilt: 'AFRICAN FOLK TALES * Lane * PETER LUNN'. Back cover blank.

Copies consulted BL and NLS.

Later releases WFL.

Notes Category: Fairy. Scarcity: 3.

PL68 **Snowdrops** **and other fairy tales**   by Ida Burrow, illustrated by Philip Gough, April 1947, [May 1947], 7/6d.

> IDA BURROW | SNOWDROPS | AND OTHER | FAIRY TALES | WITH DRAWINGS BY | PHILIP GOUGH | PETER LUNN | LONDON | 1947

Collation (183 x 123 mm): [1-6], 7-157, [158-160] in 10 x 16pp sections coded: uncoded, B-K.

Contents [1] half-title: '[at right] SNOWDROPS'; [2] frontis., reproducing illustration on p. 128; [3] title; [4] imprint; 'First published in April 1947 by | PETER LUNN (PUBLISHERS) LIMITED | 49 Chancery Lane | London WC2 | All rights reserved | Printed in Great Britain by | W S CAINES LIMITED | Andover House Broadway Plaistow | London E13'; [5] 'CONTENTS | [illustration] | [contents] | and many drawings by | PHILIP GOUGH'; [6] blank; 7-157, [158] text; [159-160] blank.

Illustrations Full-page illustration on p. [2]. Various other illustrations.

Paper White wove text paper and endpapers.

Binding (188 x 130 x 13 mm): orange cloth. Front cover blank. Spine lettered horizontally in gilt: 'Snowdrops | * | Ida | Burrow | [at bottom] Peter | Lunn'. Back cover blank.

Copy consulted NLS.

Later releases WFL.

Notes Category: Fairy. **Scarcity**: 4.

> Contains the following stories: Rellie and Rennie; The Witch in the Green Haystack; The Green Paper Boat; Snowdrops.

PL69 **The Enchanted Glen**   by Beatrice Carroll, illustrated by Clifford Webb, February 1947, [May 1947], 10/6d.

> BEATRICE CARROLL | THE | ENCHANTED | GLEN | DRAWINGS BY | CLIFFORD WEBB | PETER LUNN | LONDON 1947

Collation (186 x 123 mm): [1-6], 7-352 in 11 x 32pp sections coded: uncoded, C-H, K-N; 353-371, [372] 20pp section coded O.

Contents [1] half-title: '[at right] THE ENCHANTED GLEN'; [2] frontis., reproducing illustration on p. 75; [3] title; [4] imprint: '*First published in February 1947 by* | *Peter Lunn (Publishers) Ltd* | *49 Chancery Lane* | *London WC2* | *All rights reserved* | *Printed in Great Britain by* | *Paramount Printing Co Ltd* | *Carkers Lane Highgate Road London NW5*'; [5] contents; [6] blank; 7-371 text; [372] blank.

Illustrations Full-page illustrations on pp. [2], 27, 53, 75, 97, 115, 139, 193, 209, 257, 292, 322 and 353. Various other illustrations.

Paper White wove text paper and endpapers.

Binding (189 x 131 x 18 mm): light blue cloth. Front cover blank. Spine lettered horizontally in gilt: 'The | Enchanted | Glen | * | Beatrice | Carroll | [at bottom] Peter | Lunn'. Back cover blank.

Dustjacket (189 x 456 mm): white wove paper. Front: 'THE ENCHANTED | GLEN | [lettered at left vertically from bottom] * THE STORY BY BEATRICE CARROLL * | [lettered at right vertically from top] * DRAWINGS BY CLIFFORD WEBB * | PUBLISHED BY PETER LUNN'. Background to front is yellow, with lettering surrounding an illustration on a dark green background of two rabbits among plants in the foreground, with a path through woods behind. Spine lettered horizontally: 'The | ENCHANTED | GLEN | * | CARROLL | & | WEBB | [at bottom] PETER | LUNN'. Back: 'Other books for boys and girls | published by Peter Lunn | [advertisements for four books] | Peter Lunn | 49 Chancery Lane London'. Front flap: 'THE ENCHANTED GLEN | The fairy story of an Irish childhood | [illustration] | [synopsis] | [at right] 10s 6d net'. Back flap blank.

Later releases WFL.

Notes Category: Fairy. Scarcity: 3.

The back of the dustjacket advertises *My First Horse*, *First Animal Book*, *Horses and Riders* and *English Trees*. This book was intended for publication in October 1946, priced at 8/6d, and was to be illustrated by Clare Leighton who, like Clifford Webb, specialised in wood-engraving.

PL70 Don Quixote de la Mancha by Saavedra Miguel de Cervantes, retold by Marjorie Hill and Audrey Walton, illustrated by Robin Jacques, March 1947, [May 1947], 8/6d.

SAAVEDRA MIGUEL DE CERVANTES | Don Quixote | DE LA MANCHA | THE STORY OF HIS ADVENTURES | RETOLD | FOR CHILDREN | BY MARJORIE HILL | AND | AUDREY WALTON | PETER LUNN | LONDON | 1947

Collation (183 x 111 mm): [1-6], 7-239, [240] in 10 x 24pp sections coded A, uncoded, uncoded, D, E, uncoded, uncoded, H, uncoded, uncoded (codes are at the extreme bottom right of the page, and some have probably been trimmed off).

Contents [1] half-title: '[at right] DON QUIXOTE'; [2] frontis; [3] title; [4] imprint: '*First published in March 1947 by* | *Peter Lunn (Publishers) Ltd* | *49 Chancery Lane* | *London W C 2* | *All rights reserved* | *Printed in Great Britain by* | *Kennerley Press Ltd* | *1/4 Britannia Walk* | *London N 1*'; [5-6] contents; 7-239, [240] text (see illustration list for unnumbered pages).

Illustrations Full-page illustrations on pp. [2], [25], [45], [62], [78], [101], [128], [142], [154], [179], [199] and [219]. Two other illustrations.

Paper White wove text paper and endpapers.

Binding (188 x 116 x 17 mm): black cloth. Front cover blank. Spine lettered vertically from top in gilt: 'DON QUIXOTE * Cervantes PETER LUNN'. Back cover blank.

Dustjacket (188 x 417 mm): white surfaced wove paper. Front printed on a uniform red background: 'CERVANTES | [in white and red script] Don Quixote | [illustration, reproducing p. [142], against a white oval panel of two men on horses riding away into a landscape of trees and rocks] | Retold by Marjorie Hill and Audrey Walton | DRAWINGS BY ROBIN JACQUES'. Spine lettered horizontally: 'CERVANTES | * | DON | QUIXOTE | FOR | CHILDREN | * | [at bottom] PETER | LUNN'. Back: 'Peter Lunn has also published | the following | [in red] children's books | [advertisements for four books] | [in red] PETER LUNN | 49 Chancery Lane London'. Front flap: '[in red] Don Quixote | [synopsis] | [at right] 8s 6d net | [in red] A Peter Lunn children's book'. Back flap blank.

Later releases WFL.

Notes Category: Classic/Adventure. **Scarcity**: 4.

The back of the dustjacket has advertisements for *Alhambra Tales, Arabian Nights, Horses and Riders* and *The Enchanted Glen*. The book was translated from a French text. Audrey Walton was a professional translator and was probably mainly responsible for translating the book from French into English, with Marjorie Hill editing it into a form suitable for children.

PL71 **The Black Stallion** by Walter Farley, illustrated by Keith Ward, November 1946, [May 1947], 7/6d.

WALTER FARLEY | THE BLACK | STALLION | [illustration] | ILLUSTRATED BY | KEITH WARD | PETER LUNN | LONDON | 1946

Collation (186 x 122 mm): [i-ii], [1-6], 7-30 32pp section coded A on p. [i] and A* on p. 7; 31-158 in 4 x 32pp sections coded B-E on the first page, and B*-E* on the ninth page, of each section; 159-174 16pp section coded F; 175-203, [204-206] 32 pp section coded G on p. 175 and G* on p. 183.

Contents [1] half-title: 'THE BLACK STALLION'; [2] frontis., reproducing the illustration on p. 106; [3] title; [4] imprint: 'First published in November 1946 by | Peter Lunn (Publishers) Ltd | 49 Chancery Lane London WC2 | All rights reserved | Printed in Great Britain by | Samuel Sidders & Son Ltd | 115 Salusbury Road | London N W 6'; [5] contents; [6] 'To | Mother, Dad and Bill'; 7-203, [204] text; [205-206] blank.

Illustrations Full-page illustrations on pp. [2], 10, 18, 59, 106, 112 and 202. Various other illustrations.

Paper White wove text paper and endpapers.

Binding (191 x 128 x 12 mm): black cloth. Front cover blank. Spine lettered vertically from top in gilt: 'Black Stallion * W. Farley * [at bottom] Peter Lunn'. Back cover blank.

Dustjacket Front, spine and back are printed on a uniform yellow background. Front: '[first three lines of text are within a red panel] THE BLACK STALLION | by Walter Farley | with drawings by Keith Ward | [illustration in blue and black of a boy and a horse jumping from a boat into the sea] | [overlying bottom of illustration] A Peter Lunn book for boys and girls'. Spine lettered horizontally: 'THE | BLACK | STALLION | * | W. FARLEY | [at bottom] PETER | LUNN'. Back: 'Peter Lunn has published other | [in red] books about animals | for children of all ages | [advertisements for three books] | [in red] Peter Lunn | 49 Chancery Lane London'. Front flap: '[in red] The Black Stallion | [synopsis] | [at right] 7s6d net | [in red] A Peter Lunn children's book'. Back flap blank.

Copies consulted NLS and private collection.

Later releases [WFL].

Notes Category: Nature. Scarcity: 4.

The back of the dustjacket has advertisements for *Horses and Riders*, *How is Inky?* and *Beppo the Ox* (i.e. *Beppo*). The book was first published in America by Random House in 1941, and was the first of a series of 'Black Stallion' books. This is the only one of the series published by Peter Lunn.

PL72 The Adventure at Marston Manor by Arthur Groom, illustrated by William Stobbs, March 1947, [May 1947], 7/6d.

BY ARTHUR GROOM | THE ADVENTURE | AT | MARSTON MANOR | A NEW SCHOOLBOY STORY | WITH DRAWINGS | BY | WILLIAM STOBBS | PETER LUNN | LONDON 1947

Collation (185 x 119 mm): [i-vi], 1-202 in 13 x 16pp sections coded: uncoded, B-N; 203-210 8 pp section coded O; 211-212 single leaf tipped in to p. 210.

Contents [i] half-title: 'The Adventure at Marston Manor'; [ii] frontis; [iii] title; [iv] imprint: 'First Published in March 1947 by | Peter Lunn (Publishers) Limited | 49 Chancery Lane London WC2 | All rights reserved | Printed in Great Britain by | Gale & Polden Limited | The Wellington Press, Aldershot'; [v] contents; [vi] blank; 1-212 text.

Illustrations Full-page illustration on p. [ii]. Other illustrations on pp. 1 and 212.

Paper White wove text paper and endpapers.

Binding (190 x 126 x 13 mm): pale greenish-blue cloth. Front cover has drawing of boy carrying spoon stamped in gilt at bottom right. Spine lettered horizontally in gilt: 'The | Adventure | at | Marston | Manor | * | GROOM | [at bottom] Peter | Lunn'. Back cover blank.

Dustjacket (191 x 451 mm): white surfaced wove paper. Front is printed against a dark red background. Front: 'The Adventure at Marston Manor * [lettered vertically from top down right hand side] a new and thrilling school story by Arthur Groom'. The text surrounds an illustration in black on a yellow background of a boy and a man wrestling with a partially open door. Spine lettered horizontally against a dark red background: 'The | Adven- | ture | at | Marston | Manor | by | Arthur | Groom | [at bottom] Peter | Lunn'. Back: 'Peter Lunn has published other | [in red] adventure stories | for boys and girls | [advertisements for three books] | [in red] Peter Lunn | 49 Chancery Lane London'. Front flap: '[in red] The Adventure at Marston Manor | [synopsis] | [at right] 7s. 6d. net | [in red] a Peter Lunn Children's Book'. Back flap blank.

Notes Category: Adventure. Scarcity: 3.

The back of the dustjacket advertises Night Cargoes, The Thunderbolt Men and The Forgotten Valley (not published).

PL73 Canadian Wildwood by Don Hillson, illustrated by William Stobbs, December 1946, [May 1947], 8/6d.

DON HILLSON | CANADIAN | WILDWOOD | WITH DRAWINGS BY | WILLIAM STOBBS | [illustration] | PETER LUNN | LONDON 1946

Collation (181 x 116 mm): [1-6], 7-207, [208] in 13 x 16pp sections coded: uncoded, B-H, uncoded, K-N.

Contents [1] half-title: 'Canadian Wildwood'; [2] frontis; [3] title; [4] imprint: 'First published in December 1946 by | Peter Lunn (Publishers) Limited | 49 Chancery Lane London WC2 | All rights reserved | Printed in Great Britain by | H. O. LOESCHER LIMITED | 70 BREWER STREET LONDON W1'; [5] contents; [6] 'All characters in this book are | completely imaginary and any | coincidence of names is unintentional | [illustration]'; 7-207, [208] text (see illustration list for unnumbered pages).

Illustrations Full-page illustrations on pp. [2], [20], [45], [93] and [129]. Various other illustrations.

Paper White wove text paper and endpapers.

Binding (186 x 121 x 16 mm): pale blue-green cloth. Front cover blank. Spine lettered in gilt: 'Canadian | Wildwood | * | Don | Hillson | Peter | Lunn'. Back cover blank.

Dustjacket (187 x 418 mm): white wove paper. Front and spine are printed on a uniform blue background. Front: '[two illustrations, at the top left of a girl in a canoe, and the at the top right of men in a canoe] | [in white] CANADIAN WILDWOOD | a tale of adventure in the Frozen North | by Don Hillson with drawings by W. Stobbs | [illustration of boy against a background of snow-covered mountains]'. Spine lettered horizontally: 'Canadian | Wildwood | * | Don | Hillson | [at bottom] Peter | Lunn'. Back: 'PETER LUNN | [in blue] adventure tales | for boys and girls | [advertisements for six books] | [in blue] PETER LUNN | 49 Chancery Lane London'. Front flap: '[synopsis] | For children from 9 to 14 | [price at bottom right, clipped on copy described]'. Back flap blank.

Later releases WFL.

Notes Category: Adventure. Scarcity: 4.

The back of the dustjacket has advertisements for *Studio J Investigates*, *Mr Bosanko*, *The Angry Planet*, *The Owl and the Pussycat*, *Detectives in Greasepaint* and *The Lost Mountain*.

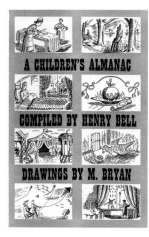

PL74 A Children's Almanac compiled and introduced by Henry Bell, illustrated by Margaret Bryan, February 1947, [June 1947], 8/6d.

COMPILED BY HENRY BELL | A CHILDREN'S | ALMANAC | WITH DECORATIONS | BY MARGARET BRYAN | [illustration] | PETER LUNN | LONDON: 1947

Collation (182 x 118 mm): [1-4], 5-191, [192] in 12 x 16pp sections coded: uncoded, B-C, uncoded, E-M.

Contents [1] half-title: 'A CHILDREN'S ALMANAC'; [2] frontis; [3] title; [4] imprint: '*First published in February 1947* | *by Peter Lunn (Publishers) Limited* | *49 Chancery Lane London WC2* | *All rights reserved* | *Printed in Great Britain by Balding & Mansell Ltd* | *London and Wisbech*'; 5-174 text, within which pp. [18], [47], [86], [88], [130], [132] are blank. See illustration list for other unnumbered pages; [175], 176-189 index with notes; [190], 191 acknowledgements; [192] blank.

Illustrations Full-page illustrations in black on single-colour backgrounds on pp. [2], [17], [47], 74, [87], 123, [131] and 167. Various other illustrations on single-colour backgrounds.

Paper White wove text paper and endpapers.

Binding (188 x 127 x 18 mm): green cloth. Front cover blank. Spine lettered horizontally in gilt: '*A* | *Child* | *ren's* | *Almanac* | * | *Henry* | *Bell* | *and* | *M. Bryan* | [at bottom] *Peter* | *Lunn*'. Back cover blank.

Dustjacket (185 x 392 mm): white surfaced wove paper. Front and spine are printed on a uniform pale orange background. The eight illustrations on the front are in black on white rectangular panels. Front: '[illustration of two maids making clothes] [illustration of woman in a bonnet in a wood] | A CHILDREN'S ALMANAC | [illustration of girl in bed looking out of window] [illustration of a flaming Christmas pudding] | COMPILED BY HENRY BELL | [illustration of circus tent and caravans] [illustration of bird pecking at flower] | DRAWINGS BY M. BRYAN | [illustration of children flying kites] [illustration of boy looking at lamplighter in street outside]'. Spine lettered horizontally: '*A* | *Child-* | *ren's* | *Almanac* | * | *Henry* | *Bell* | *and* | *M. Bryan* | [at bottom] *Peter* | *Lunn*'. Back: 'Peter Lunn has published other | [in pale orange] CHILDREN'S BOOKS | Titles include | [advertisements for three books] | [in pale orange] PETER LUNN | 49 Chancery Lane London'. Front flap: '[synopsis] | [at right] 8s 6d net'. Back flap blank.

Later releases [WFL].

Notes Category: Educational. **Scarcity:** 4.

The back of the dustjacket has advertisements for *Alhambra Tales*, *Arabian Nights* and *The Enchanted Glen*. The copy described also has a wrap-around banner of greyish surfaced wove paper (64 x 419 mm) lettered on the front in blue: 'An Anthology of the Seasons | mainly for Children'.

PL75 Black Sunset by Michael Challenger, illustrated by William Stobbs, February 1947, [June 1947], 8/6d.

MICHAEL CHALLENGER | BLACK | SUNSET | *WITH DRAWINGS BY* | *WILLIAM STOBBS* | PETER LUNN | LONDON 1947

Collation (184 x 122mm): [1-6], 7-208 in 13 x 16pp sections coded: uncoded, B-D, uncoded, F-N; 209-218, [219-220] 12pp section coded O.

Contents [1] half-title: 'BLACK SUNSET'; [2] frontis, reproducing illustration on p. [110]; [3] title; [4] imprint: '*First published in February 1947 by* | PETER LUNN (PUBLISHERS) LIMITED | 49 CHANCERY LANE LONDON WC2 | *All rights reserved* | *Printed in Great Britain by* | COOPER SCANNELL & CO LTD | 6 ELDON STREET LONDON EC2'; [5] contents; [6] blank; 7-218 text (see illustration list for unnumbered pages); [219-220] blank.

Illustrations Full-page illustrations on various single-colour backgrounds on pp. [65], [90], [105], [110] and [166]. Various other illustrations on single-colour backgrounds.

Paper White wove text and endpapers.

Binding (191 x 132 x 18 mm): orange-brown cloth. Front cover blank. Spine lettered vertically from top in gilt: 'BLACK SUNSET Challenger PETER LUNN '. Back cover blank.

Copy consulted BL.

Later releases WFL.

Notes Category: Adventure. **Scarcity:** 3.

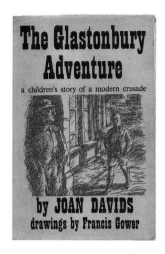

PL76 The Glastonbury Adventure by Joan Davids, illustrated by Francis Gower, October 1946, [June 1947], 7/6d.

THE | GLASTONBURY | ADVENTURE | BY JOAN DAVIDS | DRAWINGS BY FRANCIS GOWER | PETER LUNN | LONDON | 1946

Collation (184 x 122 mm): [1-8], 9-128 in 8 x 16pp sections coded: uncoded, B-H; 129-136 8pp section coded I; 137-167, [168] in 2 x 16pp sections coded J-K.

Contents [1] half-title: 'THE GLASTONBURY ADVENTURE'; [2] frontis, reproducing illustration on p. [140]; [3] title; [4] imprint: 'First published in October 1946 by | PETER LUNN (PUBLISHERS) LIMITED | 49 CHANCERY LANE | LONDON | All rights reserved | Printed in Great Britain by | H O LOESCHER LTD | 70 BREWER STREET | LONDON'; [5] '[contents] | and many illustrations | by Francis Gower'; [6] blank; [7] list of characters in story; [8] 'To Father Paul Stacy | who told me the Glastonbury Story | with such unforgettable charm | I dedicate this book'; 9-167 text (see illustration list for unnumbered pages); [168] blank.

Illustrations Full-page illustrations on pp. [2], [22], [24], [36], [43], [57], [89], [90], [105], [113], [140], [153] and [155].

Paper White wove text paper and endpapers.

Binding (190 x 130 x 15 mm): blue cloth. Front cover blank. Spine lettered vertically from top in gilt: 'THE GLASTONBURY ADVENTURE Joan Davids * Peter Lunn'. Back cover blank.

Dustjacket (191 x 442 mm): white wove paper. Front: 'The Glastonbury | Adventure | a children's story of a modern crusade | [illustration in red of a boy in street being watched by a man in hat and spectacles] | by JOAN DAVIDS | drawings by Francis Gower'. Spine lettered horizontally: 'The | Glastonbury | Adventure | * | JOAN | DAVIDS | [at bottom] PETER | LUNN'. Back: 'Peter Lunn also publishes other | [in red] adventure stories | for children | [advertisements for four books] | [in red] PETER LUNN | 49 Chancery Lane London'. Front flap: '[synopsis] | [at bottom right] 7s 6d net'. Back flap blank.

Later releases [WFL].

Notes Category: Adventure. Scarcity: 4.

The back of the dustjacket has advertisements for *The Lost Mountain*, *Night Cargoes*, *The Hunting of Zakaroff* and *The Angry Planet*.

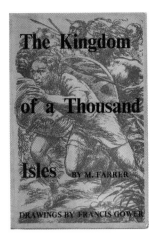

PL77 The Kingdom of a Thousand Isles by M. Farrer, illustrated by Francis Gower, January 1947, [June 1947], 8/6d.

M. FARRER | THE KINGDOM | OF A | THOUSAND ISLES | WITH DRAWINGS BY | FRANCIS GOWER | PETER LUNN | LONDON 1947

Collation (185 x 120 mm): [1-6], 7-160 in 5 x 32pp sections coded: uncoded, B-E; 161-176 16pp section uncoded; 177-208 32pp section coded G.

Contents [1] half-title: 'The Kingdom of a Thousand Isles'; [2] frontis., reproducing illustration on p. [161]; [3] title; [4] imprint: 'First published in January 1947 by | PETER LUNN (PUBLISHERS) LIMITED | 49 Chancery Lane London W C 2 | All Rights Reserved | Printed in Great Britain by | Samuel Sidders & Son Limited | 115 Salusbury Road London N W 6'; [5] contents; [6] blank; 7-208 text (see illustration list for unnumbered pages).

Illustrations Full-page illustrations on pp. [2], [15], [48], [53], [67], [84], [115], [121], [133], [145], [161], [175] and [198].

Paper White wove text paper and endpapers.

Binding (190 x 127 x 16 mm): red cloth. Front cover blank. Spine lettered vertically from top in gilt: 'The Kingdom of a Thousand Isles * Ferrer [sic] * Peter Lunn'. Back cover blank.

Dustjacket (190 x 457 mm): thickish cream wove paper. Front lettered against a background illustration in red of a boy, and warriors with spears and headdresses, running from right to left: 'The Kingdom | of a Thousand | Isles BY M. FARRER | DRAWINGS BY FRANCIS GOWER'. Spine lettered horizontally: The | Kingdom | of | 1,000 Isles | * | FARRER | [at bottom] PETER | LUNN'. Back: 'PETER LUNN | [in red] adventure stories | [in red] for boys and girls | [advertisements for three books] | [in red] PETER LUNN | 49 Chancery Lane London'. Front flap has synopsis and price at bottom right (clipped on copy described). Back flap blank.

Notes Category: Adventure. Scarcity: 3.

The back of the dustjacket has advertisements for *The Haunted Island*, *The Hunting of Zakaroff* and *The Ghost of Gordon Gregory*.

PL78 Bright is the Starlight by Peter Holley, illustrated by Ernest Wigglesworth, February 1947, [June 1947], 8/6d.

PETER HOLLEY | BRIGHT IS | THE STARLIGHT | DRAWINGS BY | ERNEST WIGGLESWORTH | PETER LUNN | LONDON : 1947

Collation (185 x 120 mm): [1-6], 7-160 in 5 x 32pp sections coded: uncoded, B, uncoded, D-E; 161-196, [197-200] 40pp section uncoded.

Contents [1] half-title: 'BRIGHT IS THE STARLIGHT'; [2] frontis, reproducing illustration on p. [61]; [3] title; [4] imprint: '*First published in February 1947 by* | PETER LUNN (PUBLISHERS) *Limited* | 49 *Chancery Lane* | *London W C 2* | *All Rights Reserved* | *Printed in Great Britain by* | *Samuel Sidders & Son Limited* | 115 *Salusbury Road* | *London NW6*'; [5] contents; [6] blank; 7-196, [197] text (see illustration list for unnumbered pages); [198-200] blank.

Illustrations Full-page illustrations on pp. [2], [29], [61], [65], [85], [117], [151] and [173]. Various other illustrations.

Paper White wove text paper and endpapers.

Binding (190 x 125 x 15 mm): orange cloth. Front cover blank. Spine lettered vertically from top in gilt: 'Bright Is The Starlight * Holley * [at bottom] Peter Lunn'. Back cover blank.

Later releases WFL.

Notes Category: Adventure. Scarcity: 4.

PL79 Song of Arizona by Frank Rhodes, illustrated by William Stobbs, June 1947, [7/6d].

FRANK RHODES | SONG OF | ARIZONA | *illustrated by* | WILLIAM STOBBS | PETER LUNN | *London* | 1947

Collation (185 x 122 mm): [1-6], 7-8 8pp section uncoded; 9-184 in 11 x 16pp sections coded B-M.

Contents [1] half-title: '*Song of Arizona*'; [2] frontis; [3] title; [4] imprint: '*First published in June 1947 by* | PETER LUNN (PUBLISHERS) LIMITED | 49 *Chancery Lane London WC2* | *All rights reserved* | *Printed in Great Britain by* | H O LOESCHER LIMITED | 70 *Brewer Street London W1*'; [5] contents; [6] '*Based on the Republic film* | SONG OF ARIZONA | *starring Roy Rogers and* | *Trigger with screen play* | *by M. Coates Webster and* | *original story by Bradford* | *Ropes, released by British* | *Lion Film Corporation Ltd.*'; 7-184 text (see illustration list for unnumbered pages).

Illustrations Full-page two-tone coloured illustration on p. [2]. Full-page illustrations on pp. [28], [54] and [127].

Paper White wove text paper and endpapers.

Binding (190 x 130 x 13 mm): green glazed cloth textured with raised dimples. Front cover blank. Spine lettered horizontally in gilt: 'Song | of | Arizona | * | Frank | Rhodes | [at bottom] Peter | Lunn'. Back cover blank.

Dustjacket (188 x 443 mm): white surfaced wove paper. Front has a coloured background illustration reproducing the frontispiece, and is of a boy in cowboy dress on a galloping horse preparing to throw a lasso, against a desert landscape. Front is lettered in script: 'Song of Arizona | by Frank Rhodes: drawings by W.Stobbs | [at bottom] a Peter Lunn book for boys & girls'. Spine is lettered horizontally in script, against a uniform orange background: 'Song | of | Arizona | by | Frank | Rhodes | [at bottom] a | Peter | Lunn | book | for | boys | and | girls'. Back: 'Peter Lunn has published other | [in orange script] adventure stories | [advertisements for two books] | [in orange script] Peter Lunn | 49 Chancery Lane London'. Front flap: '[in orange] Song of Arizona | [synopsis] | [price at right, clipped on copy described] | [at bottom, in orange] a Peter Lunn book | [in orange] for boys and girls'. Back flap: 'Another Peter Lunn book | [advertisement for a book]'.

Later releases [WFL].

Notes Category: Adventure. **Scarcity:** 4.

An advertisement in *The Ivory Trail* prices this book at 7/6d. The back of the dustjacket has advertisements for *The Thunderbolt Men* and *Great Gold Rushes*. The back flap has an advertisement for *The Young Cowboy*. A working title for the book was "Arizona Holiday", and it was advertised under this title, with the author as **George Pengelly**, in the April 1947 issue of *Publishers' Circular*. It is adapted from the film script for 'Song of Arizona', featuring Roy Rogers and his horse Trigger, released by British Lion Film Corporation.

PL80 **Beppo** by Peter Ross, [illustrations unattributed], December 1946, [June 1947], 8/6d.

BEPPO | BY PETER ROSS | [illustration] | PETER LUNN: LONDON: 1946

Collation (184 x 122 mm): [1-6], 7-208 in 13 x 16pp sections coded A-M; 209-225, [226-228] 20pp section coded N.

Contents [1] half-title: '[at right] BEPPO'; [2] blank; [3] title; [4] imprint: 'First published in December 1946 by | PETER LUNN (PUBLISHERS) LTD | 49 Chancery Lane London WC2 | All rights reserved | Printed in Great Britain by | COOPER, SCANNELL & CO LTD | 6 Eldon Street London EC2'; [5] contents; [6] 'To my nephew | GEOFFREY MARTIN | Trusting that he will not be too | critical in the years | to come'; 7-225, [226] text (pp. 56-57 unnumbered); [227-228] blank.

Illustrations Full-page illustrations on pp. 28, 181 and 192. Double-page illustration on pp. [56-57]. Various other illustrations.

Paper White wove text paper and endpapers.

Binding (190 x 129 x 21 mm): maroon cloth. Front cover blank. Spine lettered vertically from top in gilt: 'BEPPO the story of an ox * ROSS * Peter Lunn'. Back cover blank.

Dustjacket (193 x 510 mm): cream surfaced wove paper. Lettering on front is all in red, and is fitted around the edge of an illustration in brown of an ox's head in profile looking to the left. Front: '[in script] the story of an Ox | [at left] Beppo | Beppo | Beppo | [at bottom right, in script] by Peter Ross'. Spine lettered vertically from top in brown: 'Beppo the Ox * Peter Ross PETER LUNN'. Back: '[in brown] Peter Lunn has also published other | [in red] animal stories | [in brown] for boys & girls of all ages | [advertisements for three books] | [in red] Peter Lunn | [in brown] 49 Chancery Lane London'. Front flap: '[synopsis] | [at right] 8s 6d net'. Back flap blank.

Later releases WFL.

Notes Category: Nature. Scarcity: 3.

The back of the dustjacket has advertisements for *Horses and Riders*, *How is Inky?* and *The Black Stallion*. There seems to have been some uncertainty about the titling of this book: the title page has 'Beppo', the spine of the dustjacket 'Beppo the Ox', and the front of the dustjacket 'Beppo Beppo Beppo'. The WFL dustjacket has 'Beppo the Ox'. Whitaker unhelpfully refers to the book as 'Beppo the Owl'.

PL81 **Every Child's Toy Book** by Thora Stowell, illustrated by Nancy Innes, December 1946, [June 1947], 6/-.

THORA STOWELL | EVERY CHILD'S | TOY BOOK | [illustration] | ILLUSTRATED BY | NANCY INNES | PETER LUNN | LONDON 1946

Collation (184 x 118 mm): [i-vi], [1-4], 5-154 in 4 x 40pp sections; 155-196, [197-198] 44pp section. All
sections uncoded. Pages [i-ii] form the front pastedown. There is no front free endpaper.

Contents [iii-iv] blank; [v] half-title: '[at right] EVERY CHILD'S TOY BOOK'; [vi] frontis; [1] title;
[2] imprint: 'First published in December 1946 by | PETER LUNN (PUBLISHERS) LTD |
49 CHANCERY LANE LONDON | All rights reserved | Printed in Great Britain by | F. R. BRITTON
& CO LTD | SHENTON STREET LONDON'; [3-4] contents; 5-196 text; [197-198] blank.

Illustrations Full-page illustrations on pp. [vi], 62, 70, 72, 75-76, 78, 81, 87-88, 102, 105, 113, 119, 121, 135,
142, 152, 162, 164, 166-167, 171, 175, 180, 189, 191-192 and 195. Various other illustrations.

Paper White wove text paper and endpapers.

Binding (192 x 127 x 13 mm): boards covered with thick paper printed with a pattern of green
and white vertical streaks. Front cover blank. Spine lettered vertically from top in gilt:
'EVERY CHILD'S TOY BOOK * THORA STOWELL PETER LUNN'. Back cover blank.

Dustjacket (192 x 430 mm): cream wove paper. Front is lettered over an illustration in red of toys
(a bird, two dolls and an animal): 'every | child's | toy book | a guide to home toy-making |
with instructions & diagrams for | making 50 toys: by Thora Stowell | with drawings |
by Nancy Innes'. Spine lettered horizontally: 'every | child's | toy | book | STOWELL | & |
INNES | [at bottom] PETER | LUNN'. Back: 'Other Peter Lunn books | [advertisements
for six books] | PETER LUNN | 49 Chancery Lane London'. Front flap: 'Every Child's Toy
Book | [synopsis] | [at right] 6s. net | A Peter Lunn children's book'. Back flap blank.

Notes Category: Educational. **Scarcity:** 3.

The back cover has advertisements for *Detectives in Greasepaint*, *Mr Bosanko*, *Full Fathom
Five*, *Here Lies Gold*, *The Story of a Tree* and *English Trees*.

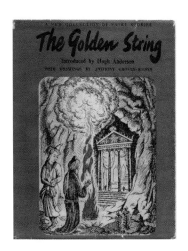

PL82 **The Golden String** introduced by Hugh Anderson,
illustrated by Anthony Groves-Raines, July 1947, 8/6d.

A NEW COLLECTION OF | FAIRY STORIES | THE GOLDEN | STRING | WITH
DRAWINGS | BY A. GROVES-RAINES | * | *I give you the end of a golden string;* | *Only wind it
into a ball,* | *It will lead you in at Heaven's gate,* | *Built in Jerusalem's wall.* | [at right] WILLIAM
BLAKE | PETER LUNN | LONDON 1947

Collation (182 x 143 mm): [1-6], 7-12 12pp section uncoded; 13-180 in 14 x 12pp sections coded B-P;
181-196 in 2 x 8pp sections coded R-S; 197-198, [199-204] 8pp section coded T.

Contents [1] half-title: 'THE GOLDEN STRING'; [2] frontis; [3] title; [4] imprint: '*Published in Great Britain by* | PETER LUNN (PUBLISHERS) LIMITED | *49 Chancery Lane London WC2* | *in July 1947* | *All rights reserved* | *Printed in Great Britain by* | W S COWELL LIMITED | *London and Ipswich*'; [5] contents; [6] blank; 7-198, [199] text (pp. 33, 83, 145 and 170 unnumbered); [200-204] blank.

Illustrations Full-page illustrations on pp. [2], [33], [83], [145] and [170]. Various other illustrations.

Paper White wove text paper and endpapers.

Binding (188 x 149 x 16mm): orange-brown cloth lettered in gilt. Front cover blank. Spine lettered horizontally: 'The Golden String | * | Hugh | Ander- | son | [at bottom] Peter | Lunn'.

Dustjacket (190 x 483 mm): white wove paper. Front and spine are lettered on a uniform red background: 'A NEW COLLECTION OF FAIRY STORIES' | [in script] The Golden String | Introduced by Hugh Anderson | WITH DRAWINGS BY ANTHONY GROVES-RAINES | [illustration in yellow, red and black of two men in Arabic clothes next to a fire in front of a palace revealed through a hole in a rock face]'. Spine lettered horizontally: 'The | Golden | String | * | Introduced | by | Hugh | Anderson | with | drawings | by | Anthony | Groves- | Raines | [at bottom] Peter | Lunn'. Back: 'Peter Lunn has published other | [in red script] CHILDREN'S BOOKS | Titles include | [advertisements for three books] | [in red script] PETER LUNN | *49 Chancery Lane London*'. Front flap: '[in red] The Golden String | [synopsis] | [in red] a Peter Lunn book | [in red] for boys and girls | [at bottom right] *8s 6d net*'. Back flap has an advertisement for a book.

Notes Category: Fairy. Scarcity: 3.

There is a variant binding in pale buff. The back of the dustjacket advertises *Alhambra Tales*, *Arabian Nights* and *The Enchanted Glen*. The back flap of the dustjacket advertises *The Dark Blanket*. The book contains the following stories: The Passport; The Dwarf with the Long Nose; The Magic Knapsacks; The Merry Musician; The Boy with the Three Dogs; The Ill-tempered Princess; The Blue Bird; The Serpent Prince; The Three Princesses of Whiteland; Alibea; The Caliph Haroun Alraschid; The Golden Duck; The Master and his Pupil. Nine of the thirteen stories were previously published as *The Three Princesses of Whiteland* (PL8) and the same type-setting appears to have been reused, and by the same printer, although the page format has changed. Chapter headings have been set in new type, and new illustrations incorporated.

PL83   Black Rock Island   by Charles Atkin, illustrated by Francis Gower, May 1947, [July 1947], 8/6d.

CHARLES ATKIN | BLACK ROCK | ISLAND | DRAWINGS BY | FRANCIS GOWER | PETER LUNN | LONDON 1947

Collation (185 x 121 mm): [1-6], 7-192 in 6 x 32pp sections coded A-B, uncoded, D-F; 193-200 8pp section coded G; 201-216 16pp section coded H.

Contents [1] half-title: '[at right] BLACK ROCK ISLAND'; [2] frontis., reproducing illustration on p. [127]; [3] title; [4] imprint: '*First published in May 1947 by* | *Peter Lunn (Publishers) Limited* | *49 Chancery Lane London W C 2* | *All rights reserved* | *Printed in Great Britain by* | *Samuel Sidders & Son Limited* | *115 Salusbury Road Kilburn* | *London N W 6*'; [5] contents; [6] blank; 7-216 text (see illustration list for unnumbered pages).

Illustrations Full-page illustrations on pp. [2], [11], [31], [39], [57], [65], [76], [121], [127], [153], [163], [197] and [211].

Paper White wove text paper and endpapers.

Binding (190 x 127 x 17 mm): light brown cloth. Front cover blank. Spine lettered horizontally in gilt: 'Black | Rock | Island | * | Charles | Atkin | [at bottom] Peter | Lunn'. Back cover blank.

Copy consulted NLS.

Later releases [WFL].

Category: Adventure. **Scarcity**: 4.

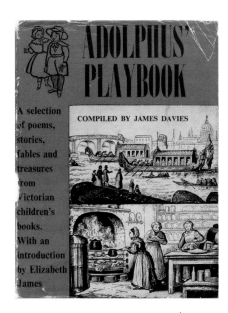

PL84 Adolphus' Playbook compiled by James Davies, June 1947, [July 1947], 9/6d.

A Selection from | Victorian Children's books | ADOLPHUS' | PLAYBOOK | with an introduction by | ELIZABETH JAMES | PETER LUNN | London 1947

Collation (239 x 184 mm): [1-10], 11-126, [127-128] in 8 x 16pp uncoded sections.

Contents [1] half-title: 'ADOLPHUS' PLAYBOOK'; [2] frontis; [3] title; [4] 'First published in June 1947 by | PETER LUNN (PUBLISHERS) LIMITED | 49 Chancery Lane London | All rights reserved | Printed in Great Britain by | WATERLOW AND SONS LIMITED | 26-27 Great Winchester Street | London EC 2'; [5] contents; [6-10] introduction and 'POSTSCRIPTUM'; 11-126 text (page 85 misnumbered as 8); [127-128] blank.

Illustrations Full-page illustrations on pp. [2], 12, 14, 16, 18, 22, 35, 37, 39, 41, 66, 68, 70, 72, 74, 76, 78, 80, 84, 86, 90, 92, 95-96 and 108. Various other illustrations.

Paper White wove text paper and endpapers. Endpapers are printed in salmon-pink with a floral design in alternating diamonds.

Binding (244 x 187 x 13 mm): crimson cloth. Front cover stamped in centre, in gilt , with an illustration of a boy and girl in old-fashioned dress. Spine lettered vertically from top in gilt: 'ADOLPHUS' PLAYBOOK FOR BOYS AND GIRLS * DAVIES [at bottom] PETER LUNN'. Back cover blank.

Dustjacket (244 x 582 mm): white surfaced wove paper. Front and spine are printed against a uniform red background. Front: '[illustration of a boy and girl in old-fashioned dress] | ADOLPHUS' | PLAYBOOK', '[at left] A selection | of poems, | stories, | fables and | treasures | from | Victorian | children's | books. | With an | introduction | by Elizabeth | James'. At centre right, against a pale blue background, illustration of barges on a river near a bridge, lettered at top left: 'COMPILED BY JAMES DAVIES'. At bottom right, against a yellow background, illustration of servants preparing food in a kitchen. Spine lettered vertically from top: 'ADOLPHUS' PLAYBOOK FOR BOYS AND GIRLS * DAVIES [at bottom] PETER LUNN'. Back: 'Peter Lunn has published other books for | [in red] BOYS & GIRLS | Titles include: | [advertisements for three books] | [in red] PETER LUNN | 49 Chancery Lane London'. Front flap: '[in red] ADOLPHUS' PLAYBOOK | [synopsis] | [in red] A Peter Lunn children's book | [at bottom right] 9s 6d net'. Back flap has an advertisement for a book.

Notes Category: Educational. **Scarcity:** 2.

The back of the dustjacket has advertisements for *Pinocchio, Arabian Nights* and *The Dark Blanket*. The back flap has an advertisement for *Hans Andersen's Fairy Tales* (PL56).

PL85 Fairy Tales with a Twist introduced [and retold] by Patrick de Heriz, illustrated by Robin Jacques, December 1946, [July 1947], 7/6d.

PATRICK DE HERIZ | *FAIRY TALES* | *WITH* | *A TWIST* | *DRAWINGS BY* | *ROBIN JACQUES* | *PETER LUNN* | *LONDON* | *1946*

Collation (229 x 151 mm): [1-8], 9-96 in 6 x 16pp sections; 97-103, [104] 8pp section. All sections uncoded.

Contents [1] half-title: 'FAIRY TALES WITH A TWIST'; [2] frontis., reproducing illustration on p. [80] in smaller size; [3] title; [4] imprint: '*Published in December 1946 by* | PETER LUNN (PUBLISHERS) LIMITED | *49 Chancery Lane London* | *All rights reserved* | *Printed by* | HARRISON AND SONS LTD. | *45 St Martin's Lane* | *WC2*'; [5] contents; [6] 'TO | JOAN PATRICIA | BECAUSE I LOVE HER, | AND BECAUSE I FIRST READ | THESE TO HER IN BED'; [8] blank; 9-11 introduction, signed at end: 'P. DE H. | May 1946'; 12-103, [104] text (see illustration list for unnumbered pages).

Illustrations Full-page illustrations on various single-colour backgrounds on pp. [2], [13], [17], [21], [43], [47], [52], [59], [77] and [80]. Various other illustrations on single colour backgrounds.

Paper White wove text paper and endpapers.

Binding (235 x 159 x 11 mm): blue cloth. Front cover stamped in gilt in centre with illustration of child on a stool reading a book. Spine lettered vertically from top in gilt: 'FAIRY TALES WITH A TWIST HERIZ & JACQUES PETER LUNN'. Back cover blank.

Copy consulted BL.

Notes Category: Fairy. Scarcity: 3.

The book contains the following stories: Puss-in-Boots; Cinderella; The Three Bears; Little Red Riding Hood; Jack the Giant Killer; The Sleeping Beauty; Jack and the Beanstalk; The House that Jack Built; Beauty and the Beast; Tom Thumb; Snow White; The Babes in the Wood; Three Little Pigs; Bluebeard.

PL86 Operation Adventure by John D. Hillaby, illustrated with photographs, May 1947, [July 1947], 8/6d.

JOHN D HILLABY | OPERATION ADVENTURE | *with many photographs* | PETER LUNN | LONDON | 1947

Collation (182 x 121 mm): [1-6], 7-16 16pp section uncoded, and with frontis tipped in to p. [3]; 17-48 in 2 x 16pp sections coded B-C; [i-ii], 49-64, [iii-iv] 20pp section coded D on p. 49, with first and last leaves for illustrations; 65-112 in 3 x 16pp sections coded E-G; [v-vi], 113-128, [vii-viii] 20pp section coded H on p. 113, with first and last leaves for illustrations; 129-190, [191-192] in 4 x 16pp sections coded I-M.

Contents [1] half-title: 'OPERATION ADVENTURE'; [2] blank; [3] title; [4] imprint: '*First published in May 1947 by* | PETER LUNN (PUBLISHERS) LIMITED | *49 Chancery Lane London WC2* | *All rights reserved* | *Printed in Great Britain by* | H O LOESCHER LIMITED | *70 Brewer Street London W1*'; [5] contents; [6] author's preface, signed 'Hampstead J.D.H.' at end; 7-190 text; [191-192] blank? (has been torn out of BL copy).

Illustrations Full-page black and white photographs. Single-sided frontis photograph tipped in to p. [3], reproducing that on p. [vii]. Double sided photographs on pp. [i-ii], [iii-iv], [v-vi] and [vii-viii].

Paper White wove text paper and endpapers. White surfaced paper for photographs.

Binding (189 x 126 x 13 mm): pale grey-green cloth. Front cover blank. Spine lettered horizontally in green: '*Operation* | *Adventure* | *John D.* | *Hillaby* | [at bottom] *Peter* | *Lunn*'. Back cover blank.

Copy consulted BL.

Notes Category: Nature. Scarcity: 4.

PL87 Summer Gypsies by Dora Nash, illustrated by Margaret Bryan, April 1947, [July 1947], 7/6d.

DORA NASH | SUMMER GYPSIES | [illustration] | *with drawings by* | MARGARET BRYAN | PETER LUNN | *London 1947*

Collation (183 x 120 mm): [1-6], 7-192 in 12 x 16pp sections coded: uncoded, B-M; 193-202, [203-204] 12pp section coded N*.

Contents [1] half-title: 'SUMMER GYPSIES'; [2] frontis., reproducing illustration on p. [143]; [3] title; [4] imprint: 'First published in April 1947 by | PETER LUNN (Publishers) LTD | 49 Chancery Lane London WC2 | *All rights reserved* | *Printed in Great Britain by* | GALE & POLDEN LIMITED | *Wellington Press Aldershot Hampshire*'; [5] contents; [6] blank; 7-202 text (see illustration list for unnumbered pages); [203-204] blank.

Illustrations Full-page illustrations on pp. [2], [20], [42], [55], [68], [83], [97], [119], [143], [159], [174]. Various other illustrations.

Paper White wove text paper and endpapers.

Binding (188 x 128 x 13 mm): light green cloth. Front cover blank. Spine lettered horizontally in gilt: 'Summer | Gypsies | Dora | Nash | [at bottom] Peter | Lunn'. Back cover blank.

Later releases WFL.

Copy consulted BL.

Notes Category: Adventure. **Scarcity**: 5.

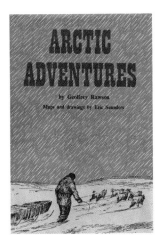

PL88 **Arctic Adventures** by Geoffrey Rawson, illustrated by Eric Saunders, April 1947, [July 1947], 9/6d.

GEOFFREY RAWSON | ARCTIC | ADVENTURES | WITH MAPS | AND DRAWINGS BY | ERIC SAUNDERS | PETER LUNN | LONDON 1947

Collation (181 x 120 mm): [1-8], 9-320 in 10 x 32pp sections coded: uncoded, C-H, K-M; 321-334, [335-336] 16 pp section coded N.

Contents [1] half-title: '[at right] ARCTIC ADVENTURES'; [2] frontis., reproducing illustration on p. 123; [3] title; [4] imprint: 'First published in April 1947 by | Peter Lunn (Publishers) Ltd | 49 Chancery Lane London WC2 | All rights reserved | Printed in Great Britain by | Paramount Printing Co Ltd | Carkers Lane Highgate Road | Kentish Town London NW5'; [5] contents and start of illustration list; [6] remainder of illustration list; [7] glossary; [8] 'Other books by the same author | ADMIRAL EARL BEATTY | BLIGH OF THE BOUNTY | SHIPS AND SEAMEN | MARY BRYANT'; 9-334 text (see illustration list for unnumbered pages); [335-336] blank.

Illustrations Full page illustrations on pp. [2], 29, 39, 63, 99, [107], 117, 123, 133, 171, [175], 201, 239, 261, 285, 293 and 317. Double-page illustrations on pp. [16-17], [48-49], [80-81], [144-145], [208-209], [240-241], [272-273] and [304-305].

Paper White wove text paper and endpapers.

Binding (186 x 129 x 25 mm): red glazed cloth textured with a wavy pattern. Front cover blank. Spine lettered horizontally in gilt: 'Arctic | Adventures | * | Geoffrey | Rawson | [at bottom] Peter | Lunn'.

Dustjacket (186 x 480 mm): white wove paper. Front is lettered on a background illustration in pale blue, black and white of a man with sledge and dogs against a snowy sky: '[in red] ARCTIC | [in red] ADVENTURES | by Geoffrey Rawson | Maps and drawings by Eric Saunders'. Spine lettered horizontally: 'Arctic | Adven- | tures | * | Rawson | [at bottom] Peter | Lunn'. Back: 'Peter Lunn has published other | [in red] instructional books | suitable for young people | [advertisements for six books] | [in red] Peter Lunn | 49 Chancery Lane London'. Front flap: '[in red] Arctic Adventures | [synopsis] | [in red] A Peter Lunn book | [price at bottom right, clipped on the copy described]'. Back flap blank.

Later releases [WFL].

Notes Category: Adventure/Educational. **Scarcity**: 4.

The back of the dustjacket has advertisements for *Here Lies Gold*, *Priest of the Legion*, *Rivers of Man*, *Pizarro of Peru*, *The World's Strange Islands* and *Children's Pets: Their Care and Welfare*. Only the first two of these were published by Peter Lunn. The final title was published by John Westhouse, as 'Your Pets: Their Care and Welfare'.

PL89 The Grand Escapade by George Pengelly, illustrated by William Stobbs, June 1947, [August 1947], 6/-.

GEORGE PENGELLY | THE | GRAND ESCAPADE | ILLUSTRATED BY | WILLIAM STOBBS | PETER LUNN | LONDON 1947

Collation (184 x 121 mm): [1-6], 7-128 in 4 x 32pp sections coded: uncoded, B-D; 129-152 24pp section coded E; 153-183, [184] 32pp section coded F.

Contents [1] half-title: '[at right] THE GRAND ESCAPADE'; [2] frontis., reproducing illustration on p. [92]; [3] title; [4] imprint: '*First published in June 1947 by* | PETER LUNN (PUBLISHERS) LIMITED | 49 *Chancery Lane London WC2* | *All rights reserved* | *Printed in Great Britain by* | SAMUEL SIDDERS & SON LIMITED | 115 *Salusbury Road London NW6*'; [5] contents; [6] 'THE GRAND ESCAPADE has been adapted from the | screen play by Geoffrey Orme and Barbara K. | Emary of the John Baxter Production, and was | released by the British Lion Film Corporation Ltd.'; 7-183 text (see illustration list for unnumbered pages); [184] blank.

Illustrations Full-page illustrations on pp. [2], [58] and [92]. Various other illustrations.

Paper White wove text paper and endpapers.

Binding (191 x 126 x 13 mm): brown glazed cloth textured with a raised dimples. Front cover blank. Spine lettered horizontally in gilt: 'The | Grand | Escap- | ade | * | Pen- | gelly | [at bottom] Peter | Lunn'. Back cover blank.

Dustjacket (190 x 435 mm): white surfaced wove paper. Front and spine are printed on a uniform red background. Front: '[illustration of three boys' heads and shoulders] | GEORGE PENGELLY | [in white script] The Grand Escapade | adapted from the film story by | GEOFFREY ORME & BARBARA K. EMARY | Illustrated by WILLIAM STOBBS | [illustration of two gipsy caravans]'. Spine lettered horizontally: 'The | Grand | Escap- | ade | * | George | Pen- | gelly | [at bottom] a | Peter | Lunn | book | for | boys | and | girls'. Back: 'Peter Lunn's other | [in red] adventure stories | for boys and girls | [advertisements for five books] | [in red] Peter Lunn | 49 Chancery Lane London'. Front flap: '[in red] THE GRAND ESCAPADE | [synopsis] | [in red] A Peter Lunn book for boys | [in red] and girls | [at bottom right] 6/- net'. Back flap: '[in red] The Phantom | [advertisement for a book]'.

Notes Category: Adventure. Scarcity: 4.

There are variant bindings in green and grey cloth. The back cover of the dustjacket has advertisements for *Studio J Investigates*, *Mr Bosanko*, *The Angry Planet*, *The Owl and the Pussycat* and *The Lost Mountain*. The back flap has an advertisement for *The Phantom*. The book is an adaptation from the 70-minute children's film 'The Grand Escapade', released by the British Lion Film Corporation in September 1946. The film was directed by John Baxter and the script written by Geoffrey Orme and Barbara Emary.

PL90 The Wandering Otter by Mortimer Batten, illustrated by David Pratt, March 1947, [September 1947], 7/6d.

MORTIMER BATTEN | THE | WANDERING | OTTER | WITH DRAWINGS BY | DAVID PRATT | [illustration] | PETER LUNN | LONDON 1947

Collation (183 x 121 mm): [1-6], 7-12 12pp section uncoded; 13-154, [155-156] in 9 x 16pp sections coded B-K.

Contents [1] half-title: 'The Wandering Otter'; [2] frontis, reproducing illustration on p. [35]; [3] title; [4] imprint: 'First published in March 1947 by | Peter Lunn (Publishers) Ltd | 49 Chancery Lane London WC2 | All rights reserved | Printed in Great Britain by | Balding & Mansell Ltd | Park Works | Wisbech'; [5] contents; [6] blank; 7-154, [155] text (see illustration list for unnumbered pages); [156] illustration. Pages [12], [36], [44], [48], [76], [86], [94], [108], [116], [128], [144] and [150] are blank.

Illustrations Full-page illustrations on pp. [2], [11], [35], [43], [47], [75], [85], [93], [107], [115], [127], [143] and [149]. Various other illustrations.

Paper White wove text paper and endpapers.

Binding (188 x 129 x 12 mm): orange cloth. Front cover blank. Spine lettered horizontally in gilt: 'The | Wandering | Otter | * | Batten | [at bottom] Peter | Lunn'. Back cover blank.

Later releases WFL.

Notes Category: Nature. Scarcity: 3.

There are variant bindings in grey and red cloth.

PL91 Pinocchio by Carlo Collodi, illustrated by Philip Gough, September 1947, 8/6d.

PINOCCHIO | A STORY OF A PUPPET | CARLO COLLODI | [illustration] | DRAWINGS BY | PHILIP GOUGH | PETER LUNN | LONDON 1947

Collation (182 x 119 mm): [i-ii], 1, [2-10], 11-236, [237-238] in 15 x 16pp sections coded: uncoded, B-H, K-Q.

Contents [i-ii] blank; 1 half-title: '[at right] PINOCCHIO'; [2] frontis; [3] title; [4] imprint: 'First published in September 1947 | PETER LUNN (Publishers) LTD | 49 Chancery Lane London | All rights reserved | Printed in Great Britain by | WEST BROTHERS | Mitcham'; [5-10] contents; 11-235, [236] text (see illustration list for unnumbered pages); [237-238] blank.

Illustrations Full-page illustrations on pp. [2], [26], [51], [55], [87] and [123]. Various other illustrations.

Paper White wove text paper and endpapers.

Binding (188 x 129 x 19 mm): crimson cloth. Front cover blank. Spine lettered horizontally in gilt: 'Pinocchio | * | Carlo | Collodi | [at bottom] Peter | Lunn'. Back cover blank.

Dustjacket (187 x 455 mm): white wove paper. Front: '[in red] PINOCCHIO [in black sloping script, overlapping end of preceding word] the story of a puppet | [at left, illustration of seated man in top hat with two puppets, near open window] [at right, lettered vertically from top in red] PINOCCHIO | [in script] by C. Collodi with illustrations | [in script] by Phillip [sic] Gough * [in red script] a Peter Lunn book'. Spine lettered vertically from top, all in script: '[in red] Pinocchio * Collodi | [illustration of dancing puppet holding umbrella] Peter Lunn'. Back: 'Peter Lunn | have also published other | [in red] children's books | [advertisements for six books] | [in red] PETER LUNN | 49 Chancery Lane London'. Front flap: '[synopsis] | [at right] 8s 6d net | [in red] a Peter Lunn book'. Back flap blank.

Later releases WFL.

Notes Category: Classic. Scarcity: 3.

The back of the dustjacket has advertisements for *Detectives in Greasepaint*, *Mr Bosanko*, *Full Fathom Five*, *Here Lies Gold*, *The Story of a Tree* and *English Trees*.

PL92 Stories from Ancient Greece introduced [and retold] by John Kent, illustrated by Ann Buckmaster, March 1947, [September 1947], 8/6d.

EDITED BY JOHN KENT | STORIES | FROM ANCIENT | GREECE | WITH DECORATIONS | BY | ANN BUCKMASTER | PETER LUNN | LONDON 1947

Collation (185 x 120 mm): [1-8], 9-223, [224] in 14 x 16pp uncoded sections.

Contents [1] half-title: 'STORIES FROM ANCIENT GREECE'; [2] frontis; [3] title; [4] imprint: '*First published in March 1947* | BY PETER LUNN (PUBLISHERS) LIMITED | *49 Chancery Lane London WC2* | *All rights reserved* | *Printed in Great Britain* | BY W S CAINES LIMITED | *193 Balaam Street London E13*'; [5] contents; [6] blank; [7] introduction, signed 'JOHN KENT' at bottom right; [8] blank; 9-223 text; [224] blank.

Illustrations Full-page illustration on p. [2]. A smaller illustration precedes each chapter heading. All illustrations are against various single colour backgrounds.

Paper White wove text paper and endpapers.

Binding (190 x 126 x 18 mm): black cloth. Centre of front cover stamped in white with a schematic illustration of a classical temple. Spine lettered vertically from top in white: 'STORIES FROM ANCIENT GREECE * PETER LUNN'. Back cover blank.

Dustjacket (190 x 455 mm): thickish white wove paper. Front and spine are printed against a uniform pale blue background. Front: 'STORIES FROM ANCIENT GREECE | [illustration in white against a black panel of young woman with an ox lying on grass] | EDITED BY JOHN KENT | [illustration in white against a black panel of a naked bearded man pushing a large stone up a hill, with sun in background] | DRAWINGS BY ANN BUCKMASTER'. Spine lettered horizontally: 'Stories | from | Ancient | Greece | * | Kent | [at bottom] Peter | Lunn'. Back: '*Peter Lunn's other* | [in pale blue] CHILDREN'S BOOKS | *include these titles:* | [advertisements for three books] | [in pale blue] PETER LUNN | 49 Chancery Lane London'. Front flap: '[in pale blue] Stories from Ancient Greece | [synopsis, reproducing the text of the introduction] | [in pale blue] A Peter Lunn Book | [in pale blue] for boys and girls | [at right] *8s 6d net*'. Back flap has an advertisement for a book.

Later releases [WFL].

Notes Category: Classic/Educational. **Scarcity**: 3.

The binding cloth and front cover motif are uniform with *Homer's Odyssey*. The back of the dustjacket has advertisements for *Alhambra Tales*, *Arabian Nights* and *The Enchanted Glen*. The back flap has an advertisement for *Homer's Odyssey*.

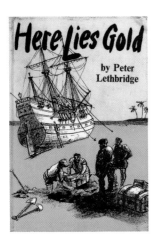

PL93 **Here Lies Gold** by Peter Lethbridge, illustrated by John Lewis, March 1947, [September 1947], 8/6d.

STORIES OF | THE WORLD'S LOST TREASURES | HERE LIES | GOLD | BY PETER LETHBRIDGE | WITH DRAWINGS | BY JOHN LEWIS | PETER LUNN | LONDON | 1947

Collation (184 x 120 mm): [1-6], 7-272 in 17 x 16pp sections coded: uncoded, B-H, uncoded, K-Q, uncoded. Page 273 is printed on the recto of the rear free endpaper.

Contents [1] half-title: [at right] HERE LIES GOLD'; [2] frontis., reproducing illustration on p. [103]; [3] title; [4] imprint: 'First published in March 1947 by | PETER LUNN (PUBLISHERS) LIMITED | 49 Chancery Lane London WC2 | All rights reserved | Printed in Great Britain by | W. S. CAINES LIMITED | Andover House Broadway Plaistow | London E13'; [5] '[contents] | and many drawings by | JOHN LEWIS'; [6] blank; 7-273 text (see illustration list for unnumbered pages).

Illustrations Full-page illustrations on pp. [2], [32], [61], [84], [103], [112], [130], [146], [164], [176], [204], [227] and [263].

Paper White wove text paper and endpapers.

Binding (188 x 128 x 21 mm): coarse-grained blue-green cloth. Front cover stamped in gilt at bottom right with an illustration of a sailing ship. Spine lettered horizontally in gilt: 'Here | Lies | Gold | * | Lethbridge | [at bottom] Peter | Lunn'. Back cover blank.

Dustjacket (190 x 469 mm): white surfaced wove paper. Front is lettered against a background illustration in blue, black and yellow of four men with treasure-chests and spades next to a beached sailing ship, with sea and palm-trees in the background. Front: '[in script] Here Lies Gold | by Peter | Lethbridge'. Spine lettered horizontally: 'Here | Lies | Gold | * | Peter | Leth- | bridge | [at bottom] Peter | Lunn'. Back: 'Peter Lunn has also published | [advertisement for a book] | [in yellow] Peter Lunn | 49 Chancery Lane London'. Front flap: '[in yellow] HERE LIES GOLD | [synopsis] | [in yellow] A Peter Lunn book for boys & girls | [at bottom right] 8s 6d net'. Back flap: 'If you like tales of men who | seek fortune in the face of | hardship you will enjoy | reading | [advertisement for a book] | [in yellow] A Peter Lunn book for boys & girls'.

Later releases WFL.

Notes Category: Adventure. **Scarcity**: 3.

The back of the dustjacket has an advertisement for Full Fathom Five. The back flap has an advertisement for Great Gold Rushes.

PL94 **The Ivory Trail** by Hugh Mackay, illustrated by Frank Baber, February 1947, [September/October 1947], 7/6d.

HUGH MACKAY | THE IVORY | TRAIL | WITH DRAWINGS BY | FRANK BABER | PETER LUNN | LONDON 1947

Collation (183 x 121 mm): [1-6], 7-160 in 5 x 32pp sections coded: uncoded, B, C, uncoded, E; 161-176 16pp section uncoded.

Contents [1] half-title: '[at top right] THE IVORY TRAIL'; [2] frontis., reproducing illustration on p. [97] in mirror-image; [3] title; [4] imprint: '*First published in February 1947 by* | PETER LUNN (PUBLISHERS) LIMITED | *49 Chancery Lane London WC2* | *All rights reserved* | *Printed in Great Britain by* | *W. S. CAINES LIMITED* | *193 Balaam Street London E 13*'; [5] contents; [6] 'THE IVORY TRAIL | *is dedicated with love to* | MY WIFE'; 7-176 text (see illustration list for unnumbered pages).

Illustrations Full-page illustrations on pp. [2], [26], [49], [65], [76], [89], [97], [121], [137], [143], [145] and [173].

Paper White wove text paper and endpapers.

Binding (189 x 128 x 18 mm): coarse-grained blue cloth. Front cover blank. Spine lettered vertically from top in gilt: 'THE IVORY TRAIL Mackay [horizontally at bottom] Peter | Lunn'. Back cover blank.

Dustjacket (190 x 469 mm): white surfaced wove paper. The front cover is lettered in red against a pale blue background edged in red, arranged around an illustration in brown of a tribesman on a horse in foreground and more tribesmen and camels in background (reproducing illustration on p. [97]). Front: 'The Ivory Trail | a story | of | Africa | by Hugh | Mackay | drawings by | Frank | Baber'. Spine lettered horizontally against a red background: 'The | Ivory | Trail | * | Hugh | Mackay | [at bottom] Peter | Lunn'. Back is printed on a pale blue background: '[in brown] Peter Lunn publishes other | [in red] adventure stories | [advertisements for three books, in brown] | [in red] PETER LUNN | [in brown] 49 Chancery Lane London'. Front flap: '[in red] all about 'The Ivory Trail' | [synopsis, in brown] | [in red] A Peter Lunn book for boys and girls' | [in brown, at bottom right] 7s 6d net'. Back flap: '[in red] SONG OF ARIZONA | [advertisement for a book, in brown] | [in red] A Peter Lunn book for boys and girls'.

Notes Category: Adventure. **Scarcity**: 4.

The back of the dustjacket has advertisements for *The Haunted Island*, *The Hunting of Zakaroff* and *The Ghost of Gordon Gregory*. The back flap has an advertisement for *Song of Arizona*.

PL95 China Coast Pirates by Donald Moore, illustrated by Laurence Scarfe, December 1946, [September 1947], 8/6d.

DONALD MOORE | CHINA COAST | PIRATES | DRAWINGS BY | LAURENCE SCARFE | [illustration] | PETER LUNN | LONDON 1946

Collation   (185 x 122 mm): [1-6], 7-128 in 8 x 16pp sections coded: uncoded, B, uncoded, D-H; 129-160 32pp section coded I; 161-183, [184] 24pp section uncoded.

Contents   [1] half-title: '[at right] *China Coast Pirates*'; [2] frontis; [3] title; [4] imprint: '*First Published in December 1946 by | Peter Lunn (Publishers) Ltd. | 49 Chancery Lane London WC2 | All rights reserved | Printed in Great Britain by | Samuel Sidders & Son Ltd. | 115 Salusbury Road London NW6*'; [5] '[contents] | and many drawings by | LAURENCE SCARFE'; [6] blank; 7-183, [184] text (see illustration list for unnumbered pages).

Illustrations   Full-page illustrations on pp. [2], [11], [33], [39], [55], [75], [86], [106], [131], [150], [161] and [182].

Paper   White wove text paper and endpapers.

Binding   (190 x 126 x 12 mm): mustard-yellow cloth. Front cover blank. Spine lettered horizontally in black: '*China | Coast | Pirates | by | Donald | Moore | [at bottom] Peter | Lunn*'. Back cover blank.

Dustjacket   (190 x 437 mm): white surfaced wove paper. Front and spine are printed on a uniform red background. Front: '[in script] *China Coast Pirates* | by Donald Moore: drawings by Laurence Scarfe | [at left, against a background panel illustrating in blue and black an airman floating in a choppy sea being approached by a junk] A thrilling | boys' story | of a dangerous | Secret Service | mission | in Northern | China'. Spine lettered horizontally: '*China | Coast | Pirates* | * Donald | Moore | [at bottom] Peter | Lunn'. Back: 'Peter Lunn publishes other | [in red] adventure stories | for boys and girls | [advertisements for three books] | [in red] Peter Lunn | 49 Chancery Lane London'. Front flap: '[in red] China Coast Pirates | [synopsis] | [in red, at left] A Peter Lunn book | [in red, at right] for boys and girls | [at right] 8s 6d net'. Back flap has an advertisement for a book.

Notes   Category: Adventure. **Scarcity:** 4.

The back cover of the dustjacket has advertisements for *The Lost Mountain*, *Night Cargoes* and *The Hunting of Zakaroff*. The back flap has an advertisement for *Bright is the Starlight*.

PL96 12 Adventures of the Celebrated Baron Munchausen

[by Rudolph Raspe, and others], selected, introduced and illustrated by Brian Robb, June 1947, [September 1947], 7/6d.

[in crescent formation] 12 ADVENTURES OF THE | CELEBRATED | BARON MUNCHAUSEN | *selected and illustrated by* | BRIAN ROBB | PETER LUNN | 1947

Collation (184 x 122 mm): [1-4], 5-8 8pp section uncoded; 9-88 in 5 x 16pp sections coded B-F; 89-104, [105-108] 20pp section coded G.

Contents [1] half-title: '[in script, contained within the outline of a man with a hat and raised sword astride a horse] 12 | ADVENTURES | OF THE | CELEBRATED | BARON | MUNCHAUSEN'; [2-3] double-page illustration with the right-hand page overlaid with the title; [4] imprint: '[all in script contained within a drawing of a piece of unfurled cloth tied at the right-hand end] First published in June 1947 by | PETER LUNN (PUBLISHERS) LIMITED | 49 CHANCERY LANE LONDON WC2. | Printed in Great Britain by | SAMUEL SIDDERS LIMITED | 115 SALUSBURY ROAD LONDON NW6 | for | [illustration of an insect standing on one leg reading a book]; 5-104 text (including contents list on pp. 10-12); [105] illustration of balloon with man in basket below, incorporating text 'THE END'; [106-108] blank.

Illustrations Full-page illustrations on pp. [9], [35] (carrying over to p. 34), [42] (carrying over to p. [43]), [49] (carrying over to p. 48), [51], [67], [75] (carrying over to p. 74), [92] and [101]. Double-page illustrations on pp. [2-3], [22-23] (in landscape orientation), [28-29] and [96-97]. Various other illustrations, many carrying over two pages. The front and rear endpapers are printed identically as a double-page spread with: 'A PICTURE OF THE GLOBE | Drawn to the direction of the late BARON MUNCHAUSEN in order to | facilitate the study of his travels and adventures | [illustration of a globe with stylised numbered hands pointing to locations, linking to captions to the left and right of the globe] | correctly drawn to scale on the BARON'S own projection'.

Paper White wove text paper and endpapers.

Binding (188 x 128 x 11 mm): beige cloth. Front cover is stamped in gilt with an outline of a man with a hat and raised sword astride a horse, the horse composed from stylised lettering 'MUNCHAUSEN'. Spine lettered vertically from top in gilt: 'BRIAN ROBB . BARON MUNCHAUSEN . PETER LUNN'. Back cover blank.

Dustjacket (188 x 457 mm): white surfaced wove paper. Front, spine, back and both flaps are printed against a uniform yellow background. Front: '12 ADVENTURES | [illustration in black and red of a uniformed man with raised sword astride a horse which has its front legs raised, looking at his reflection in a mirror]'. The mirror, man and horse stand on a chest which incorporates the following text, in a variety of styles and orientation of lettering: 'OF | THE CELEBRATED BARON | [in red] MUNCHAUSEN | SELECTED AND ILLUSTRATED | by | Brian Robb | PETER LUNN | 1947'. Spine lettered vertically from top 'BRIAN ROBB . BARON MUNCHAUSEN . PETER LUNN'. Back has an illustration of an affidavit confirming the truth of Munchausen's tales, reproducing the illustration on p. [9]. Front flap: '[in red] Baron Munchausen | Selected and illustrated by | BRIAN ROBB | [synopsis] | [at bottom right] 7s 6d net'. Back flap: '[in red] Other Peter Lunn books | [advertisements for three books]'.

Later releases Reissued in August 1950 at 2/6d.

Notes Category: Classic. Scarcity: 1.

There is a variant binding in red cloth. The back flap has advertisements for *The Owl and the Pussycat*, *Don Quixote de la Mancha* and *The Glastonbury Adventure*. Another version of this book with the same text and illustrations was published in 1978 by Deutsch.

The book comprises short extracts from 10 of the 35 chapters of the 1793 English publication of the Munchausen stories, which is the most complete. Chapters 1-12 in this volume are taken, respectively, from chapters II, II, IV, V, V, VI, VII, VIII, IX, XVII, XVIII and XXXIV of the original work. The work has quite a complicated history of publication and attribution of authorship is uncertain. The earliest edition (which was in English – it was only later translated into German) was *Baron Munchausen's Narrative of his Marvellous Travels and Campaigns in Russia* (Smith, 1785), and this is an incredibly rare 48-page booklet containing only chapters II to VI of the 1793 edition. An 'intermediate' edition, containing chapters I to XX appeared in 1786. The authorship of these editions was not stated. Subsequent research has suggested that chapters II to VI were indeed by Raspe, the remainder of chapters I-XX possibly by Raspe, and the remainder probably by another hand.

PL97 The Master of Magic by Michael Stone, illustrated by H. W. Hailstone, May 1947, [September 1947], 6/-.

MICHAEL STONE | THE MASTER OF MAGIC | *with illustrations by* | H.W.HAILSTONE | PETER LUNN | *London* | 1947

Collation (185 x 120 mm): [1-6], 7-160 in 5 x 32pp sections coded: uncoded, B-E; 161-184 24pp section coded F; 185-213, [214-216] 32pp section coded G.

Contents [1] half-title: 'The Master of Magic'; [2] frontis; [3] title; [4] imprint: 'First published in May 1947 by | PETER LUNN (PUBLISHERS) LIMITED | 49 Chancery Lane London WC2 | All rights reserved | Printed in Great Britain by | SAMUEL SIDDERS & SON LIMITED | 115 Salusbury Road London NW6'; [5] contents; [6] 'For | MICHAEL EGAN'; 7-213 text (see illustration list for unnumbered pages).

Illustrations Full-page illustrations on pp. [2], [28], [87] and [107]. Various other illustrations.

Paper White wove text paper and endpapers.

Binding (190 x 128 x 12 mm): maroon glazed cloth textured with a wavy pattern. Front cover blank. Spine lettered horizontally in gilt: 'The | Master | of | Magic | * | Stone | [at bottom] Peter | Lunn'. Back cover blank.

Dustjacket Front is printed on a uniform pale blue background. Front: 'The | Master of Magic | Michael Stone | [at left, lettered vertically from bottom] An amusing tale for boys & girls [illustration framed in red of two boys at mouth of a cave looking at a man with bag over shoulder and a dog] [at right, lettered vertically from top] Illustrated by H. W. Hailstone'. Spine lettered horizontally: 'The | Master | of | Magic | * | Michael | Stone | [at bottom] a | Peter | Lunn | Book | for | boys | and | girls'. Back: 'Peter Lunn has also published | [advertisement for a book] | [in red] PETER LUNN | 49 Chancery Lane London'. Front flap: '[in red] The Master of Magic | [synopsis] | [in red] A Peter Lunn book for | [in red] boys & girls | [?price at bottom right]'. Back flap has an advertisement for a book.

Copies consulted BL and private collection.

Notes Category: Adventure. **Scarcity**: 4.

There is a variant binding in green cloth. The back of the dustjacket has an advertisement for *The Ghost of Gordon Gregory*. The back flap has an advertisement for *The Adventure at Marston Manor*.

PL98 **The Champion** by Gordon Grimsley, illustrated by Frank Baber, October 1947, 8/6d.

GORDON GRIMSLEY | THE CHAMPION | *With illustrations by* | FRANK BABER | PETER LUNN | LONDON 1947

Collation (183 x 121 mm): [1-6], 7-192 in 12 x 16pp sections coded: uncoded, B-M; 193-203, [204] 12pp section coded N on p. 193 and N* on p. 195.

Contents [1] half-title: 'THE CHAMPION'; [2] frontis; [3] title; [4] imprint: '*First published in October 1947 by* | PETER LUNN (PUBLISHERS) LIMITED | *49 Chancery Lane London WC2* | *All rights reserved* | *Printed in Great Britain by* | SPEEDEE PRESS SERVICES LIMITED | *206 Union Street SE1*'; [5] contents; [6] blank; 7-203, [204] text (see illustration list for unnumbered pages).

Illustrations Full-page illustrations on pp. [2], [32], [72], [107], [137], [175] and [196]. Various other illustrations.

Paper White wove text paper and endpapers.

Binding (189 x 130 x 19 mm): green cloth. Front cover blank. Spine lettered horizontally in gilt: 'The | Champion | * | Grimsley | [at bottom] Peter | Lunn'. Back cover blank.

Dustjacket (191 x 499 mm): white surfaced wove paper. Front has text on a red panel at top: '[in white script] The Champion | [in brown] BY GORDON GRIMSLEY'. Below panel is an illustration in brown against a pale blue background of two boxers and referee. Spine lettered horizontally: '[in red] The | Champion | [in brown] * | Gordon | Grimsley | [at bottom] a | Peter | Lunn | book | for | boys | and | girls'. Back: '[in brown] Peter Lunn has published other | [in red] adventure stories | [in brown] Titles include | [advertisements for three books] | [in red] Peter Lunn | [in brown] 49 Chancery Lane London'. Front flap: '[in red] The Champion | [in brown] synopsis | [at right] 8s 6d net | [in red] A Peter Lunn book | [in red] for boys and girls'. Back flap has an advertisement for a book.

Later releases Reissued in September 1950 at 3/6d.

Notes Category: Adventure. Scarcity: 4.

The back of the dustjacket advertises *The Lost Mountain*, *Night Cargoes* and *The Hunting of Zakaroff*. The back flap of the dustjacket advertises *The Grand Escapade*.

PL99 English Trees written and illustrated by Nora Kay, August 1947, [October 1947], 7/6d.

ENGLISH TREES | [illustration] | *Written and illustrated* | by NORA KAY | *Introduced by* | RICHARD St BARBE BAKER | PETER LUNN . LONDON

Collation (182 x 122 mm): [i-ii], [1-6], 7-91, [92-94] in 6 x 16pp sections coded: uncoded, B-F. Pages [i-ii] form the front pastedown and pages [93-94] the rear pastedown. There are no free endpapers.

Contents [1] half-title: 'ENGLISH TREES'; [2] frontis., reproducing illustration on p. 15; [3] title; [4] imprint: '*First published in August 1947 by* | PETER LUNN (PUBLISHERS) LIMITED | *49 Chancery Lane London WC2* | *All rights reserved* | *Printed in Great Britain by* | SAMUEL SIDDERS AND SON LIMITED | 115 *Salusbury Road London NW6*'; [5-6] contents; 7-91 text; [92] blank. The title page, and the text of the book (excluding the introduction on pp. 7-11), is all in italic script.

Illustrations Full-page illustrations in green and black (of the trees) on p. [2] and on all right-hand pages from pp. 13 to 91. Small green and black illustrations (of the leaves) accompanying the text on all corresponding left-hand pages.

Paper White wove text paper and endpapers.

Binding (190 x 128 x 8 mm): green cloth. Front cover stamped in gilt with an illustration of a conifer. Spine lettered vertically from top in gilt: '*ENGLISH TREES * NORA KAY PETER LUNN*'. Back cover blank.

Dustjacket (192 x 445 mm): white surfaced wove paper. Front and spine are printed against a uniform yellow background. Front: '[in green script] ENGLISH | [in green script] TREES | [illustration in green and black of an oak tree above with leaves and acorns below]'. There are two columns of text on each side of the illustration. At left: 'Drawings | and | descriptions | of over | 50 trees | by | Nora Kay | Preface by | Richard | St. Barbe | Baker'. At right: 'A new | Peter | Lunn | book | for | boys | and | girls | of all | ages'. Spine lettered vertically from top: '[in green] ENGLISH TREES | * | [lettered horizontally] Nora | Kay | [at bottom] A | Peter | Lunn | book | for | boys | & | girls'. Back: '[in green] Peter Lunn | [in green] has also published | [advertisements for three books] | [in green] PETER LUNN | 49 Chancery Lane London'. Front flap: '[in green] English Trees | [synopsis] | [in green] A Peter Lunn book | [in green] for boys and girls | [at bottom right] 7s 6d net'. Back flap: 'Another Peter Lunn book | [advertisement for a book]'.

Notes Category: Educational/Nature. **Scarcity**: 3.

The back of the dustjacket has advertisements for *Horses and Riders, How is Inky?* and *Beppo*. The back flap has an advertisement for *The Wandering Otter*. The book is introduced by Richard St. Barbe Baker, stated to be 'Founder of The Men of the Trees'.

PL100 God of Brazil by Edward Buckingham, illustrated by Philip Gough, November 1947, 6/-.

GOD OF | BRAZIL | BY | EDWARD BUCKINGHAM | *with illustrations by* | PHILIP GOUGH | PETER LUNN | *London 1947*

Collation (183 x 121 mm): [1-6], 7-192 in 6 x 32pp sections coded: uncoded, B-F on first page of each section and: uncoded, B1, C1, uncoded, E1 and F on the third page of each section; 193, [194-196] 4pp section uncoded.

Contents [1] half-title: '[at right] *God of Brazil*'; [2-3] double-page illustration integrated with title on p. [3]; [4] imprint: '*First published in November 1947 by* | PETER LUNN (PUBLISHERS) LIMITED | *49 Chancery Lane London W C 2* | *All rights reserved* | *Printed in Great Britain by* | WILLIAMS-COOK LIMITED | *Brunel Road Acton W 3*'; [5] contents; [6] blank; 7-193, [194] text (see illustration list for unnumbered pages); [195-196] blank.

Illustrations Full-page illustrations on pp. [21], [47], [61], [72], [83], [130], [147], [163], [177] and [186]. Double-page illustrations on pp. [2-3] and [98-99]. One other illustration on p. 7.

Paper White wove text paper and endpapers.

Binding (187 x 130 x 12 mm): blue cloth. Front cover blank. Spine lettered horizontally in gilt: 'God of | Brazil | * | Edward | Buck- | ingham | [at bottom] Peter | Lunn'. Back cover blank.

Dustjacket (187 x 453 mm): white surfaced wove paper. Front and spine are printed on a uniform yellow background. Front: '[in red, in crescent formation] GOD OF BRAZIL | [at left, lettered vertically from bottom] a thrilling story of adventure | [illustration in black and white within panel bordered in red of various figures in plumed headdresses before the statue of a god] | [at right lettered vertically from top] in the unknown Matto Grosso | by Edward Buckingham | with drawings by Philip Gough'. Spine lettered horizontally: 'God | of | Brazil | * | Edward | Buck- | ingham | [at bottom] a | Peter | Lunn | book | for | boys | and | girls'. Back: 'a few of Peter Lunn's | [in red] adventure stories | for boys & girls | [advertisements for three books] | [in red] Peter Lunn | 49 Chancery Lane London'.

Front flap: '[in red] God of Brazil | [synopsis] | * | [in red] A Peter Lunn book | [in red] for boys and girls | [at bottom right] 7s 6d net'. The back flap has an advertisement for a book.

Later releases WFL.

Notes Category: Adventure. **Scarcity**: 4.

On the copy described, the '7s 6d net' price on the front flap has been overlaid with a printed label for '6s od net', probably by the publisher. The back of the dustjacket has advertisements for *The Haunted Island*, *The Hunting of Zakaroff* and *The Ghost of Gordon Gregory*. The back flap has an advertisement for *Black Sunset*.

PL101 The Silver Florin and other stories by William Hauff, illustrated by Philip Gough, November 1947, [7/6d].

THE SILVER FLORIN | *and other stories* | *by* | WILLIAM HAUFF | *illustrated by* | PHILIP GOUGH | PETER LUNN | LONDON | 1947

Collation (182 x 122 mm): [1-6], 7-218, [219-224] in 14 x 16pp sections coded: uncoded, B-P (pp. [221-224] form the rear endpaper and pastedown).

Contents [1] half-title: 'THE SILVER FLORIN'; [2] frontis; [3] title; [4] imprint: '*First published in November 1947 by* | PETER LUNN (PUBLISHERS) LIMITED | *49 Chancery Lane London WC2* | *All rights reserved* | Printed in Great Britain by | CAINES . BROADWAY . PLAISTOW . LONDON . E13'; [5] contents; [6] blank; 7-218 text (see illustration list for unnumbered pages); [219] illustration; [220] blank. Pages [30], [66] and [206] are also blank.

Illustrations Full-page illustrations on pp. [2], [113] and [219]. Various other illustrations.

Paper White wove text paper and endpapers.

Binding (190 x 130 x 21 mm): ochre cloth. Front cover blank. Spine lettered horizontally in gilt: 'THE | SILVER | FLORIN | WILLIAM | HAUFF'. Back cover blank.

Dustjacket (190 x 459 mm): white surfaced wove paper. The front and spine are printed on a background which shades gradually from red at the top to blue at the bottom. Front: '[coloured illustration of man in hat and wig astride a rearing horse] | [in purple Gothic] The Silver Florin | [in red] FAIRY STORIES BY HAUFF | [coloured illustration of a man and woman dancing in front of a seated audience]'. Spine lettered horizontally: 'HAUFF | [in purple Gothic] The | Silver | Florin | [at bottom, in purple] Peter | Lunn'.

Back: 'Peter Lunn has published other | [in red] CHILDREN'S BOOKS | Titles include | [advertisements for two books] | [in red] PETER LUNN | 49 Chancery Lane London'. Front flap: '[in red] The Silver Florin | [synopsis] | [in red] A Peter Lunn Book | [in red] for children | [price at bottom right, clipped on copy described]'. Back flap: 'Another Peter Lunn Book | [advertisement for a book] | [in red] A Peter Lunn Book'.

Notes Category: Fairy. **Scarcity:** 3.

The print-run was 5100. Advertised at 7/6d in the July 1947 issue of *Publishers' Circular*. Smith reports having seen two versions of the dustjacket. The book contains the following stories: The Silver Florin; Longnose the Dwarf; The Story of Little Mook; How the Caliph became a Stork; The Adventures of Said; The Heart of Stone; The Ghost Ship. The back of the dustjacket has advertisements for *Fairy Tales with a Twist* and *Pinocchio*. The back flap has an advertisement for *Adolphus' Playbook*.

PL102 The Thunderbolt Men by David S. MacArthur, illustrated by William Stobbs, February 1947, [November 1947], 8/6d.

David S. MacArthur | THE | THUNDERBOLT | MEN | *with many drawings by* | William Stobbs | Peter Lunn | London 1947

Collation (191 x 124 mm): [1-6], 7-216 in 9 x 24pp sections; 217-229, [230-232] 16pp section. All sections uncoded.

Contents [1] half-title: 'THE THUNDERBOLT MEN'; [2] frontis., reproducing illustration on p. [74]; [3] title; [4] imprint: 'First published in February 1947 by | Peter Lunn (Publishers) Limited | 49 Chancery Lane, London, W.C.2 | All rights reserved | Printed in Great Britain by | CLARIDGE, LEWIS & JORDAN LIMITED | 68/70 Wardour Street London W 1'; [5] contents; [6] blank; 7-229 text (see illustration list for unnumbered pages); [230-232] blank.

Illustrations Full-page illustrations on pp. [2], [10], 14, [21], [57], [74], [104], [112], [122], [156], [173], [195], [212], [219] and 224. Various other illustrations.

Paper White wove text paper and endpapers.

Binding (196 x 135 x 13 mm): blue cloth. Front cover blank. Spine lettered horizontally in gilt: 'The | Thunder- | bolt | Men | * | Mac | Arthur | [at bottom] Peter | Lunn'. Back cover blank.

Dustjacket (195 x 479 mm): white surfaced wove paper. Front has three illustrations within pale blue panels together with black text, all on a red background. Illustration at top left is of a boy and a girl, at top right of two helmeted men, and at bottom of a flotilla of boats with sails. The central text panel has: '[in script] THE THUNDERBOLT MEN | A story of adventure by David MacArthur | with illustrations by William Stobbs'. Spine lettered horizontally: 'The | Thunderbolt | Men | * | MacArthur | [at bottom] A | Peter | Lunn | book'. Back: 'Peter Lunn publishes other | [in red] adventure stories | for boys and girls | [advertisements for five books] | [in red] Peter Lunn | 49 Chancery Lane London'. Front flap: '[in red] The Thunderbolt Men | [synopsis] | [in red] A Peter Lunn book for boys and | [in red] girls | [at right] 8s 6d net'. Back flap has an advertisement for a book.

Later releases Reissued in August 1950 at 5/-.

Notes Category: Adventure. **Scarcity:** 3.

The print-run was 5500. The back of the dustjacket advertises *The Haunted Island*, *Detectives in Greasepaint*, *Mr Bosanko*, *Full Fathom Five* and *Here Lies Gold*. The back flap advertises 'The Captives of Black Rock Island' (working title of *Black Rock Island*).

PL103 The Picture Frame by Pieter van Oostkerke, illustrated with colour plates, July 1947, [November 1947], [17/6d].

THE | PICTURE FRAME | *WITH TWELVE REPRODUCTIONS* | OF FAMOUS PAINTINGS | BY WORLD-FAMOUS ARTISTS | PIETER VAN OOSTKERKE | PETER LUNN | LONDON | 1947

Collation (280 x 219 mm): [1-8], 9-18 16pp uncoded section with a single leaf for frontis tipped in to p. [3], and [11-12] as a plate; 19-38 16pp section coded B, with [21-22] and [31-32] as plates; 39-57 16pp section coded C with [41-42], [49-50] and [59-60] as plates; 61-80 16pp section coded D, with [69-70] and [77-78] as plates; 81-98 16pp section coded E with [89-90] as plate; 99-118 16pp section coded F, with [103-104] and [111-112] as plates; 119-127, [128] 8pp section coded G with [121-122] as plate. All plates are coloured reproductions and are tipped in to the following page, with the reproduction on the verso, and the recto blank.

Contents [1] half-title: 'The Picture Frame'; [2] blank; [3] title; [4] imprint: 'First published in July 1947 by | PETER LUNN (PUBLISHERS) LIMITED | 49 Chancery Lane London WC2 | All rights reserved | Printed in Great Britain by the | KENNERLEY PRESS LIMITED | 1-4 Britannia Walk City Road | London N1'; [5] contents; [6] blank; [7-8] list of plates; 9-127 text, in double columns; [128] blank. The following pages are blank and unnumbered: 20, 30, 40, 48, 58, 68, 76, 88, 100, 110 and 120.

Illustrations Full-page coloured reproductions of paintings on: frontis (reproducing plate on p. [22]) and pp. [12], [22], [32], [42], [50], [60], [70], [78], [90], [104], [112] and [122].

Paper White cartridge text paper and endpapers. White surfaced paper for plates.

Binding (287 x 224 x 13 mm): beige cloth. Front cover has illustration at bottom right of a knight stamped in blue, on a horse stamped in white. Spine lettered in blue '[rule] | [lettered vertically from top] THE PICTURE FRAME [lettered horizontally at bottom] PETER | LUNN | [rule]'. Back cover blank.

Copy consulted BL.

Later releases Reissued in July 1950 at 7/6d.

Notes Category: Educational. Scarcity: 5.

Advertised at 12/6d in the November 1947 issue of *Publishers' Circular*, although a number of other advertisements state that it was published at 17/6d. The pictures illustrated and described are: Mr and Mrs Arnolfini (Jan van Eyck); Lady Jean (George Bellows); The Madonna of the Rose Garden (Memling school); Hunters in the Snow (Peter Bruegel); The Weeping Madonna (Dirk Bouts); The Maids of Honour (Diego Rodriguez de Silva y Velasquez); St. George and the Dragon (Raphael); Portrait of a Man (Hans Memling); By the Seashore (Renoir); Madonna and Child (Dirk Bouts); The Madonna of Martin van Nieuwenhoven (Hans Memling); The Ince Hall Madonna (Jan van Eyck).

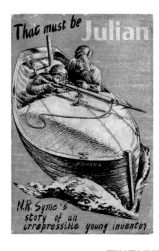

PL104 That Must Be Julian by N. R. Syme, illustrated by William Stobbs, July 1947, [November 1947], 8/6d.

THAT MUST | BE JULIAN | BY N R SYME | *with illustrations* | *by William Stobbs* | PETER LUNN | LONDON 1947

Collation (183 x 122 mm): [1-6], 7-205, [206-208] in 13 x 16pp sections coded: uncoded, uncoded, C-H, uncoded, K, uncoded, M-N.

Contents [1] half-title: 'THAT MUST BE JULIAN'; [2] frontis., reproducing illustration on p. [78]; [3] title; [4] imprint: '*First published in July 1947 by* | PETER LUNN (PUBLISHERS) LIMITED | 49 Chancery Lane London W C | *All rights reserved* | *Printed in Great Britain by* | H O LOESCHER LIMITED | 70 Brewer Street London W'; [5] contents; [6] '*Dedicated to my young nephew Julian who,* | *strange as it may seem, is an alarmingly* | *real person*'; 7-205 text (see illustration list for unnumbered pages); [206-208] blank.

Illustrations Full-page illustrations on pp. [2], [17], [60], [78], [149] and [196]. Various other illustrations.

Paper White wove text paper and endpapers.

Binding (188 x 131 x 18 mm): blue cloth. Front cover blank. Spine lettered horizontally in gilt: 'That | must be | Julian | * | N. R. | SYME | [at bottom] Peter | Lunn'. Back cover blank.

Dustjacket (187 x 463 mm): white wove paper. The front is lettered against an illustration in black, white and greenish blue of two boys in a motor boat, one looking through the sight on a harpoon mounted on the front of the boat. Front: '[in upwards sloping script] That must be [in white lettering] Julian | [at bottom, all in script] N.R. Syme's | story of an | irrepressible young inventor'. Spine lettered horizontally: 'That | Must | Be | Julian | * | N. R. | Syme | [at bottom] a | Peter | Lunn | book | for | boys | and | girls'.

Back: '[in greenish blue] Another 'Master Mind' | story on the way! | [illustration within a rectangular black border of two cablegrams] | [in greenish blue] 'Julian Strikes Lucky' | [in greenish blue] N. R. SYME | to be published by Peter Lunn'. Front flap: '[in greenish blue] THAT MUST BE JULIAN | [synopsis] | [in greenish blue] A PETER LUNN BOOK | [in greenish blue] FOR BOYS AND GIRLS | [at bottom right] 8s 6d net'. Back flap: '[in greenish blue] FULL FATHOM FIVE | [advertisement for a book]'.

Later releases   [WFL]. Also reissued in September 1950 at 3/6d (this may be the WFL issue).

Notes   Category: Adventure. Scarcity: 4.

The back of the dustjacket has an advertisement for *Julian Strikes Lucky* (not published). The back flap has an advertisement for *Full Fathom Five*.

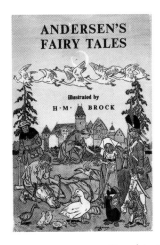

PL105   Hans Andersen's Fairy Tales   third edition, by Hans Andersen, illustrated by H. M. Brock, 1947, [?December 1947], [7/6d].

Hans | Andersen's | Fairy Tales | with illustrations by | H . M . BROCK | PETER LUNN | LONDON | 1947

Collation   (183 x 119 mm): [1-6], 7-24 24pp section uncoded, with a single leaf for frontispiece tipped in to p. [2]; 25-40 16pp section coded B; 41-64 24pp section uncoded; 65-80 16pp section coded D; 81-104 24pp section coded E; 105-120 16pp section coded F; 121-144 24pp section coded G; 145-160 16pp section coded H; 161-184 24pp section coded I; 185-200 16pp section coded K; 201-212 12pp section coded L; 213-224 12pp section uncoded.

Contents   [1] half-title: 'HANS ANDERSEN'S FAIRY TALES'; [2] blank; [3] title; [4] imprint: '*First published in 1947 by* | PETER LUNN (PUBLISHERS) LIMITED | 49 *Chancery Lane London WC2* | *All rights reserved* | *Printed in Great Britain by* | SAMUEL SIDDERS AND SON LIMITED | 115 *Salusbury Road London NW6*'; [5] contents; [6] blank; 7-224 text (within which pp. [20], [34], [62], [86], [110], [140], [154], [176], [218] are blank. See illustration list for other unnumbered pages).

Illustrations   Full-page colour frontispiece tipped in to page [2]. Full-page illustrations on pp. [19], [33], [61], [85], [109], [139], [153], [175] and [217].

Paper   White wove text paper and endpapers. White surfaced wove paper for frontispiece.

Binding   (188 x 126 x 18 mm): pale grey-green cloth. Front cover stamped in gilt in centre with illustration of a bird singing on a perch and moon in background. Spine lettered horizontally in gilt: 'FAIRY | TALES | * | Hans | Andersen | [at bottom] Peter | Lunn'. Back cover blank.

Dustjacket (187 x 440 mm): white surfaced wove paper. Front is lettered on a background colour illustration, reproducing the frontispiece, of various characters from the stories on a grassy area, against a yellow sky with swans in flight. Front: 'ANDERSEN'S | FAIRY TALES | illustrated by | H . M . BROCK'. Spine lettered horizontally: 'FAIRY | TALES | * | Hans | Andersen | [at bottom] Peter | Lunn'. Back: 'PETER LUNN | announces | another fine Gift Book for Modern Children | illustrated by H. M. Brock | [advertisement for a book] | PETER LUNN | 49 Chancery Lane | London'. Front flap has synopsis, and price at the bottom right (clipped on the copy described). Black flap blank.

Later releases [WFL]. Whitaker records a reissue of the Andersen Fairy Tales in October 1949, at 5/-. It is not clear whether this is a reissue of this book, or of PL56.

Notes Category: Classic/Fairy. **Scarcity:** 2.

The print-run was 20,406 (unusually large for Lunn). Advertised at 7/6d in the November 1947 issue of *Publishers' Circular*. The book was not bound until late November, and was probably intended for the Christmas market. The book contains a different selection of stories from PL1 and PL56: The Steadfast Tin Soldier; The Tinder Box; The Darning Needle; The Red Shoes; The Ugly Duckling; Little Claus and Big Claus; The Little Mermaid; The Emperor's New Clothes; The Wild Swans; The Match-Girl; The Travelling Companion; The Candles; The Flying Trunk; The Happy Family; The Goloshes of Fortune; Thumbelina; The Nightingale. The back of the dustjacket has an advertisement for *The Children's Omnibus*.

PL106 Woodheap Cats by Dennis Barry, illustrated by William Wood, November 1947, [?December 1947], 8/6d.

DENNIS BARRY | WOODHEAP | CATS | with illustrations by | WILLIAM WOOD | PETER LUNN | London | 1947

Collation (180 x 120 mm): [1-6], 7-160 in 5 x 32pp sections coded: uncoded, B-E on first, and uncoded, B*-E* on third page of each section; 161-176 16pp section coded F; 177-205, [206-208] 32pp section coded G on first and G* on third page of section.

Contents [1] half-title: 'WOODHEAP CATS'; [2] frontis., reproducing p. [204]; [3] title; [4] imprint: 'First published in November 1947 by | PETER LUNN (PUBLISHERS) LIMITED | 49 Chancery Lane London WC2 | All rights reserved | Printed in Great Britain by | WATERLOW AND SONS LIMITED | London and Dunstable'. [5] contents; [6] blank; 7-205: text (see list of illustrations for unnumbered pages); [206-208] blank.

Illustrations Full-page illustrations on pp [2], [11], [23], [53], [71], [87], [119], [139], [179], [195] and [204]. Various other illustrations.

Paper White wove text and endpapers.

Binding (186 x 127 x 22 mm): red cloth. Front cover stamped in gilt with illustration of a cat at bottom right. Spine lettered horizontally in gilt: 'Woodheap | Cats | * | Dennis | Barry | [at bottom] Peter | Lunn'. Back cover blank.

Dustjacket (187 x 457 mm): white surfaced wove paper. Front and spine are printed on a uniform dull yellow background. Front: '[in crescent formation] Woodheap Cats | [illustration of a cat facing to its right, sitting on a blanket (?)] | An animal story by Dennis Barry'. Spine lettered horizontally: 'Woodheap | Cats | * | [at bottom] Peter | Lunn'. Back: 'Peter Lunn has published other | nature books | for boys and girls | [advertisements for three books] | Peter Lunn | 49 Chancery Lane London'. Front flap: '[synopsis] | [at bottom right] 8s 6d net'. Back flap blank.

Copies consulted BL and my own copy.

Later releases WFL.

Notes Category: Nature. **Scarcity:** 3.

Although Whitaker has a publication date of April 1948 for this book, this is contradicted by the BL copy's accession stamp of 22 Dec 1947. The back of the dustjacket has advertisements for *Horses and Riders, How is Inky?* and 'Beppo the Ox' (i.e. *Beppo*).

PL107 Pasha by Donald Henderson, illustrated by C. H. Oates, September 1947, [December 1947], 7/6d.

DONALD HENDERSON | PASHA | *with drawings by* | C. H. OATES | [illustration] | PETER LUNN | LONDON 1947

Collation (185 x 122 mm): [1-6], 7-188, [189-192] in 6 x 32 pp sections coded: uncoded, B-F.

Contents [1] half-title: '[at top right] PASHA'; [2] frontis; [3] title; [4] imprint: '*First published in September 1947 by* | Peter Lunn (Publishers) Ltd | 49 Chancery Lane | W C 2 | All rights reserved | Printed in Great Britain by | Kennerley Press Ltd | 1/4 Britannia Walk | London N 1'; [5] contents; [6] 'For | COLIN LANDELS HENDERSON'; 7-188, [189-191] text (see illustration list for blank and unnumbered pages); [192] blank.

Illustrations Full-page illustrations on pp. [2], [25], [69], [83], [145], [175] and [189]. The verso of each full-page illustration (except the frontispiece) is blank. Various other illustrations.

Paper White wove text paper and endpapers.

Binding (190 x 129 x 17 mm): blue cloth. Front cover blank. Spine lettered and stamped horizontally in gilt: 'Pasha | [illustration of dog] | Hender- | son | [at bottom] Peter | Lunn'. Back cover blank.

Dustjacket (190 x 456 mm): white surfaced wove paper. Front, spine and back are printed on a uniform deep yellow background. Front: '[in script] PASHA [all in red script] the story of | A DOG | by Donald Henderson | drawings by | C. H. Oates | [illustration, reproducing p. [25], of a small dog emerging from a pile of bricks and wood]. Spine lettered horizontally: 'Pasha | * | Donald | Henderson | [at bottom] Peter | Lunn'. Back: 'Peter Lunn publishes other | [in red] animal stories | Titles include | [advertisements for three books] | [in red] PETER LUNN | 49 Chancery Lane London'. Front flap: '[in red] Pasha | [in red] the story of a dog | [synopsis] | [in red] A Peter Lunn book | [in red] for boys and girls | [at bottom right] 7s 6d net'. Back flap: '[in red] The Wandering Otter | [advertisement for a book] | [in red] A Peter Lunn book | [in red] for boys and girls'.

Notes Category: Nature. Scarcity: 3.

The back cover has advertisements for *First Animal Book*, 'Beppo the Ox' (i.e. *Beppo*) and *The Black Stallion*. The back flap has an advertisement for *The Wandering Otter*.

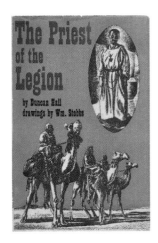

PL108 **The Priest of the Legion** by Duncan Hall, illustrated by William Stobbs, December 1947, [February 1948], 7/6d.

DUNCAN HALL | THE PRIEST | OF | THE LEGION | DRAWINGS BY | WILLIAM STOBBS | PETER LUNN | LONDON 1947

Collation (185 x 121 mm): [1-6], 7-160 in 10 x 16pp sections coded: uncoded, B-H, K-L; 161-180 20pp section coded M.

Contents [1] half-title: 'THE PRIEST OF THE LEGION'; [2] frontis., reproducing illustration on p. [60]; [3] title; [4] imprint: 'First published in December 1947 by | PETER LUNN (PUBLISHERS) LTD | 49 Chancery Lane London WC | All rights reserved | Printed in Great Britain by | West Brothers Mitcham Surrey'; [5] contents; [6] blank; 7-180 text (see illustration list for unnumbered pages).

Illustrations Full-page illustrations on pp. [2], [24], [47], [60], [88], [111], [132] and [163]. Various other illustrations.

Paper White wove text paper and endpapers.

Binding (190 x 128 x 13 mm): red cloth. Front cover blank. Spine lettered horizontally in gilt: 'The | Priest | of the | Legion | * | Duncan | Hall | [at bottom] Peter | Lunn'. Back cover blank.

Dustjacket (190 x 445 mm): white wove paper. Front is printed on a uniform pale blue background: '[at top left, in red] The Priest | [in red] of the | [in red] Legion | by Duncan Hall | drawings by Wm. Stobbs'. To right of lettering is an illustration in brown and white within an oval panel of a standing priest. At bottom is an illustration in brown and white of three men in Arab dress astride camels. Spine lettered horizontally in red: 'THE | PRIEST | OF | THE | LEGION | * | D. HALL | [at bottom] PETER | LUNN'. Back: '[in brown] Peter Lunn publishes other | [in red] adventure stories | [in brown] Titles include | [advertisements for four books] | [in red] PETER LUNN | [in brown] 49 Chancery Lane London'. Front flap: '[in red] The Priest of the Legion | [synopsis] | [in red] a Peter Lunn book | [at bottom right] 7s 6d net'. Back flap blank.

Later releases Reissued in September 1950 at 2/6d.

Notes Category: Adventure. **Scarcity**: 2.

The back of the dustjacket has advertisements for *Night Cargoes*, *Mr Bosanko*, *The Owl and the Pussycat* and *The Haunted Island*.

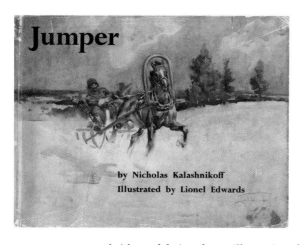

PL109 Jumper by Nicholas Kalashnikoff, illustrated by Lionel Edwards, 1948, [February 1948], 9/6d.

[with word designed as an illustration of a horse jumping fences] Jumper | by Nicholas Kalashnikoff | WITH DRAWINGS BY | Lionel Edwards | PETER LUNN . LONDON . 1948

Collation (185 x 244 mm): [1-4], 5-94, [95-96] in 6 x 16pp sections coded A-F. A leaf for frontispiece is tipped in to p. [2].

Contents [1] half-title: '[at right, with word designed as an illustration of a horse jumping fences] Jumper'; [2] blank; [3] title; [4] imprint: 'First published in 1948 by | Peter Lunn (Publishers) Limited | 49 Chancery Lane London | *All rights reserved* | Printed in Great Britain by | Kennerley Press Limited | 1-4 Britannia Walk London N I'; 5 author details; [6] blank; 7 illustrator details; [8] blank; [9] illustration; [10] blank; 11-94, [95] text in double columns (see illustration list for unnumbered pages); [96] blank. The following pages are also unnumbered: 28, 34, 37, 53, 60, 69 and 84.

131

Illustrations Coloured frontispiece on verso of leaf tipped in to p. [2]. Full-page illustrations on pp. [9], [22], [36], [51], [75], [88] and [91]. Double-page illustration on pp. [54-55]. Various other illustrations.

Paper White wove text paper and endpapers. White surfaced wove paper for frontispiece.

Binding (190 x 250 x 11 mm): green cloth. Front cover stamped in gilt at bottom right with an illustration of a horse. Spine lettered vertically from top in gilt: 'Jumper * Nicholas Kalashnikoff & Lionel Edwards * [at bottom] Peter Lunn'. Back cover blank.

Dustjacket (189 x 702 mm): white surfaced wove paper. Front is lettered against a coloured illustration, reproducing the frontispiece, of a man in fur hat driving a sledge pulled by a horse over a snowy landscape: '[at top left] Jumper | [at bottom right] by Nicholas Kalashnikoff | Illustrated by Lionel Edwards'. Spine lettered vertically from top: 'Jumper * Nicholas Kalashnikoff & Lionel Edwards * [at bottom] Peter Lunn'. Back is printed against a uniform yellow background, with text at left, fitted around a coloured illustration at right of a carriage and riders pulled by two horses against a wooded background: 'If you like Jumper you will certainly like My First Horse | with drawings by Lionel Edwards | one of the most delightful | and original books for | young horsemen | and horsewomen | published during | recent years. Read | about the early | experiences of famous | riders: Siegfried Sassoon, | Vic Oliver, A. F. Tschiffely, | Cynthia Asquith, Laurian Jones and Lionel Edwards, too.'. Front flap: '[synopsis] | [at bottom right] 9s 6d net'. Back flap has an advertisement for a book.

Later releases Reissued in October 1950 at 5/-.

Notes Category: Nature. Scarcity: 1.

There are variant bindings in blue, orange, brown and red cloth. The back cover and back flap of the dustjacket both advertise *My First Horse*. The book was first published by Scribners in 1944. In 1963, Oxford University Press published a new edition illustrated by Victor Ambrus.

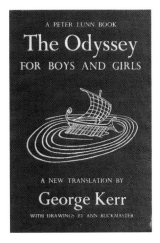

PL110 Homer's Odyssey retold by George Kerr, illustrated by Ann Buckmaster, June 1947, [February 1948], 8/6d.

Homer's | Odyssey | A NEW TRANSLATION | FOR CHILDREN | BY GEORGE KERR M.A. | WITH DRAWINGS BY | ANN BUCKMASTER | PETER LUNN | LONDON 1947

Collation	(184 x 122 mm): [1-4], 5-8, [9], 10-16 16pp section uncoded; [17-18],19-256 in 15 x 16pp sections coded: B, uncoded, D-Q.
Contents	[1] half-title: 'HOMER'S ODYSSEY FOR CHILDREN'; [2] frontis; [3] title; [4] imprint: '*First published in June 1947 by* | PETER LUNN (PUBLISHERS) LIMITED | 49 CHANCERY LANE LONDON WC | *All rights reserved* | *Printed in Great Britain by* | H O LOESCHER LIMITED | 70 BREWER STREET | LONDON WI'; 5-8 contents; [9] 'To | JENIFER and LORNA | who thought it a good idea.'; 10-256 text. Pages 17, 33, 51, 65, 81, 97, 111, 129, 141, 153, 171, 183, 195, 207, 217, 229 and 241 are unnumbered. Pages 18, 34, 50, 52, 66, 80, 82, 98, 112, 128, 130, 142, 152, 154, 170, 172, 182, 184, 194, 196, 206, 208, 218, 228, 230, 240 and 242 are blank and unnumbered.
Illustrations	Full-page illustration on p. [2]. Various other illustrations.
Paper	White wove text paper and endpapers.
Binding	(190 x 130 x 24 mm): black cloth. Centre of front cover stamped in white with a schematic illustration of a classical temple. Spine lettered horizontally in white: 'The | Odyssey | * | George | Kerr | [at bottom] Peter | Lunn'. Back cover blank.
Dustjacket	(189 x 448 mm): white surfaced wove paper. Front and spine are printed in white on a uniform blue background. Front: 'A PETER LUNN BOOK | The Odyssey | FOR BOYS AND GIRLS | [stylised illustration of sailing-boat in a whirlpool] | A NEW TRANSLATION BY | George Kerr | WITH DRAWINGS BY ANN BUCKMASTER'. Spine lettered horizontally: 'The | Odyssey | for | Boys | & | Girls | * | George | Kerr | [at bottom] Peter | Lunn'. Back: 'Peter Lunn | has published another | classic volume | [advertisement for a book lettered in blue and black] | [in blue] Peter Lunn | 49 Chancery Lane London'. Front flap: '[in blue] The Odyssey | [synopsis] | [in blue] A Peter Lunn book | [in blue] for boys and girls | [at bottom right] 8s 6d net'. Back flap: 'Another Peter Lunn book | [advertisement for a book lettered in blue and black] | [in blue] A Peter Lunn book | [in blue] for boys and girls'.
Later releases	Reissued in October 1950 at 3/6d.
Notes	Category: Classic/Educational. **Scarcity**: 4.
	The binding cloth and front cover motif are uniform with *Stories from Ancient Greece*. The back cover has an advertisement for *Stories from Ancient Greece*. The back flap has an advertisement for *The Legends of St Francis*, described as 'retold by Nora Wydenbruck' (i.e. **Nora Purtscher**). A new edition illustrated by John Verney was published by Warne in 1958.

PL111 **The Legends of St. Francis** retold by Alfons and Nora Purtscher, October 1947, [March 1948], 7/6d.

The | Legends of | St. Francis | RETOLD BY | ALFONS AND NORA | PURTSCHER | PETER LUNN | LONDON | 1947

Collation (183 x 120 mm): [1-6], 7-32 32pp uncoded section with a single leaf for frontispiece tipped in to p. [2]; 33-192 in 5 x 32pp sections coded B-F; 193-202, [203-204] 12pp section coded G on first and G* on third page of section.

Contents [1] half-title: 'The Legends of St. Francis'; [2] blank; [3] title; [4] imprint: 'First published in October 1947 by | PETER LUNN (PUBLISHERS) LIMITED | 49 Chancery Lane London WC2 | *All rights reserved* | Printed in Great Britain by | GALE & POLDEN LIMITED | Wellington Press Aldershot Hampshire'; [5-6] contents; 7-202 text; [203-204] blank.

Illustrations Full-page colour illustration tipped in to p. [2], signed 'Purtscher' at bottom right. No other illustrations

Paper White wove text paper and endpapers. White surfaced paper for frontispiece.

Binding (189 x 127 x 15 mm): pale yellow cloth. Front cover blank. Spine lettered horizontally in gilt: 'The | Legends | of | Saint | Francis | * Alfons | and | Nora | Purts- | cher | [at bottom] Peter | Lunn'. Back cover blank.

Dustjacket (190 x 433 mm): white surfaced wove paper. Front: '[at top] *The Legends of* | *St Francis* | [at bottom] ALFONS *and* NORA PURTSCHER'. Background to lettering is an illustration of St Francis with five animals on a mountain background, in shades of red and blue, reproducing the frontispiece. Spine lettered horizontally: 'The | Legends | of | Saint | Francis | * | Alfons | and | Nora | Purt- | scher | [at bottom] A | Peter | Lunn | book | for | boys | and | girls'. Back: 'Peter Lunn publishes other books for | [in red] *boys and girls* | *which include:* | [advertisements for two books] | [in red] *Peter Lunn* | *49 Chancery Lane London*'. Front flap: '[in red] The Legends of St Francis | [synopsis] | [in red] A Peter Lunn book for boys and girls'. Price is at bottom right (clipped on the copy described). Back flap has an advertisement for a book.

Later releases Reissued in August 1950 at 3/6d.

Notes Category: Classic/Educational. **Scarcity:** 4.

The back cover advertises *The Odyssey and Stories from Ancient Greece*. The back flap advertises *The Glastonbury Adventure* (author stated to be 'Joan Edwards'). **Alfons Purtscher** was an artist and probably contributed the frontispiece, but it is not clear whether he also collaborated with Nora on the text.

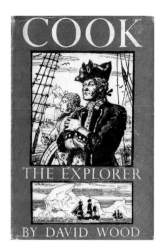

PL112 Cook the Explorer by David Wood, illustrated by John Worsley and Eric Saunders, September 1947, [March 1948], 8/6d.

Cook | The Explorer | by DAVID WOOD | ILLUSTRATED BY | JOHN WORSLEY | WITH FOUR MAPS BY | ERIC SAUNDERS | PETER LUNN | LONDON | 1947

Collation (184 x 120 mm): [1-6], 7-216, [217-224] in 14 x 16pp sections coded: uncoded, B-O.

Contents [1] half-title: 'COOK THE EXPLORER'; [2] frontis., reproducing illustration on p. [179]; [3] title; [4] imprint: 'First published in September 1947 by | PETER LUNN (PUBLISHERS) LIMITED | 49 Chancery Lane London WC2 | All rights reserved | Printed in Great Britain by | CAINES . BROADWAY . PLAISTOW . LONDON . E13'; [5] contents; [6] blank; 7-216, [217] text (see illustration list for unnumbered pages); [218] illustration; [219-224] blank. The following pages are also blank and unnumbered: 10, 22, 44, 50, 62, 86, 114, 152, 180 and 206.

Illustrations Full-page illustrations on pp. [2], [9], [21], [43], [49], [61], [85], [113], [151], [179], [205] and [218].

Paper White wove text paper and endpapers.

Binding (190 x 129 x 19 mm): green cloth textured with raised dimples. Front cover blank. Spine lettered horizontally in gilt: 'Cook | the | Explorer | * | David | Wood | [at bottom] Peter | Lunn'. Back cover blank.

Dustjacket (189 x 464 mm): white surfaced wove paper. Front and spine are printed on a uniform blue background. Front is lettered in white: 'COOK | [illustration of a sailor and a man in naval uniform on the deck of a sailing-ship] | THE EXPLORER | [illustration of two sailing-ships at sea with icebergs in the background] | BY DAVID WOOD'. Spine lettered horizontally: 'Cook | the | Explorer | * | David | Wood | [at bottom] a | Peter | Lunn | book | for | boys | and | girls'. Back: 'Peter Lunn has also published | [advertisement for a book] | [in blue] PETER LUNN | 49 Chancery Lane London'. Front flap: '[in blue] Cook the Explorer | [synopsis] | [in blue] A Peter Lunn book | [in blue] for boys and girls | [price at bottom right, clipped on copy described]'. Back flap: 'Another Peter Lunn | title on exploration | [advertisement for a book]'.

Later releases Reissued in September 1950 at 2/6d.

Notes Category: Adventure/Educational. **Scarcity**: 3.

The back of the dustjacket has an advertisement for *Voyage to Chivalry*. The back flap has an advertisement for *Arctic Adventures*.

PL113 Great Gold Rushes by I. M. Holmes, illustrated by Robin Jacques, December 1947, [July 1948], 8/6d.

I . M . HOLMES | GREAT | GOLD RUSHES | ILLUSTRATED BY | ROBIN JACQUES | PETER LUNN | London | 1947

Collation (185 x 121 mm): [i-ii] single leaf tipped on to p. [1]; [1-4], 5-16 16pp section uncoded; 17-208 in 6 x 32pp sections coded B-G; 209-246, [247-248] 40pp section coded H.

Contents [i] half-title: '[at right] *Great Gold Rushes*'; [ii] frontis; [1] title; [2] imprint: '*First published in December 1947 by* | PETER LUNN (PUBLISHERS) LIMITED | *49 Chancery Lane London W C 2* | *All rights reserved* | *Printed in Great Britain by* | KENNERLEY PRESS LIMITED | *1-4 Britannia Walk City Road* | *London N 1*'; [3] contents; [4] blank; 5-246, [247] text (see illustration list for unnumbered pages); [248] blank.

Illustrations Full-page coloured illustration on p. [ii]. Full-page illustrations on pp. [29] and [181]. Various other illustrations.

Paper White wove text paper and endpapers.

Binding (190 x 129 x 21 mm): orange cloth. Front cover is stamped in gilt at bottom right with illustration of horse next to dismounted rider. Spine lettered horizontally in gilt: 'Great | Gold | Rushes | * | Holmes | [at bottom] Peter | Lunn'. Back cover blank.

Dustjacket (191 x 469 mm): white surfaced wove paper. Front and spine are printed on a uniform red background. Front: '[in script] Great Gold Rushes | I . M . Holmes | [coloured illustration of a man riding a horse within a hilly landscape, reproducing the frontispiece] | illustrated by Robin Jacques'. Spine lettered horizontally 'Great | Gold | Rushes | * | I . M . | Holmes | [at bottom] a | Peter | Lunn | book | for | boys | and | girls'. Back: 'Peter Lunn has also published | [advertisement for a book] | [in red] Peter Lunn | 49 Chancery Lane London'. Front flap: '[in red] Great Gold Rushes | [synopsis] | [in red] A Peter Lunn book for boys and girls | [at bottom right] 8s 6d net'. Back flap: 'Another Peter Lunn book | [advertisement for a book]'.

Copies consulted My own copy and private collection.

Notes Category: Adventure/Educational. Scarcity: 3.

The print-run was 4324. The back of the dustjacket has an advertisement for *Suez and Panama* (not published). The back flap has an advertisement for *Here Lies Gold*.

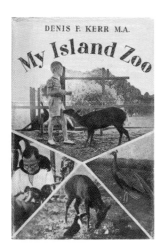

PL114 My Island Zoo by Denis F. Kerr, illustrated with photographs, June 1947, [July 1948], 6/-.

DENIS F. KERR M.A. | My | Island Zoo | [illustration] | WITH MANY PHOTOGRAPHS | PETER LUNN | LONDON 1947

Collation (186 x 122 mm): [i-vi], [1-6], 7, [8], 9-26 32pp uncoded section with a leaf for frontispiece tipped in to p. [2] (pp. [i-ii] form the front pastedown, and there is no front free endpaper); [vii-viii], 27-58, [ix-x] 36pp section coded B on p. 27; [xi-xiv], 59-90, [xv-xviii] 40pp section coded C on p. 59; 91-122 32pp section coded D.

Contents [iii-vi] blank; [1] half-title: 'MY ISLAND ZOO'; [2] blank; [3] title; [4] imprint: 'First published in June 1947 by | PETER LUNN (PUBLISHERS) LIMITED | 49 Chancery Lane London WC2 | *All rights reserved* | Printed in Great Britain by | W S CAINES LIMITED | Andover House Broadway Plaistow | London E13'; [5] contents; [6] blank; 7 foreword; [8] blank; 9-122 text.

Illustrations Black and white photographs with captions between pages [2] and [3] (one photograph), and on pp [vii-viii] (two photographs), [ix-xiv] (11 photographs) and [xv-xviii] (four photographs).

Paper White wove text paper and endpapers. White surfaced paper for photographs.

Binding (190 x 129 x 13 mm): buff cloth. Front cover blank. Spine lettered horizontally in gilt: 'My | Island | Zoo | * | Kerr | [at bottom] Peter | Lunn'. Back cover blank.

Dustjacket (191 x 495 mm): white surfaced wove paper. Front and spine are printed against a uniform yellow background. Front: '[in red] DENIS F. KERR M.A. | [in red, in a crescent formation] My Island Zoo'. Below the lettering are four photographs arranged in a circular formation separated by yellow bands: at top, boy with agouti, peacock and peahen; at left, man with various animals; at right, peacock; at bottom, deer and toucan. Spine lettered vertically in red from top: 'KERR * MY ISLAND ZOO [at bottom] PETER LUNN'. Back: 'PETER LUNN ANNOUNCES | [advertisement for a book, lettered in black and red] | [in red] PETER LUNN | [in red] 49 CHANCERY LANE LONDON'. Front flap: '[in red] MY ISLAND ZOO | [synopsis] | [at bottom right] 6s net'. Back flap blank.

Notes Category: Nature/Educational. **Scarcity**: 4.

The back of the dustjacket has an advertisement for *The Fables of Aesop and Others* (not published). A working title for this book was 'Some Creature Friends of Mine'.

PL115 The Children's Omnibus compiled by John Keir Cross, illustrated by H. M. Brock, n.d., [?1948], 15/-.

THE | CHILDREN'S | OMNIBUS | Lewis Carroll Hans Andersen | Charles Dickens Edward Lear | Mrs. J. H. Ewing Charles Kingsley | W. M. Thackeray The Brothers Grimm | Nathaniel Hawthorne Charles & Mary Lamb | Shakespeare Coleridge | Browning Southey | Cowper Poe | COMPILED BY | JOHN KEIR CROSS | ILLUSTRATED BY | H. M. BROCK | PETER LUNN | London

Collation   (182 x 116 mm): [1-6], 7-288 in 18 x 16pp sections coded: uncoded, B-S; 289-735, [736] in 14 x 32pp sections coded T, U, X-Z, 2A-2I. A leaf for the frontispiece is tipped in to p. [3].

Contents   [1] half-title: 'THE CHILDREN'S OMNIBUS'; [2] 'Books by John Keir Cross | THE OTHER PASSENGER | THE MAN IN MOONLIGHT | THE WHITE MAGIC | For Children | THE ANGRY PLANET | THE OWL AND THE PUSSYCAT | and the Studio J series: | STUDIO J INVESTIGATES | DETECTIVES IN GREASEPAINT | MR. BOSANKO'; [3] title; [4] imprint: 'PETER LUNN (PUBLISHERS) LIMITED | 49 Chancery Lane London WC2 | All rights reserved | Printed in Great Britain by | GALE & POLDEN LIMITED | The Wellington Press | Aldershot Hampshire'; [5-6] '[contents] | With some limericks by EDWARD LEAR and | many illustrations by H. M. BROCK throughout'; 7-8 introduction, signed 'JKC' at bottom right; [9] illustration; [10] illustration; 11-735, [736] text (see illustration list for unnumbered pages).

Illustrations   Full-page coloured illustration tipped in to p. [3]. Full-page illustrations on pp. [9-10], [61], [174], [205-206], [258], [364], [389-390], [445], [479-480], [489], [589], [607-608], [615-616] and [673]. Various other illustrations.

Paper   Thin white wove text paper. White wove endpapers.

Binding   (187 x 125 x 30 mm): brown cloth. Front cover stamped in gilt at bottom right with illustration of girl kneeling in front of an armchair reading a book. Spine lettered horizontally in gilt: 'The | Children's | Omnibus | * | John | Keir Cross | and | H. M. Brock | [at bottom] Peter | Lunn'. Back cover blank.

Dustjacket (189 x 432 mm): white surfaced wove paper. Front is lettered against a background coloured illustration of eight characters from the stories in the book on grass next to the sea with a ship in the background: 'THE | CHILDREN'S OMNIBUS | * | by | John Keir Cross | and H. M. Brock | Carroll Shakespeare Andersen | Dickens Lear Kingsley | Thackeray Grimm Lamb | Hawthorne Coleridge Browning'. Spine lettered horizontally against a uniform yellow background: 'THE | CHILDREN'S | OMNIBUS | Carroll | Dickens | Thackeray | Lear | Lamb | Cowper | Browning | Southey | Hawthorne | Coleridge | * | PETER | LUNN'. Back is lettered within a frame of oval portraits of six authors: 'In | THE | CHILDREN'S OMNIBUS | *Peter Lunn presents* | [list of stories] | and many other | stories and poems | by the masters. | Each item is | complete and unabridged | 736 pages'. Front flap: '[synopsis] | [at bottom right] 15s net'. Back flap blank.

Later releases Reissued in July 1950 at 7/6d.

Notes Category: Classic/Fairy. **Scarcity:** 3.

Contains the following stories: Alice's Adventures in Wonderland; The Ugly Duckling; The Pied Piper; Three Tales of the Wise Men of Gotham; The Akhond of Swat; Pegasus; The Rose and the Ring; Rumpelstiltskin; Some Incidents in the Life of the Famous Tyll Owlglass; The Diverting History of John Gilpin; Snowdrop; The Battle of Blenheim; The Argonauts; It was a Lover and his Lass; The Rime of the Ancient Mariner; The Gorgon's Head; A Midsummer Night's Dream; Jackanapes; The First Nowell; The Bells; A Christmas Carol in Prose. Some of these stories were repackaged by Lunn into the two volumes *Alice's Adventures in Wonderland* and *The Rose and the Ring*.

PL116 Alice's Adventures in Wonderland by Lewis Carroll, with other stories and poems, illustrated by H. M. Brock, n.d., [?1948], [7/6d].

Illustrations Two tipped-in coloured plates. Four black and white illustrations.

Binding Green cloth. Front and back covers blank. Titled on spine in gilt.

Dustjacket Front, spine and back of dustjacket printed on a uniform green background. Front cover: 'ALICE IN WONDERLAND | By | LEWIS CARROLL | [coloured illustration of three children at play, kneeling on the floor of a room, onlaid to cover] | *Illustrations by H. M. Brock*'.

Notes Category: Classic/Fairy/Educational. **Scarcity:** 5.

This book is described as 'The Lunn Readers Number 1', and is a companion volume to *The Rose and the Ring* ('The Lunn Readers Number 2'). Both are a repackaging of material from *The Children's Omnibus*. This book contains the following stories and poems: Alice's Adventures in Wonderland; The Ugly Duckling; Three Tales of the Wise Men of Gotham; The Akhond of Swat; The Diverting History of John Gilpin. A book catalogue reports the illustration on the dustjacket as being by Lilian Govey, although as pointed out in the entry for *The Rose and the Ring*, the same illustration was probably not consistently used.

I have been unable to view a copy of this book. The above description contains information about which I am reasonably certain, and is based on an image I have seen of the dustjacket, and booksellers' catalogue entries. Much of the missing information, however, can be deduced with some confidence from the entry for *The Rose and the Ring*, since they were clearly designed to be in the same format.

PL117 The Rose and the Ring by W.M. Thackeray with other stories and poems, illustrated by H. M. Brock, n.d., [?1948], 7/6d.

THE LUNN READERS | NUMBER TWO | THE ROSE AND THE RING | by | W. M. Thackeray | with other Stories and Poems | THE ILLUSTRATIONS ARE BY H. M. BROCK | EVERY ITEM IS COMPLETE AND UNABRIDGED | [illustration] | PETER LUNN | LONDON

Collation   (182 x 117 mm): [1-4], 5-144 in 9 x 16pp sections coded: uncoded, B-I; 145-152 8pp section coded K; 153-165, [166-168] 16pp section coded L.

Contents   [1] half-title: 'THE ROSE AND THE RING | with other | Stories and Poems'; [2] frontis; [3] title; [4] contents, and imprint at bottom: 'PUBLISHED BY PETER LUNN (PUBLISHERS) LIMITED | 49 CHANCERY LANE LONDON WC2 AND PRINTED BY | GALE AND POLDEN LIMITED OF ALDERSHOT'; 5-165, [166] text (see illustration list for unnumbered pages); [167-168] blank.

Illustrations   Full page coloured illustrations tipped in to pp.11 and 141 (but see Notes below). Full-page illustrations on pp. [2], [56] and [150]. Various other illustrations.

Paper   White wove text paper and endpapers. White surfaced wove paper for tipped-in illustrations.

Binding   (189 x 122 x 14 mm): red cloth. Front cover blank. Spine lettered horizontally in gilt: 'THE | ROSE | AND | THE | RING | [at bottom] WITH | OTHER | STORIES | AND | POEMS'. Back cover blank.

Dustjacket   (191 x 478 mm): white surfaced wove paper. The front, spine and back are printed on a uniform pink background. Front: 'THE ROSE AND THE RING | By | W. M. THACKERAY | [coloured illustration (trimmed-down copy of the illustration tipped in to p. 141) onlaid to the cover, of young girl and boy walking down a street in front of a toy shop (but see Notes below)] | Illustrations by H. M. Brock'. Spine lettered horizontally: 'THE | ROSE | AND | THE | RING | * | W. | M. | T | H | A | C | K | E | R | Y | * | With | Other | Stories | and | Poems'. Back blank. Front flap: '[synopsis] | [at bottom right] 7/6 net.'. Back flap blank. The dustjacket has been recycled from paper stock already printed for another purpose.

The verso has three coloured panel illustrations of horses, each with five farmyard animals below and titles in red: 'A Wayside Halt', 'Two's Company' and 'Good Morning'.

Notes Category: Classic/Fairy/Educational. **Scarcity**: 4.

This is a companion volume to *Alice in Wonderland* ('The Lunn Readers Number 1'), and both are a repackaging of material from *The Children's Omnibus*. This book contains the following stories and poems: The Rose and the Ring; Rumplestiltskin; Snowdrop; The First Nowell; The Akhond of Swat; The Pied Piper of Hamelin.

I seen have two copies of this book, and the description above is based on one of them. The other differs in respect of the coloured illustrations. The illustration tipped in to p.11 is absent, and is replaced by a different illustration tipped in to p.25. Furthermore, the pictorial onlay on the front of the dustjacket is different (two girls arranging daffodils on a table) – an illustration which does not appear inside the book. There is no evidence in either book of illustrations having loosened and becoming lost. This suggests that a standard set of illustrations already printed for other publications were re-used, but not in a consistent way, to embellish this book.

The illustrations used were not by Brock, nor do they seem to have any connection with the text. Signatures on two of the illustrations indicate they were by Gordon Browne and Millicent Sowerby respectively. The dustjacket of the second copy is also recycled, and the verso of both is identical.

3

The authors
and illustrators

This section has a twofold purpose. Most importantly, it provides short biographical sketches of the authors and illustrators who worked on the Peter Lunn books. Secondly, in the final part of each entry, it provides an easy way of establishing with which book(s) a particular author or illustrator was involved.

Although the name of each individual and the books involved will always appear, in some cases no biographical sketch is given. This will be the case either where I have been unable to find out anything about the person concerned, or where a classic author is so well known (e.g. Hans Andersen, Robert Louis Stevenson), and life details are easily available from other sources, that it seemed pointless to repeat the information. The authors and illustrators are arranged in alphabetical order of surname, referring to the name as it appears in the book, even if this was a pseudonym. Where the same person acted as both an author and illustrator, the biographical entry appears only in the author entry.

Each entry comprises

- **Title of the entry** This is the name of the individual as it appears in the book. Other names by which he or she was known appear next to the main name, identified as *rn* (real name), *ps* (pseudonym) or *aka* ('also known as'). Where doubt exists I have preceded the alternative name with a question mark.

- **Biographical sketch.**

- **List of titles** for which the person was responsible. Each entry here contains the title, the date of publication as it appears in the book and the key to the book within the bibliography section, e.g. '*Full Fathom Five* (November 1946, PL55)'. In the case of unfulfilled books, these appear at the end of the entry, in the form: '*Children Next Door* (unpublished)'.

AUTHOR BIOGRAPHIES

HANS CHRISTIAN ANDERSEN

Fairy Tales (first edition, 1943, PL1)
Hans Andersen's Fairy Tales (second edition, January 1947, PL56)
Hans Andersen's Fairy Tales (third edition, 1947, PL105)

HUGH ANDERSON

(as editor)
Selected Tales from the Arabian Nights (November 1946, PL57)
The Golden String (July 1947, PL82)
A Zoo in your House (unpublished)

BRUCE ANGRAVE   Bruce Angrave was born in Leicester in 1912 into a family of artists, the son of Charles Angrave, a photographer and graphic artist. He soon learned to draw strip cartoons, and seems also to have been fascinated by machinery. This interest later developed into a rather Arts and Crafts-like aversion to mechanisation which is evident in *Lord Dragline the Dragon* and *The Mechanical Emperor*. As a young man he moved to London to study at various art schools, and found work in advertising agencies in London and New York. While working in America, he invented (and patented) a form of paper sculpture which used no adhesives, producing sculptures of prominent figures such as Roosevelt, Beaverbrook and Stalin. He also became a freelance illustrator of books and periodicals (he did many cover designs for *London Opinion* and *Radio Times*), and designed posters for London Transport. His work for Peter Lunn and John Westhouse during the war was primarily as an illustrator, although he also wrote accompanying text for two Lunn picture-books. *Lucy Maroon* was the first children's book he illustrated. Some of his most remarkable and surreal illustrations were for **John Keir Cross's** collection of macabre stories *The Other Passenger* (Westhouse, 1944). He published a number of books of cartoons of cats with more or less humorous titles such as 'Magnifi-cat' and 'Pa-purr-back cat-alog'. Angrave continues to reserve a small place in the hearts of Sherlock Holmes enthusiasts for the caricature of Holmes which embellishes the front of the catalogue of the Sherlock Holmes Exhibition staged for the Festival of Britain in 1951. He died in London in 1983.

(as author and illustrator)
Lord Dragline the Dragon (1944, PL18)
The Mechanical Emperor (May 1945, PL24)

(as illustrator)
Lucy Maroon (July 1944, PL11)
Mr Bosanko (August 1944, PL14)

ALFRED ASSOLLANT   Alfred Assollant was a French author born in Aubusson in 1827. He began his career by teaching history in Paris where his staunch Republican views (which seem to have steered the course of his life) led to conflict with his employers. He travelled to America hoping to find a more agreeable political climate, but returned soon afterwards to France, disillusioned, and wrote *Scènes de la vie des Etats-Unis*, published in Paris in 1858. For a period thereafter he published some children's books, before becoming an increasingly frustrated writer of political works. He died in obscurity in Paris in

1896. One of his most popular children's books was *The Fantastic History of the Celebrated Pierrot* (1860), which was first published in English in a translation by A. G. Munro (Sampson Low, Marston and Co., 1875). It was subtitled 'written by the Magician Alcofribas and translated from the Sogdian by Alfred Assollant', although it was of course written by Assollant himself. It is a lively and enjoyable book, populated by delightful figures such as King Vantipran and Prince Horribilis. The 1875 edition is a handsomely bound volume with engagingly humorous line-engravings by Yan' Dargent. The version Peter Lunn had planned to publish was the same translation, but with illustrations by **William Stobbs**.

> *The Fantastic History of the Celebrated Pierrot* (unpublished)

CHARLES ATKIN

> *Black Rock Island* (May 1947, PL83)

JOSEPH AVRACH   Artist, author, translator, broadcaster and jazz expert, Joseph (Joe) Avrach was a multi-talented and colourful figure. He was born in 1905 in Lódz, Poland, into a Jewish family. As a teenager, he left home and travelled to Berlin where, between mushroom-picking expeditions in the surrounding forests with his brother Emile, he studied painting. He remained in Berlin until the 1930s, and illustrated two books published in 1935 by Erwin Löwe: *Das Jüdische ABC* (written by his half-brother Bernhardt Cohn) and *Mirjams Wundergarten*, whose subtitles translate as 'a guide to Jewish knowledge' and 'a book for Jewish children'. Having briefly run an artists' coffee-house in Berlin until it was broken up by a Nazi gang, he then joined the tide of central European Jews who emigrated to other countries at this time, by smuggling himself into England under the cover of a German cultural trip. Soon after he first arrived in London, he met a glamorous young Yorkshire art student called Beryl Sanderson on the banks of the Serpentine, and they later married. Joe was granted British citizenship in 1950, having escaped the fate of many of his relatives who perished in the concentration camps.

Although Avrach was a talented painter of pastel portraits, artists did not find it easy to make a living at that time, and he needed to find other work. This he found at Bush House, broadcasting anti-Nazi propaganda on the BBC's German Service throughout the war. He maintained contact with many other émigrés, and it is likely that this is how he came to know David Gottlieb. He seems to have been closely involved with Gottlieb's children's book publishing venture from its inception in 1943, and was one of his most prolific contributors, writing seven books and illustrating a further six by other authors. However, we may guess that not all of Avrach's illustrations for Peter Lunn were regarded as wholly satisfactory since three of these books (including his own book *The Ginger Gang*) were reissued shortly afterwards with new illustrations. He also found work translating a number of books from German, including Gerd Ruge's *Pasternak – a Pictorial Biography* (Thames and Hudson, 1959) which he co-translated with his wife Beryl, and Gustav Buescher's *Geheimnisvolle Tiefen* which appeared in Britain as *The Boys' Book of the Earth Beneath Us* (Burke, 1960). Avrach even made one foray into the adult detective fiction market. His book *Murder in Oil* is set amongst a 'sinister colony of artists in Chelsea' and was published in 1948 under Gottlieb's Westhouse imprint. It is now a forgotten work, and seems to have been his only attempt to write in this genre. During the war, he hosted a radio programme called 'Jazz with Joe', broadcast every Saturday from Bush House, as part of the BBC's morale-boosting propaganda effort. After the war, he worked on as a journalist, jazz broadcaster and chat show host until he was in his sixties. Joe and Beryl continued to live in Streatham, South London, until Joe's death in 1981.

> (as author and illustrator)
> *The Ginger Gang* (first edition October 1943, PL2)
> *Peter the Sailor* (1943, PL4)

(as author)

Timbu the Monkey (October 1944, PL17)

Ferry to Adventure (September 1944, PL19)

The Parade on the Cliff (April 1945, PL23)

Old Dave's Hut (December 1945, PL30)

The Ginger Gang (second edition May 1946, PL34)

Crooked Lane (August 1946, PL44)

(as illustrator)

The Magic Zoo (1943, PL3)

Treasure Island (1943, PL7)

The Three Princesses of Whiteland (November 1943, PL8)

Studio J Investigates (first edition, April 1944, PL13)

Detectives in Greasepaint (first edition, May 1944, PL12)

The Lion and the Vulture (June 1944, PL15)

E[LIZABETH] W[HITEMORE] BAKER

Elizabeth Baker, an American academic, was born in 1882. She gained a Master's degree in Sociology from the University of Chicago in 1912 on 'The Social and Economic Condition of Women Teachers in the United States', and went on to publish widely in academic and teaching journals on topics related to the literacy of adults and children among various social groups in the United States. One such work was a report of a survey undertaken on English language teaching in elementary schools in Dallas, Texas, in 1927, and this probably gave her some of the background to her children's book *Stocky, Boy of West Texas* (John C. Winston, 1945), set in nineteenth century Texas. This was published by Peter Lunn as *The Young Cowboy* a year later. Her only other children's book seems to have been *Sonny-Boy Sim*, a short 31-page illustrated story about Sim and his dog Homer, published in 1948 by Rand McNally

The Young Cowboy (June 1946, PL41)

DENNIS BARRY

Woodheap Cats (November 1947, PL106)

[HARRY] MORTIMER BATTEN

Wildlife enthusiast and photographer, Mortimer Batten was born Henry Mortimer Batten in 1888. His birth was registered in Wharfedale, Yorkshire, although Lofts and Adley[6] state that he was born in Singapore, and educated at Oakham Public School. He came to write and lecture widely on animal and bird life, with a particular emphasis on Britain and Canada. His work was aimed at both the adult and children's markets, both as books and as contributions to magazines such as *Blackwood's*, *Little Folks* and *The Captain*. Batten had travelled to Canada before the Great War, where work as a forest ranger gave him much of the experience and background for his later writings. Some of his earliest books were published in Canada just before he returned to Britain around 1920. One of his most admired children's books (later published as a Puffin Story Book) was *Starlight* (Chambers, 1936) which tells the story of a Canadian timber-wolf, and pulls few punches in describing the crueller

---

[6] Lofts, William O.G. and Adley, D.J. *The Men Behind Boys' Fiction*. London: Howard Baker, 1970, p. 51.

aspects of survival in the wild. *The Wandering Otter*, despite its beautiful wood-engravings by **David Pratt**, never achieved the same readership. The book's sympathetic treatment of the tribulations of the otter-kit Negeet sits rather strangely with Batten's admission to young correspondents in *Little Folks*[7] that 'he used to be a whip-in to a pack of otter hounds which hunted mountain rivers, and it was great fun.' Batten contributed two animal stories to **Hugh Anderson**'s compilation *A Zoo in your House* (Yates, 1951).

Batten was a keen motor-cyclist, and was editor of *The Motor Cycle* magazine during the 1920s. This mode of transport allowed him to reach remote spots carrying the heavy photographic gear needed to take many memorable close-ups of animals and birds. He is also credited with inventing a novel method for photographing nocturnal animals. This involved first transfixing them in the glare of his car headlights, which had flash-guns mounted next to them, and then triggering both flash and camera from inside the car. Batten lived in the Scottish Highlands for the later part of his life, but died in Vancouver in 1958.

The Wandering Otter (March 1947, PL90)

HENRY BELL (*?rn* JOHN KEIR CROSS)   According to the synopsis of *A Children's Almanac*, Henry Bell was 'well known for his sincere and sympathetic work for young readers'. If this was true, I have been unable to find any evidence of children's books previously published under this name, although Henry Bell did edit a volume of 'stories for young and old' called *Youth*, published by John Westhouse in 1947, illustrated by **Robin Jacques**. I think it is likely that Henry Bell was a pseudonym for **John Keir Cross**, although I admit to having no hard evidence which proves it. If one compares the prefaces to *A Children's Almanac* and *The Children's Omnibus*, it is difficult not to be struck by the similarity in style, and in particular the rather unusual approach to punctuation which is evident in both. Also, Keir Cross often collaborated with Jacques, and admired his work. Finally, if Keir Cross did decide to use a pseudonym, there are good reasons why he might have chosen 'Henry Bell' (see entry for **John Keir Cross**).

(as compiler)
A Children's Almanac (February 1947, PL74)

HELEN BINYON   Helen Binyon was one of three daughters of (Robert) Laurence Binyon, a poet and art historian, and Cicely Margaret Binyon (Powell), an artist. Helen and her twin sister Margaret (with whom she later collaborated on a number of children's books for Oxford University Press) were born in 1904 in London. Her other sister Nicholete was to become an accomplished calligrapher. After leaving school, Helen studied widely in the fields of art and design, including watercolour, engraving and wood carving, and in 1949 she began teaching at the Bath Academy of Art, where she developed a consuming interest and involvement with puppetry. There she put on marionette performances, held puppetry classes for teachers, and was later to publish *Puppetry Today* (Studio Vista, 1966). After her retirement, she conducted a survey of professional puppetry in England on behalf of the Arts Council. She died in 1979, and is buried at St Mary's Church, Aldworth, in Berkshire.

(as writer and illustrator)
Children Next Door (unpublished)

AUDREY BLAIR   A radio actress who was married to **John Keir Cross**.

The Sampler Story (March 1945, PL21)

[7] Batten, H.M. 'The Little Folks Pine Martens.' *Little Folks*, 1931, April, p. 154.

OSWELL BLAKESTON (*rn* HENRY JOSEPH HASSLACHER)   British film critic and director, artist, author, and poet, Oswell Blakeston was born Henry Hasslacher into an Austrian wine-importing family in 1907. He ran away from home as a teenager and eventually found work as a clapper boy at Gaumont film studios, working for David Lean, and this launched a career in the film industry, first as editor and later as a director. With the American photographer Francis Brugière, he is credited with having produced in the 1920s the first truly abstract film 'Light Rhythms'. He later became a prolific author of volumes of poetry, cookery books and travel writing, as well as ten detective novels (on four of which he collaborated with Roger Burford under the joint pseudonym 'Simon'). He adopted the name Oswell Blakeston, derived from the author Osbert Sitwell and his mother's family name Blakiston.

Blakeston was a homosexual who maintained a lifelong partnership with the artist Max Chapman, to whom *Danger in Provence* is dedicated as his collaborator. David Buckman's obituary of Chapman in *The Independent* (November 30th 1999) records that this collaboration resulted in them both being arrested in Venice during the war as Russian spies. The story goes that one particularly hot evening, while they were composing *Danger in Provence* on a typewriter on the roof of the building, the security services believed them to be transmitting Morse messages. Chapman collaborated with Blakeston on a number of other books, often as illustrator or photographer. Blakeston and Chapman moved widely in literary circles, and were friends of Dylan Thomas and M. P. Shiel among others. Blakeston's friendship with Shiel led to him receiving a surprising honorific – that of Duke of Redonda, a tiny island in the Leeward group inhabited mainly by a colony of feral goats. Shiel (whose family came from Montserrat) was the first King of Redonda – a title which was for some reason unilaterally conferred on him when he was 15 by his father. Blakeston died in 1985.

> *Danger in Provence* (December 1946, PL52)

R[OLF] A. BRANDT   Rolf Brandt was a British artist born in Germany in 1906, one of four sons of the manager of the Hamburg branch of the Brandt & Sons Bank, originally founded in London by Rolf's grandfather. Rolf was the younger brother of Bill Brandt, one of the greatest of British twentieth-century photographers, with whom he had a close relationship throughout his life. As boys, both received training in drawing at Hamburg, and despite their family background showed no interest in banking as a career. In Austria in 1927 Bill and Rolf became friendly with a Danish teenager Ester Bonnesen, and she and Rolf married and settled in Dessau, where Rolf studied at the Bauhaus as a contemporary of artists such as Kadinsky and Klee. The rise of Nazism in the 1930s led both Rolf and Bill to move to London (they were already British citizens) in 1933. Here Rolf began a career as book illustrator in a distinctive surrealist style, developing a relationship during the war with Gottlieb's publishing houses. **John Keir Cross** described his work as 'Rabellaisian' in a review in *Graphis* magazine[8]. He also remarked that: 'Brandt has been criticized for being "horrible". He is not horrible: the people who find his work horrible are horrible' (hardly Keir Cross's finest literary moment). Some of Brandt's best work in this genre are to be found in the several volumes he illustrated for John Westhouse. When Lunn and Westhouse became bankrupt in 1948, the event seems to have marked an end to Brandt's interest in book illustration; collage had been a long-standing interest and from the 1950s he concentrated on this and abstract painting. He also became an influential teacher at the London College of Printing until the 1970s. He died in 1986, three years after Bill's death. A retrospective exhibition of his work, called 'Apparitions', was held in the Royal Festival Hall in 1988.

---

[8] Cross, John Keir. 'The Book Illustrations of R.A. Brandt.' *Graphis*, 1946, 2(15), pp. 374-379.

(as author and illustrator)
The Man with the Red Umbrella (March 1946, PL32)
The Story of a Tree (April 1946, PL35, with **Stephen Macfarlane**)

(as illustrator)
Fairy Tales by the Brothers Grimm (March 1944, PL6)
The Fisherman's Son (March 1944, PL10)
Why the Sea is Salt (March 1946, PL36)

EDWARD BUCKINGHAM

God of Brazil (November 1947, PL100)

IDA BURROW
Ida Burrow also wrote *Eiderdown Country* (Pixie Press, 1946), a young children's fairy story.

The Dark Blanket (November 1946, PL64)
Snowdrops (April 1947, PL68)

SAM [ARTHUR] CAMPBELL
Sam Campbell was born in Watseka, Illinois, in 1895, and became a writer, lecturer, photographer and ardent wildlife conservationist. When he was a child, his family moved to Chicago, but every summer they visited Sam's mother's parents' 120-acre farm in northern Wisconsin, where Sam developed his love of wildlife. Following the death of his mother Kittie, Sam and his remaining family moved to the farm at Three Lakes, and the property became known as 'The Sanctuary of Wegimind'. Wegimind (a Native American word for 'mother') had been Sam's pet name for his mother. In Three Lakes, Sam began to develop a religio-spiritual philosophy of life in which the forces of nature figured strongly, and he later discussed these ideas in a book of essays called *Nature's Messages* (Rand McNally, 1952). In 1941 he married Giny Adams, and soon afterwards published *How's Inky* (Bobbs-Merrill, 1943), the first of what became a series of twelve nature books called the 'Forest Life' series, re-published in America quite recently by the AB Publishing Company. (The first three of the series were published by Peter Lunn, though in a different order.) Many of the characters who appear in Campbell's books are based on his real life family and friends. During the 1940s and 1950s, he became an increasingly well-known writer, broadcaster and lecturer on conservation matters, and was referred to as 'the philosopher of the forest'. He died in 1962. Shandelle Henderson has published a biography entitled *Sam Campbell: Philosopher of the Forest* (Brushton, 2001).

The Island Sanctuary (December 1945, PL27)
Eeny, Meeny, Miney Mo (April 1946, PL37)
How is Inky? (1946, PL45)

BEATRICE CARROLL (*aka* LADY DUNCAN OF JORDANSTONE)
Beatrice Carroll was born into a well-off family in County Cork in 1910 and her childhood was set against the background of the Troubles of the 1920s. Her early life was clearly an influence on *The Enchanted Glen*, which is described as 'The Fairy Story of an Irish Childhood'. She worked initially in theatre in Dublin, then married and moved to Manchester where she worked for the BBC During the war, she played the part of Larry the Lamb in Uncle Mac's 'Toytown', broadcast on the BBC's Home Service. She moved to Scotland in 1945, and three years after the death of her first husband in 1963, she married Sir James Duncan of Jordanstone. She died in 2003.

The Enchanted Glen (February 1947, PL69)

Lewis Carroll (*rn* Charles Lutwidge Dodgson)

Alice's Adventures in Wonderland ([?1948], PL116)

Through the Looking-Glass (unpublished)

Nicholas Cavanagh (*?rn* William Stobbs)

Night Cargoes (September 1946, PL42)

Sister to the Mermaid (November 1946, PL58)

Saavedra Miguel de Cervantes

Don Quixote de la Mancha (March 1947, PL70)

Michael Challenger

Black Sunset (February 1947, PL75)

Carlo Collodi (*rn* Carlo Lorenzini)

Carlo Lorenzini was born in Florence in 1826, and is now known almost exclusively for his children's classic *Pinocchio*. The pseudonym was derived from the name of his mother's home town. At various periods of his life he was a journalist, editor of a leading newspaper, senior government official involved in educational reform, and military hero. When he retired he gave himself over to writing books for children, including a translation of Perrault's tales and series of humorous stories which, in the manner of the times, often had a hidden agenda of instructing the young. *Pinocchio* first saw print as an 1881 serial in the magazine *Giornale dei Bambini*, and soon became a best-seller when published in book form in 1883. Lorenzini never married, and died in 1890. After his death, his brother Paulo wrote a sequel called *The Heart of Pinocchio*, and a certain Eugenio Cherubini wrote another sequel with the intriguing title *Pinocchio in Africa*.

Pinocchio (September 1947, PL91)

Nancy [Salkeld] Conran (*ps* Nancy Salkeld)

Nancy Conran published an article 'The Open Door' in the magazine *Holiday Parade* (Westhouse, [1947]) under the name Nancy Salkeld, and had also been commissioned to write a further article for a Westhouse book which never appeared. She described herself variously as an author and a journalist. Brief details about her in *Holiday Parade* state that she was a doctor's wife, and that 'her first novel will appear shortly'. I can find no record of it ever having appeared, and it is possible that this was a reference to *Cousin from France* and which may therefore not have been a children's book, despite her claim for the manuscript being against Lunn rather than Westhouse.

Cousin from France (unpublished)

John Keir Cross (*ps* Stephen Macfarlane, *?*Henry Bell, Susan Morley)

John Keir Cross was a Scottish author, musician and radio dramatist, born in Carluke, Lanarkshire, in 1914. His autobiography *Aspect of Life* (Selwyn and Blount, 1937) is an entertaining and reflective account of his childhood, and of his later rejection of a 'safe' career in the insurance business to take to the road as a travelling musician and ventriloquist. (He also shared with the present writer the distinction of being a descendant of Henry Bell, who built *The Comet*, Britain's first steam-boat.) He recalls his creativity at school, where he wrote stories and poems and composed pieces of music. Later, to relieve the tedium of office work, he imagined himself as a Martian, newly arrived on Earth. His autobiography ends at the point he gravitated to London in 1936. There he joined the BBC in 1937, as a writer and producer of radio plays and occasional musical compositions.

In the 1940s his writing career took off, with no fewer than six children's books published by Peter Lunn in the year 1944, under the pseudonym **Stephen Macfarlane**. Undoubtedly his best two works for children, *The Angry Planet* and *The Owl and the Pussycat*, were published under his own name, with superb illustrations by **Robin Jacques**. At about this time, Keir Cross left the BBC and became a freelance writer, although he continued to work with the BBC as radio producer and dramatist for most of his life, even contributing to episodes of 'The Archers' in the 1960s. He also wrote adult fiction (often in the science fiction/fantasy genres) including three books published by John Westhouse. The most notable of these is *The Other Passenger* (Westhouse, 1944), containing 18 genuinely creepy tales, enhanced by **Bruce Angrave**'s remarkable surreal illustrations. Keir Cross also tried his hand at art criticism, with articles for art magazines on his collaborators **Robin Jacques** and **Rolf Brandt**, although they read more like eulogies than critical assessments. It is unfortunate that Keir Cross never extended his autobiographical effort with an account of his years in London, since this would probably have thrown considerable light on his relationship with Gottlieb's publishing houses. We know that this was more than a casual one, since he was a director of Peter Lunn for a period during 1948.

Keir Cross married the radio actress **Audrey Blair**, and they moved from London to run a farm near Totnes, in Devon, where they remained until Keir Cross's sudden death in 1967. Before his death, he had become friends with Bruce Montgomery (real name of the crime writer Edmund Crispin) and something of the flavour of John and Audrey's rather chaotic alcohol-fuelled life in Devon can be gleaned from amusing anecdotes in David Whittle's *Bruce Montgomery/Edmund Crispin: A Life in Music and Books* (Ashgate, 2007). A note by one of Keir Cross's colleagues in *The Times* after his death recalled him as 'a most charming colleague, and in every way an outstanding and delightful personality'.

See also the entry for **Henry Bell**.

> *The Angry Planet* (first edition, October 1945, PL28)
> *Jack Robinson* (December 1945, PL26)
> *Detectives in Greasepaint* (second edition, May 1946, PL40)
> *The Owl and the Pussycat* (May 1946, PL39)
> *The Angry Planet* (second edition, July 1946, PL38)
> *Studio J Investigates* (second edition, August 1946, PL46)
>
> (as compiler)
> *The Children's Omnibus* (n.d.[?1948], PL115)

JOAN DAVIDS (*rn* JOAN EVELYNE HEWITT)   Joan Davids was born in London in 1912 and educated in Eastbourne, Surrey. She later lived in Windsor, and was a contributor to the BBC's Children's Hour. She seems to have written only one other book, *A Pity Beyond All Telling* (Constable, 1956) which is a romantic novel. The advertisement on the back flap of *Legends of St Francis* has her name as 'Joan Edwards'.

> *The Glastonbury Adventure* (October 1946, PL76)

JAMES DAVIES

(as compiler)
Adolphus' Playbook (June 1947, PL84)

DANIEL DEFOE

Robinson Crusoe (1943, PL5)

DAISY ECKERSLEY   First wife of artist **Tom Eckersley**, with whom she collaborated on *Cat O' Nine Lives*.

Cat O' Nine Lives (July 1946, PL48)

CHARLES [EGERTON] EDEN   I have discovered Charles Eden's middle name from the claim he

put in to the Receiver for the balance of the payment due to him for the manuscript of *Suez and Panama*. He gave an address in Westminster. The only person of this name I have been able to find referred to elsewhere was a London barrister who published *Questions Answered on Making and Proving Wills* (Jordan and Sons, 1947).

Suez and Panama (unpublished)

LIONEL [DALHOUSIE ROBERTSON] EDWARDS   Lionel Edwards was an artist who made his name

from illustrating horses and hunting scenes with remarkable skill, and his work as a watercolourist came to be particularly admired. He was born in 1878 in the Clifton area of Bristol, the youngest of the eight children of James and Harriet Edwards. He spent much of his childhood in north Wales, where he appears to have had little interest in anything other than country pursuits and drawing. His mother encouraged his evident artistic gifts, which were presumed to have derived from his maternal grandmother who had been a talented artist. After some training as a young man at art schools in London, including at Frank Calderon's School of Animal Painting, Edwards began to have drawings and watercolours accepted by magazines such as *Country Life*. His contribution to *Horses and Riders* gives some insight into his life in London as an artist and horse-owner in central London in the 1890s. When he was in his late 20s he married Ethel Ashness Wells, the daughter of a brewer. They moved home a number of times, but always to districts where they could pursue their love of fox-hunting - Lionel usually armed with sketch-pad and pencil. He was briefly a reporter for *The Graphic* in Spain in 1910. After the war, during which Lionel was a Remount Purchasing Officer in the army, he and Ethel finally moved to West Tytherley, near Salisbury, where Lionel died in 1966.

Edwards illustrated many books and articles during his life, and was also commissioned to paint stand-alone works, almost invariably with equestrian themes. He also wrote in an engaging and lucid style, often providing the text to accompany his own illustrations. In later years, he was reported to be 'a quiet gentle man who looked like an old soldier'.

(as editor and illustrator)
Horses and Riders (September 1946, PL53)

(as contributor and illustrator)
My First Horse (March 1947, PL63)

154

(as illustrator)
Flame (September 1945, PL25)
Black Beauty (August 1946, PL50)
Jumper (1948, PL109)

WALTER [LORIMER] FARLEY   Walter Farley's life, from a very young age until he died, was devoted to horses. He rode them, bred them, and he wrote about them. He was born in Syracuse, New York, in 1915, the son of Walter (an assistant hotel manager) and Isabelle. He was brought up in New York City, where he began writing at the age of eleven and also spent a lot of time frequenting race-tracks. *The Black Stallion* was published in 1941, while Farley was still an undergraduate, and immediately became popular with young readers. Farley did army service during the war, and between 1942 and 1946 he was a reporter for the army magazine *Yank*. He married Rosemary Lutz in 1945, and they had four children. Farley died in Florida in 1989.

For nearly fifty years after the publication of his first book, Farley wrote more stories as part of what became known as the 'Black Stallion' series, finally reaching 21 titles. The last of these, *The Young Black Stallion*, was co-written with his son Steve, who continued the series after his father's death. The 'Black Stallion' books have given rise to something of a cult following in America, and there is now a 'Black Stallion' web-site, which also promotes literacy programmes for children – an activity with which Farley himself was involved during his later life. Farley's books were also widely published in other countries, including Britain, where they were published quite recently as paperbacks by Knight Books. Whether Peter Lunn would have gone on to publish more than the first of the series we do not know. Farley published around a dozen other books, all concerned with horses. Back in the 1930s, his first editor had told him that 'he could never make a living writing children's books'.

   The Black Stallion (November 1946, PL71)

M. FARRER   It is possible that this author was Mary Farrer, a children's writer who retold a number of famous stories as 'The Academy Series', a series of 48-page card-covered booklets, published by the Studely Press between 1947 and 1948 and illustrated by Jennetta Vise.

   The Kingdom of a Thousand Isles (January 1947, PL77)

CYRUS FISHER (*rn* DARWIN LEORA TEILHET, *ps* CYRUS T. FISHER)   Cyrus Fisher was the pseudonym of American author Darwin L. Teilhet, born in 1904 in Illinois. Under his real name, he wrote a number of detective novels during the thirties and forties, the best-known of which feature his series detective Baron Von Kaz. Some of these were in collaboration with his wife Hildegarde (Tolman). Barzun and Taylor[9] are dismissive of the quality of Teilhet's work in this field, and note that his career 'seems to boil down to the feat of having once given a lecture on Marxism with three other people'.

If Barzun and Taylor had been a little more assiduous with their research, they would have discovered that Teilhet actually led a rather colourful life. His family had roots in France, and he travelled there regularly as a child. He worked as a juggler in a French circus, learnt to fly, and when he was 20,

   [9] Barzun, Jacques and Taylor, Wendell Hertig. *A Catalogue of Crime.* New York: Harper & Row, 1971, p. 498.

returned to France to build a glider. Teilhet was encouraged to try writing for children by the American children's author Howard Pease, and his first children's book, *Skwee-Gee*, was published by Doubleday, Doran & Co. in 1940. During the war, he worked as an intelligence officer in Britain and America. In 1946, he published *The Avion my Uncle Flew*, which he wrote under the pseudonym Cyrus T. Fisher. Cyrus Fisher Tolman was a Professor of Geology at Stanford who died a few years before the book was published, and I take it that he was Teilhet's father-in-law and that he gave Teilhet the idea for his pseudonym. It is obvious how Teilhet's early experiences in France supplied the background for *The Avion my Uncle Flew*, but his involvement with a circus also gave him material for his next children's book *Ab Carmody's Treasure* (Henry Holt, 1948). This book is set in Guatemala, and tries to teach the reader some Spanish in the same way that *Avion* taught them French. Teilhet was also involved for a period in pineapple farming in Hawaii, which provides the background for his last children's book *The Hawaiian Sword* (Funk and Wagnalls, 1956), in which he makes a rather half-hearted attempt to introduce the reader to Hawaiian vocabulary.

Teilhet also tackled more serious issues in his writing. During a spell in Germany in the 1920s he had witnessed, and been outraged by, the rise of Nazism and its treatment of the Jewish population. One of his crime novels, *The Talking Sparrow Murders* (Morrow, 1934) is set in Heidelberg against this background. Teilhet died in 1964 in California.

> *The Avion my Uncle Flew* (December 1946, PL65)

THE BROTHERS GRIMM

> *Fairy Tales by the Brothers Grimm* (March 1944, PL6)

GORDON GRIMSLEY (*rn* ARTHUR GROOM)

> *The Champion* (October 1947, PL98)

ARTHUR [WILLIAM] GROOM (*ps* GORDON GRIMSLEY, *plus many other pseudonyms*)

Arthur Groom was born in 1898 in Hove, Sussex, the son of William and Emily Groom, and was educated in Croydon, Surrey. At 17, he began a career in banking, and was sent to the West Indies. During a holiday he spent time looking for natural diamonds in British Guiana and managed to find a few which he later sold in Hatton Garden to finance the purchase of a typewriter. He worked for London Underground for six years, before launching his career as a writer. In later years he also lectured and broadcast, with a particular interest in Scouting, and in children's affairs generally. His interest in the outdoor life is reflected in *The Bearded Stranger* which is a (misguided) attempt to amalgamate a story of boys pursued by a homicidal criminal gang with detailed tips on how to run a camping expedition. During his life, Groom was a highly prolific writer of boys' magazine stories as well as books. These also included a few girls' stories and original books based on TV Western series such as *Roy Rogers* and *Wagon Train*. His output has been variously estimated at figures from one to four hundred books, but the loss of many publishers' records during the war, and the fact that he wrote under so many pseudonyms, make it difficult to have much confidence in any estimate. He was a two-finger typist who stated that he completed a 60,000 word story in about three weeks. Groom lived in Cornwall for a few years (where he said his heart thereafter always remained) before settling 'with his wife, daughter, cat and television set' in a farmhouse in Gloucestershire. (The name **Gordon Grimsley**, under which he wrote *The Champion*, was derived from Marjorie Grimsley, whom he married in 1928.) Groom was also a lay Church of England preacher, and at a height of 6ft 5in one imagines he must have cut a formidable figure behind the pulpit. He had little liking for the material to be found in the newly arriving American comics, although be did express approval of two 'factual' ones his daughter had obtained entitled 'The Old Testament' and 'The New Testament'. Groom died in 1964.

> *The Ghost of Gordon Gregory* (November 1946, PL60)
> *The Bearded Stranger* (March 1947, PL59)
> *The Adventure at Marston Manor* (March 1947, PL72)

DUNCAN HALL

> *The Priest of the Legion* (December 1947, PL108)

EDMUND HARDY

> *Voyage to Chivalry* (April 1947, PL66)

WILLIAM HAUFF (*rn* WILHELM HAUFF)

Wilhelm Hauff ('William' seems to have been an uncalled-for Anglicisation of his name by an editor at Peter Lunn) was born in Stuttgart in 1802, one of the four children of August and Hedwig Hauff. When Wilhelm was four, the family moved to Tübingen, where his father died three years later. His mother then moved, with the children, to live with her parents. A fortunate outcome of this sad event was that Wilhelm then had a free run of his grandfather's library, well stocked with the works of classic authors, including the early novels of Sir Walter Scott. (One of Hauff's later literary ambitions was 'to become the German Walter Scott'.) At the age of 15, Hauff began a course of theological study which led to him becoming a student at the Protestant theological college of Tübinger Stift. Here he developed a taste for radical student politics and joined a fraternity which in 1924 became the subject of an investigation for alleged anti-patriotic activities. In spite of this he was awarded a doctorate the same year, and thereafter he pursued his real desire to become a literary figure. Sadly, this was to be a short pursuit, since late in 1827 Hauff was to die of 'nerve fever' (possibly encephalitis) surrounded by his student friends. His death came some nine months after his marriage to Luise, and eight days after the birth of his child. It is remarkable how prolific he was during this short period of literary activity, although much of his work was published posthumously. He is best remembered for two works: *Lichtenstein: A Romantic Saga from the History of Wurttemberg* (a historical romance) published by Franckh in 1826, and his *Märchen* (Fairy Tales) published by Metzler the same year, from which *Mukrah the Dwarf* and the stories in *The Silver Florin* are drawn.

> *Mukrah the Dwarf* (December 1944, PL22)
> *The Silver Florin* (November 1947, PL101)

DONALD [LANDELS] HENDERSON (*ps* D. H. LANDELS, STEPHANIE LANDELS)

Donald Henderson, author and playwright, was born in 1905 in Brentford, Middlesex. During the 1930s and 1940s he wrote around a dozen crime fiction novels, both under his own name and the pseudonym D. H. Landels. *Pasha* seems to have been his only children's book. He married in 1942, and *Pasha* is dedicated to his son Colin, who was born in 1945. Tragically, Henderson died a month or two before the book was published, at the age of 41.

> *Pasha* (September 1947, PL107)

PATRICK DE HERIZ (*rn* WALTER SIDNEY SCOTT)   Walter Sidney Scott, who described himself as a 'Clerk in Holy Orders', was primarily an anthologist and editor, although he also wrote a few books. He lived in Selborne, Hampshire, a district beloved of Gilbert White (also a clergyman) who published his famous *Natural History and Antiquities of Selborne* in 1789. Scott himself edited different versions of this work , including one published by the Folio Society in 1962. Scott was clearly a man of letters as well as of the cloth, and his introduction to *Fairy Tales with a Twist* is arguably rather too learned for a children's book. The only other book published under the name Patrick de Heriz appears to have been *La Belle O'Morphi*, a short biography of Louis XV's teenage Irish mistress Marie Louise O'Morphi, issued in a limited edition of 750 by the Golden Cockerel Press in 1947. In fact, most of Scott's work appears under his own name, and his first published work appears to have been a small pamphlet *Prayers and Intercessions in Times of War*, privately published in 1939. He later edited three volumes of correspondence between Percy Bysshe Shelley and his friends, one of whom was Thomas Jefferson Hope, from whom Scott's wife Margaret was descended. He wrote or edited four volumes published by Westhouse, including one of works by John Donne, and a biography of Gilbert White. Scott was also a cat-lover: he compiled an anthology called *A Clowder of Cats* for Westhouse in 1946, dedicated to his three cats 'from their Master'. The final item, 'Puss-in-Boots by Patrick de Heriz', is headed 'The Best Cat of All'.

> *Fairy Tales with a Twist* (December 1946, PL85)

MARJORIE HILL

> (as adapter)
> *Don Quixote de la Mancha* (March 1947, PL70, with **Audrey Walton**)

JOHN D. HILLABY   John Hillaby, travel writer and editor, was born in 1917 in Pontefract, the son of a printer. He is best known as a writer of books about outdoor life, particularly those describing his two main passions: angling and walking. *Within the Streams* (Harvey and Blythe, 1949), written at much the same time as he wrote *Operation Adventure* for Peter Lunn, describes an angling career beginning at the age of 14 on the Leeds and Liverpool Canal at Kirkstall, and following streams and rivers to end up in the Hebrides. However, he is probably best known for his accounts of walking tours (often alone) throughout the world, such as *Journey to the Jade Sea* and *Journey through Britain*, both published by Constable in the 1960s. He was an active campaigner for the maintenance of public rights-of-way. Hillaby also edited two magazines (similar in format and content to *Lilliput*) called *Holiday Parade* and *Autumn Parade*, both published in 1947 by John Westhouse. He died in York in 1996.

> *Operation Adventure* (May 1947, PL86)

DON HILLSON   Between 1939 and 1950, Don Hillson wrote a number of books for children about outdoor life in Canada, many of which he illustrated himself. He also published a fictionalised biography of Captain Cook called *Heart of Oak* (Schofield and Sims, 1948).

> *Canadian Wildwood* (December 1946, PL73)

GLADYS HIRST

> *Roundabout House* (unpublished)

PETER HOLLEY   Holley also wrote another war-time children's adventure story called *Adventure in France* (Werner Laurie, [1949]).

> *Bright is the Starlight* (February 1947, PL78)

I. M. HOLMES   I have been unable to find out anything about this author except that he or she was the same person who wrote *In Africa's Service* (a biography for children of Mary Kingsley, the niece of Charles Kingsley). This was published in 1949 by the Saturn Press, but was originally to have been published by Peter Lunn.

> *Great Gold Rushes* (December 1947, PL113)
> *In Africa's Service* (unpublished)

WASHINGTON IRVING

> *Alhambra Tales* (November 1946, PL54)

NICHOLAS KALASHNIKOFF   Nicholas Kalashnikoff, soldier and writer, was born Nikolai Kalashnikoff in 1888 in Minusinsk, Siberia, the son of a farmer and a part-Tartar mother. He was educated at Irkutsk, and later studied history and philosophy in Moscow. As a young man, he felt inclined to a military career and took part in the 1905 rebellion, leading to his being exiled in Siberia by the Czarist regime. There, work as a newspaper correspondent gave him the opportunity to travel widely across the country. He served in the Russian army during the Great War, and afterwards led campaigns on behalf of the Siberian Territorial Government. From 1920 to 1922 he worked for the Siberian Cooperative Association in Harbin, China, before emigrating to the United States, where he married Elizabeth Lawrence, an editor at Harper's publishing house. His early days in Siberia provided him with the background for *Jumper* and a number of other books: *Toyon: a Dog of the North and his People* (Harper and Row 1950), *The Defender* (Scribners, 1951) – a story about Turgen, a mountain shepherd who protects endangered wild rams in Siberia – and the autobiographical *My Friend Yakub* (OUP, 1961). *The Defender* won a Newbery Honor medal in 1952. Kalashnikoff died in 1961.

> *Jumper* (1948, PL109)

NORA KAY   Nora Kay was a craft artist and designer, specialising in lino-cuts, cut paper and calligraphy. She was brought up in Buckinghamshire, and attended Wycombe High School, St Martin's School of Art and the Royal College of Art. She went on to teach art and she carried out a variety of design commissions. She had a particular interest in italic script, and her expertise in this area can be judged from the text of *English Trees*.

> (as author and illustrator)
> *English Trees* (August 1947, PL99)

JOHN KENT

> (as editor)
> *Stories from Ancient Greece* (March 1947, PL92)

Denis F[rancis] Kerr   Denis Kerr was a younger brother of **George Kerr**, who retold *Homer's Odyssey* for Peter Lunn. Denis was born in Ipswich in 1911, but moved quite soon to Treeton, in Yorkshire, where his father had been appointed vicar. There Denis came to know Gabrielle Scovell, the daughter of the vicar of the neighbouring parish of Rawmarsh, and whom Denis was later to marry. (Gabrielle was a descendant of George Scovell who gained fame by deciphering Napoleon's secret code during the Peninsular War.) Denis was sent to Haileybury College in Hertfordshire, and later gained an M.A. in History at Cambridge. Emerging at a time of economic depression, he briefly worked for P&O as assistant purser on trips to Australia, before joining George in London to look for other work, based at a flat near Covent Garden. It is probably during this time that he and George first made contact with Gottlieb, in the years before he launched his publishing venture.

In 1936 Denis was offered a job in Trinidad, and he and Gabrielle decided to marry and leave for the British West Indies. Here, while Denis was working for Regent Oil (later Texaco), they set up in the grounds of their house the 'Island Zoo' which Denis wrote about for Peter Lunn. Denis had developed an affinity for animals during his childhood, and although ambitions to keep pets while at school were frustrated by authority, he did keep two doves (Michael and Sheila) while at university. They became the core of a larger collection kept in a home-built aviary in London, and Michael and Sheila even accompanied Denis to Trinidad. *My Island Zoo* (originally to have been called 'Some Creature Friends of Mine') seems to have been written more to instruct than to entertain. For example, it describes in exhaustive detail: a menu suitable for rearing puppies, the measurements to the nearest half-inch of every conceivable dimension of the body of a caiman he had just shot, and a description of how best to kill a rabbit which one imagines would unnerve even the most hardened youngster.

Denis and Gabrielle remained in Trinidad during the war, when Denis ran a shore battery defending a strategically important oil refinery at Pointe-à-Pierre. After Denis had given up running the zoo, he and Gabrielle (who was a talented musician) set up the Southern Light Orchestra and Choir. This was an inclusive and multi-racial venture which they pursued with great passion and success, and it culminated in Denis being awarded the Humming Bird Gold Medal for services to music in Trinidad and Tobago in 1970. When he and Gabrielle retired and returned to England in 1975 to live in a bungalow at Slimbridge in Gloucestershire, Denis became a lay preacher, and together they set up and ran the church choir. Denis died in 1989, and he and Gabrielle now lie together alongside the path used by William Tyndale when he attended the same church.

> *My Island Zoo* (June 1947, PL114)

George [Pengelley] Kerr (*ps* **George Pengelly, ?Frank Rhodes**)   George Kerr was born in London in 1901, the son of William and Elizabeth Kerr. He was one of five sons and a daughter brought up in the family rectory in Ipswich, where his father was the vicar of St Peter's Church. The youngest of George's brothers was **Denis Kerr**, who wrote *My Island Zoo*. Although George himself just missed being involved in the First World War, his older brother Edward was killed as a lieutenant at Ypres, an event which greatly affected the family. (When William later became vicar of Treeton Parish Church in Yorkshire, he dedicated the fittings of the Brampton Chapel to the memory of Edward.) After George had gained a first class honours degree in Classics at Cambridge, his wealthy uncle, who owned the Kerr Shipping Line based in the Caribbean, paid for George to travel around the world. In the early 1930s Wright and Brown published three light-hearted volumes by Kerr entitled *Life's Little Pleasures*, *Life's Little Problems* and *Little Journeys*, the last of which describes anecdotes from this period of travel, during which he visited Japan (where he worked as a teacher), China, Egypt and the Philippines. When he returned to England he tried his hand at various types of work including teaching, stockbroking and journalism. He gained a flying certificate in 1929, and gave his profession at that time as 'Editor'. In 1931 he married Olive Mary Hatch, to whom *Little Journeys* is dedicated.

During the Second World War, Kerr became a Wing-Commander in the RAF and was posted to Canada to train pilots who were flying overseas. (In 1948, he wrote *Time's Forelock*, published by the Shell Petroleum Company, which was an account of Shell's contribution to aviation during the war, illustrated by **Laurence Scarfe**.) By this time George had two daughters, and Olive and the girls were sent to America in 1940 on the last available boat, a small cargo boat of the Kerr Shipping Line. They returned to England in 1943, to be welcomed by flying bombs. After the war George worked as a financial journalist, and the family moved to Frensham in Surrey, before finally settling in Kensington in 1956. Following a long marriage, George and Olive died in 1976, within hours of each other.

Under the name **George Pengelly**, Kerr also adapted the children's film *The Grand Escapade* to book form for Peter Lunn, and he was probably the adapter of the film *Song of Arizona*, under the name **Frank Rhodes**.

   Homer's Odyssey (June 1947, PL110)

YOTI LANE (*ps* MARK MAYO)   Yoti Lane was an actress, journalist and drama critic, born in Kilmore, Ireland. She worked in Dublin as a journalist for a number of years, and acted, produced and wrote scripts for the Dublin Studio Theatre, as well as writing short stories for the newspaper and magazine markets. As an author, she has only a handful of books to her credit. The first of these seems to have been *African Folk Tales*, which was based on stories told to her by African acquaintances, including Kwame N'krumah (later to become the first President of Ghana), written down for the first time by Lane, and published by Peter Lunn. She later published two manuals for aspiring actors: *Stage Make-up* (Hutchinson, 1950) and *If You Would Act* (Hutchinson, 1951). Lane also had a strong interest in psychology, particularly as applied to drama, and much of her thinking on this was brought together in *The Psychology of the Actor* (Secker and Warburg, 1959). The only other book she appears to have published, under the pseudonym Mark Mayo, was a psychological novel *Red, Yellow and Green* (Peter Davies, 1952) which a contemporary review described as 'cherished by the staffs of psychiatric hospitals'.

   African Folk Tales (November 1946, PL67)

PETER LETHBRIDGE (*rn* RONALD SYME)   After a fruitless attempt to uncover information about this author, the preface to *Here Lies Gold* finally alerted me to the fact that the incidents of early life which the author mentions (such as '[fishing] for schnapper off the coast of Western Australia') were very similar to those of Ronald Syme. I was also aware of an item called 'Here Lies Gold' published in *Eagle Annual No. 1* under the name Ronald Syme, and comparison of the text with the Lunn volume makes it quite clear that the former is a shortened and simplified version of the latter. Sections of text have been adopted almost verbatim. The name 'Lethbridge' was probably suggested to Syme by John Lethbridge, an eighteenth-century diver for treasure from Devon who invented a sort of hybrid diving-bell/armoured diving suit, and whose exploits are recounted by Syme in *Full Fathom Five*. A few other children's books were published under the name Peter Lethbridge, including *The Holiday Adventurers* (Museum Press, 1947) – a Blytonesque tale set on the Cornish coast and bristling with smuggling, treasure and secret passages.

   Here Lies Gold (March 1947, PL93)

DAVID S. MACARTHUR (*aka* DAVID FORBES LORNE)   The Thunderbolt Men appears to be the only book written by MacArthur under this name. According to the dustjacket of the book, under the name David Forbes Lorne he wrote extensively for radio, contributing both to the adult programme of the BBC, as well as supplying stories, plays and serials for Children's Hour. I have been unable to establish which (if either) of these names was his real one.

   The Thunderbolt Men (February 1947, PL102)

STEPHEN MACFARLANE (*rn* JOHN KEIR CROSS)
   Studio J Investigates (first edition, April 1944, PL13)
   Detectives in Greasepaint (first edition, May 1944, PL12)
   Lucy Maroon (July 1944, PL11)
   Mr Bosanko (August 1944, PL14)
   The Strange Tale of Sally and Arnold (August 1944, PL16)
   The Blue Egg (December 1944, PL20)
   The Story of a Tree (April 1946, PL35)
   Arbuthnot the Goldfish (unpublished)

[MAJOR] HUGH [A. D.] MACKAY   The synopsis on the dustjacket of *The Ivory Trail* states that Mackay knew Africa well, and we know that in 1948 he was a married military man, and resident in Pietermaritzburg, Natal. He appears to have published no other book in Britain, although he may plausibly be identified with the 'Captain Hugh Mackay' who collaborated on the book *Our Feathered Friends* by W. J. Vorster (Fishwick, Durban, 1938). He may also have written *Songs of the Services: a book of light verse* (Lawlers, Port Elizabeth, 1941).

   The Ivory Trail (February 1947, PL94)

W. B. MACMILLAN   Macmillan also wrote another children's mystery thriller *Riddle of the Burning Castles* (Pictorial Art, 1947), a slim 32-page booklet priced at 6d.

   The Hunting of Zakaroff (September 1946, PL49)

JO[AN GRENVILLE] MANTON (*aka* JO GITTINGS, JO MANTON GITTINGS)   Jo Manton was born in 1919 in Hertfordshire, the daughter of artist Grenville Manton. She attended Cambridge University before moving to work for the BBC from 1942-1949, as a programme planner and a writer and producer of school history broadcasts. It was during this period that she wrote *The Story of Titania and Oberon* for Peter Lunn. She published a further book in collaboration with the illustrator **Phyllis Bray**, called *The Enchanted Ship* in 1950, published by Oxford University Press. In 1949, she married Robert Gittings, who at the time was also working for the BBC as a writer and producer, and later became well known as a poet and literary biographer. Jo also went on to write biographies, some in collaboration with Robert. She died in Chichester in 1997, five years after Robert's death.

   The Story of Titania and Oberon (September 1945, PL33)

162

DONALD MOORE   Donald Moore was born in 1923 in Loughborough, Leicestershire and he was educated locally. During the war, he travelled to China, and his experiences in Shanghai provided the background for *China Coast Pirates*, his only children's book. In 1946 he, his wife (who worked in the book trade) and his daughters moved to Singapore. Moore had been charged with representing leading British publishers, and promoting the sale of British books in the Far East. In fact he remained in Singapore for most of his life, and in 1954, he set up his own publishing company, Donald Moore Ltd, becoming a director of Heinemann (Asia) Ltd in 1959. He did much to promote cultural development in Singapore, and some flavour of his activities during the 1950s can found in a travel diary published as *Far Eastern Agent* (Hodder and Stoughton, 1953) describing a three-month trip to Malaya, Indonesia, Thailand, Hong Kong and Japan. He appears also to have been a capable photographer, and examples of his work appear in *We Live in Singapore* (Hodder and Stoughton, 1955).

> *China Coast Pirates* (December 1946, PL95)

SYDNEY MOORHOUSE   Sydney Moorhouse was an author and journalist born in Huddersfield, Yorkshire, in 1909. Before and after the war, he wrote a number of guide-books for walkers covering areas in Lancashire and Yorkshire, and many articles on countryside-related topics for newspapers and magazines, including children's magazines such as *Boy's Own Paper*. During the war, he was a flight-lieutenant in the RAF, operating from a base in the Cocos Islands as Public Relations Officer for south-east Asia, reporting on naval operations. This would no doubt have given him background material for *The World's Strange Islands*. Immediately after the war he was living in Lancaster, but he later moved to Morecambe. Moorhouse was a Fellow of both the Royal Geographical Society and the Zoological Society, and contributed articles to journals in both fields. He was also a keen philatelist, and a member of the Circus Fans Association. Although *I Find the Past* was never published, a cut-down version entitled 'Digging up the Past' did appear in Westhouse's magazine *Holiday Parade*.

> *The World's Strange Islands* (unpublished)
>
> *I Find the Past* (unpublished)

P[ercival] H[orace] Muir (AKA PERCY MUIR)   Percy Muir was an author, antiquarian bookseller and bibliographer of Scottish descent born in 1894 in Poplar, East London. He began to work for the London antiquarian bookseller and publisher Elkin Mathews in 1930 and was already a director of the company when he married Barbara Gowing in 1937. He was a close friend of A. J. A. Symons and of Ian Fleming, and for many years advised and assisted Fleming in his building of a collection of 'milestone books'. As war loomed, Percy, Barbara (and Elkin Mathews itself) retreated to a Tudor cottage in Takeley, Essex, where they were to bring up a son and daughter, and almost single-handedly nurse the Elkin Mathews business through difficult times. The arrival of Stansted Airport drove them in 1970 to the coastal village of Blakeney in Norfolk, where they remained until Percy's death in 1979, after which Barbara and their son David continued to run the Elkin Mathews firm as partners.

Muir became well-known in book-collecting circles for two important works he wrote: *English Children's Books 1600-1900* (Batsford, 1954) and *Victorian Illustrated Books* (Batsford, 1971), and he had a significant personal collection of Victorian children's books, parlour games and automata. He was also a central figure in the politics of the antiquarian book trade; in 1946 he became president of the Antiquarian Booksellers Association (ABA) and during his period of office was instrumental in the ABA's attempts to clear its stables of dealers who routinely, though illegally, participated in book auction rings. He was later a founder member and president of the International League of Antiquarian Booksellers

(ILAB). Under her pen-name Barbara Kaye, his wife was to publish *The Company We Kept* (Werner Shaw, 1986) and *Second Impression* (Oak Knoll Press, 1995) which were in a sense continuations of Percy's own autobiography *Minding My Own Business* (Chatto and Windus, 1956), and contain many insights into the workings of the international antiquarian book trade.

> (as editor)
> *Alhambra Tales* (November 1946, PL54)

DORA NASH

> *Summer Gypsies* (April 1947, PL87)

SYLVIA NORTON

The only other book Norton seems to have published was *Meet Mr Buggley* (Haddock and Baines, 1947). This is another children's picture book, which concludes with the information that she wrote it at Hedgerley (a village in Buckinghamshire).

> *The Magic Zoo* (1943, PL3)

PIETER VAN OOSTKERKE (*rn* (BARON) JOSEPH VAN DER ELST)

Baron Joseph van der Elst was a diplomat, art critic and collector of Flemish art, born in Ixelles, Belgium in 1896. He was a prominent figure in diplomatic circles, and became Belgium's ambassador to Italy. His interest in art was not easily engendered, and he recalled that he and his brothers were 'more mulish than most boys' and had to be more or less dragged by their father through 'every Museum in Europe'. Nevertheless, he was to become a knowledgeable and enthusiastic collector of Flemish Renaissance art, and he wrote a book on the subject, entitled *The Last Flowering of the Middle Ages* (Doubleday, 1944). This was to have been published in Britain by Westhouse, but in fact it never appeared. His children's art book *The Picture Frame* grew out of van der Elst's habit of showing his own children (two daughters and a son) reproductions of art just before bedtime, when he would weave invented stories around the figures in the paintings. It is an unusual type of book, and I am unaware of any other which aims to foster children's interest in art in this way. The name Pieter van Oostkerke, under which van der Elst wrote it, was derived from Kasteel van Oostkerke, a fourteenth century castle in the West Flemish town of Damme, which he bought in 1938 and renovated after the war. He died in 1971.

> *The Picture Frame* (July 1947, PL103)

GEORGE PENGELLY (*rn* GEORGE KERR)

> *The Grand Escapade* (June 1947, PL89)

JOHN H. PERNULL

> *Pizarro of Peru* (unpublished)

ALFONS PURTSCHER: *see* NORA PURTSCHER.

NORA [FRIEDERIKE MARIA] PURTSCHER (*aka* NORA WYDENBRUCK, (COUNTESS) NORA PURTSCHER-WYDENBRUCK)

Nora Wydenbruck, writer, artist and spiritualist, was born in London in 1894, where her father, Count Cristoph Anton Wydenbruck, was first secretary at the Austrian Embassy. When she was still a baby, her father was re-assigned to duties in Japan, and she and her mother returned to her parents' native Austria. Here she spent her childhood in Castle Meiselberg, a period described in her autobiography *An Austrian Background* (Methuen, 1932). She seems to have been a rebellious and somewhat hysterical teenager. When threatened with being sent to a boarding-school, she went on hunger-strike, but had quickly to abandon it after being force-fed by a tube through her nose, in the manner of the Suffragettes. After leaving school, she travelled in Italy and then 'came out' in Vienna in 1912. She married the Austrian animal and landscape painter **Alfons Purtscher** in 1919, and they moved to a villa on the edge of a lake in Carinthia, where Nora gave birth to a daughter and a son. It was during this period that Nora developed an interest in spiritualism and regularly attended séances with a group of friends. Alfons was sceptical to begin with, but having been persuaded to attend a séance where, according to Nora, he and his chair were lifted bodily into the air and a strong hand shook him vigorously and rained blows all over his body, he too became a believer. In 1926, Alfons and she moved to London, leaving the children in Austria, and there began a rather unhappy period living in straitened financial circumstances in boarding-houses in Bayswater and Paddington, while Alfons tried to earn a living from painting and Nora wrote articles and short stories and did some translation work. Eventually their situation improved, and they were able to buy a property, and were reunited with their children. Nora was a member of the executive council for the International Institute for Psychical Research during the 1930s.

Although *The Legends of St Francis* was her only book published by Lunn, Westhouse published *Gothic Twilight* (1946) and *Doctor Mesmer* (1947). The latter book reflects her interest in psychic investigation. Although she published a number of other books, much of her literary output remains unpublished and is preserved in the Robert Musil Archive. She died in 1959, survived for three years by Alfons.

The Legends of St Francis (October 1947, PL111, with **Alfons Purtscher**)

Rudolph [Erich] Raspe

Linguist, gemmologist, art historian and mining engineer, Rudolph Raspe appears also to have been a man possessed of a flexible moral code, leading him at several times during his colourful career into situations where he felt it prudent to move quickly on from one country to another. He was born in Hanover in 1737, and educated at the universities of Leipzig and Göttingen. He was later put in charge of a collection of medals and gems owned by Frederick II, Landgrave of Hesse, some of which he pilfered and sold to boost his personal finances. He fled to England in 1755, where he published *An Account of some German Volcanos and their Productions* (Lockyer Davis, 1776) – a book which probably did little to improve his financial situation. After a spell in debtors' prison in 1780, he is next found in 1782 working as an assayer for the Dolcoath mines in Cornwall. In 1785, he published (anonymously) the first of various versions of the Munchausen stories. (The issues surrounding authorship of this and later versions is discussed in the notes to the entry for PL96.) Baron Münchhausen (1720-1797) was a real person, whom Raspe may well have met in Göttingen, but Raspe's tales evidently drew on (and embellished) tales from earlier folklore, as well as real individuals and events.

By 1791, Raspe was prospecting for minerals at the estate of Ulbster in Scotland. Although he initially appeared to have been successful in this venture, he was exposed as having 'planted' specimens he had previously collected in Cornwall, and was obliged to decamp to Ireland. He continued here as a mining engineer, but died in 1794, either of typhoid in Killarney or of scarlet fever in Donegal, depending on which source one consults. The accuracy of some of the more florid details of Raspe's life has been questioned by John Carswell in his erudite introduction to a 1948 edition of *Munchausen*[10].

12 Adventures of the Celebrated Baron Munchausen (June 1947, PL96)

[10] Raspe, R.E. et al. *Baron Munchausen*. London: Cresset Press, 1948.

GEOFFREY RAWSON   Naval officer, journalist and writer, Geoffrey Rawson was born in 1886, the son of Charles, a tea-planter, and Kate Rawson, and he was christened in Leytonstone, Essex, on 14th October 1888. At the age of nine his guardians (his parents were apparently abroad at this time) enrolled him as a 'Blue-coat boy' at the preparatory school for Christ's Hospital, in Hertford, before he moved to the main school in Newgate Street, London. His memories of life at Christ's Hospital, including the Tudor-style dress of blue skirt and bright yellow stockings which he had to wear, are related in his autobiographical work *Sea Prelude* (Blackwood, 1958). On leaving school, he began a long period of naval training, beginning on a school ship H.M.S. *Worcester*, moored at Greenhithe. He then spent several years sailing around the world aboard the Aberdeen barque *Inversnaid* before securing a commission as a sub-lieutenant in the Royal Indian Marine, working on troop ships between India and Burma. He later served in the Persian Gulf, where one of his ship-mates was Lieutenant Bowers (who perished on Scott's Antarctic expedition). By the time of his retirement from the navy, he had achieved the rank of Lieutenant-Commander in the Royal Navy. During 1930s, he settled in Melbourne, Australia, and this also marked the most active period of his career as a writer and journalist. He published a number of non-fiction books, mainly biographies of nautical figures such as Admiral Beatty and Captain Bligh, and some accounts of exploration. *Arctic Adventures* seems to have been his only book aimed at children. Rawson died in 1969.

Arctic Adventures (April 1947, PL88)

FRANK RHODES (*?rn* GEORGE KERR)   Frank Rhodes was probably another pseudonym for George Kerr. *Song of Arizona* (under the title 'Arizona Holiday') was given advance advertising as written by **George Pengelly** in the April 1947 issue of *Publishers' Circular*.

Song of Arizona (June 1947, PL79)

PETER ROSS

Beppo (December 1946, PL80)

ANNA SEWELL   Anna Sewell was born in Great Yarmouth in 1820 to Isaac and Mary Sewell (Wright) who were Quakers. Isaac appears to have been in financial difficulties at this time, and the family moved to London where Anna's brother Philip was born in 1822. While the family was living in Stoke Newington, Anna, previously educated by her mother at home, was allowed to attend school. When she was fourteen she slipped on the way back from school and badly sprained both ankles. Unfortunately this injury was not correctly treated, and she was unable to walk without a crutch for the rest of her life, despite various attempts (including a vigorous course of bleeding) to cure her. She seems, however, to have maintained a kindly and optimistic outlook throughout her life. Following Isaac in his quest for settled employment, the family moved first to Brighton, then Lancing (where Anna developed her love of horses), then Wick in Gloucestershire, finally settling in 1867 in Old Catton, now a suburb of Norwich. It was here that Anna, now bedridden, started to write what was to be her only book *Black Beauty*. It was finally sold to Jarrolds for £40, and published at the end of 1877, only a few months before Anna died. She was buried at the Quaker burial ground at Lamas, near Norwich. Isaac was to die only a few months later.

Anna's mother Mary was a deeply religious woman who published several books of poems and stories (often assisted by Anna) which contained strong moral messages. When Anna came to write *Black Beauty*, it was to have a moral message of its own: that horses, and animals in general, should be more humanely treated. Although now regarded as a children's book, it was originally aimed at horse owners. It was phenomenally successful, and is now considered to have had a genuine impact on standards of animal welfare at the time. It is sad that Anna did not live long enough to realise the full extent of her achievement.

> *Black Beauty* (August 1946, PL50)

ROBERT LOUIS STEVENSON

> *Treasure Island* (1943, PL7)

BRENDA STOBBS
Brenda Stobbs (Dunn) was the first wife of **William Stobbs**. They married in 1938, had two sons, but later divorced.

> *Lilybelle* (n.d. [March 1946], PL31, with **William Stobbs**)

WILLIAM STOBBS (*?ps* NICHOLAS CAVANAGH)
William Stobbs, artist, writer and car enthusiast, was a Northerner, born in 1914 to William and Margaret Stobbs (Urquhart) in South Shields. His fame rests largely on his distinctive style of line illustration which embellished and enlivened over a hundred children's books, around a third of which are picture-books written by himself. Many of the others, for older children, were in collaboration with **N. R. Syme**. A lot of his books and illustrations have nautical themes, drawing inspiration from his own childhood on the North Sea coast. Stobbs attended Durham School of Art in 1933, and emerged with degrees in Art History and Fine Art just before the start of the war. In 1938, he married Brenda Dunn, with whom he was to collaborate on *Lilybelle*. Stobbs had a talent for engineering as well as art and helped to develop the Merlin engine as a draughtsman for Rolls-Royce in 1939, and after the war he worked briefly for the car manufacturer Alvis.

Like **Robin Jacques**, Stobbs' long and distinguished career as a book illustrator was launched by Peter Lunn just after the war (he also did illustration work for John Westhouse). Two of the books he illustrated for Peter Lunn (*Night Cargoes* and *Sister to the Mermaid*) were written by "Nicholas Cavanagh", which I believe was probably a pen-name for Stobbs himself. A Stobbs obituary (unattributed) in *The Times* for May 6th 2000 implies that Stobbs was indeed the author as well as the illustrator of these books, although the article contains enough careless errors of fact to make one hesitant in accepting this unreservedly. However, it does seem quite likely that these nautical stories were written by Stobbs, and the dedications in the books tend to support this. *Night Cargoes* is dedicated 'To Michael', and Stobbs did have a son Michael with whom he collaborated on *The Best Cars* (Pelham, 1981) and who may well have been a young boy at about this time. *Sister to the Mermaid* is dedicated 'To Our Parents', which is a rather odd dedication for a single-authorship book, unless this was a private joke by Stobbs/Cavanagh.

In the decades following the war, Stobbs' reputation as a sought-after illustrator led to many commissions and two Kate Greenaway awards. He combined this work with teaching graphic design at the London School of Printing, and later as the Principal of the Maidstone School of Art. In 1971 he married Joanna Stubbs (*sic*) with whom he had two sons and four daughters. He also collaborated with her on two children's picture-books. After his retirement from teaching, Stobbs exploited some very different areas of expertise, publishing a number of books on automobiles, as well as one on French cheeses (*A Guide to the Cheeses of France*, Apple Press, 1984), which he stated was an outcome of 'thirty years or more of travelling around France'. He died in Hawkhurst, Kent, in 2000.

(as author)
Lilybelle (n.d. [March 1946], PL31, with **Brenda Stobbs**)

(as illustrator)
Night Cargoes (September 1946, PL42)
Sister to the Mermaid (November 1946, PL58)
Canadian Wildwood (December 1946, PL73)
Black Sunset (February 1947, PL75)
The Thunderbolt Men (February 1947, PL102)
The Adventure at Marston Manor (March 1947, PL72)
Song of Arizona (June 1947, PL79)
The Grand Escapade (June 1947, PL89)
That Must be Julian (July 1947, PL104)
The Priest of the Legion (December 1947, PL108)
The Fantastic History of the Celebrated Pierrot (unpublished)
Granton Guineas (unpublished)
In Africa's Service (unpublished)
A Journey into Time (unpublished)
Julian Strikes Lucky (unpublished)
Mystery Mine (unpublished)
Pizarro of Peru (unpublished)
Pizarro's Empire (unpublished)

MICHAEL STONE (*rn* MAURICE WILLIAM CRANSTON)   Maurice Cranston, journalist, author and a political philosopher of international standing, was of Scottish ancestry, but born in Tottenham in 1920 and brought up by two of his aunts in Tunbridge Wells. He began training as a journalist until the war claimed his time in civil defence tasks (he was a conscientious objector). He became increasingly drawn to philosophy after the war, and began to publish books and articles on political aspects of philosophy, such as the ethics of war and human rights. His academic career gathered pace, and he graduated at Oxford in 1948, eventually becoming professor of political science at the London School of Economics in 1969. He published major biographies of John Locke in 1957 and Jean-Jacques Rousseau in 1983. For most of his academic life, he supplemented his salary through journalism and broadcasting, with frequent contributions on the BBC's World Service. In 1958, he rather impressively married Baroness Maximiliana von und zu Fraunberg, and they had two sons. Cranston died in 1993, shortly after making a radio broadcast.

Although the vast majority of Cranston's considerable body of publications was academic, he had his lighter publishing moments. Just after the war, he wrote two humorous detective novels: *Tomorrow We'll be Sober* and *Philosopher's Hemlock*, both published by Westhouse in 1946. *The Master of Magic* is as far as I am aware his only children's book.

The Master of Magic (May 1947, PL97)

THORA STOWELL (*rn* ALICE MARY DICKEN)   Thora Stowell was the pseudonym of Alice Mary Dicken, who was born Alice Mary Ogden in Calcutta in 1885. She was the eldest daughter of William

Ogden, a civil service administrator involved with the Indian railways, and Emily Mary Ogden (Stowell). Alice had four sisters and a brother, all of whom were born, and spent their childhood, in Simla. Some of Alice's forebears came from the Isle of Man and settled in India before the 1850s, and the Manx journal *Mannin* contained occasional reports of her activities during the First World War. At some time before or during the war, Alice went to Egypt; there is a record of a 'Thora Stowell' involved in Red Cross work at Aboukir in 1914. In 1917, in Cairo, she married a Cambridge graduate teacher of mathematics Charles Vernon Dicken. Charles then began working for the Egyptian Civil Service, and while living in Cairo they had two children. Also at this time Alice published *The Anglo-Egyptian Cookery Book* (Whitehead Morris, 1923) which is a rare volume containing a compilation of Egyptian and Indian recipes 'adapted' for the European palate. She is also recorded as a correspondent of the *Egyptian Gazette*, writing articles about native life in Egypt. During the 1920s and 1930s she wrote a number of other books of fiction and poetry, and wild-life books for children. In 1944, she published *I Made My Own Dolls* (a book in very similar vein to *Every Child's Toy Book*). This was published by Thacker & Co. in Bombay, as a charitable venture in support of the Red Cross Fun Fairs during the war (it included patterns for a golliwog, and for a fat lady modelled on one of her own dolls called 'Hetty the Hun'). Alice died in Brighton in 1974, having survived Charles by 20 years.

Every Child's Toy Book (December 1946, PL81)

JOHN SYLVESTER (*rn* HECTOR HAWTON)

Journalist, author and Humanist scholar, Hector Hawton was born in Plymouth in 1901, and was educated there. On leaving school he began a career in journalism, working for local newspapers, and between the wars also wrote romantic fiction for several national dailies. He went on to write juvenile fiction under the pseudonym John Sylvester. This took the form of short story and serial contributions to many of the best-known boys' magazines (including one for the *Sexton Blake Library*), as well as books such as those published by Peter Lunn, and three science-fiction tales published by Ward Lock: *Master of the World* (1949), *The Black Dragon* (1950) and *The Flying Saucer* (1952). Hawton also wrote fifteen detective novels under his real name, most of which were published by Ward Lock. In other circles, Hawton was better known as a prominent figure in the Humanist movement, and he was a Director of the Rationalist Press Association. He died in North London in 1975.

The Lost Mountain (July 1946, PL43)
The Phantom (November 1946, PL61)
A Journey into Time (unpublished)

N[EVILLE] R[ONALD] SYME (*ps* PETER LETHBRIDGE)

Ronald Syme was born Neville Rowland (sic) Syme in Ormskirk, Lancashire in 1910, to David and Ida Florence Syme. Although born in England, he and his three siblings spent much of their childhood in County Galway, and Syme later stated himself to be 'of pure Irish origin'. His parents appear to have been well-to-do, and lived in an eighteenth century home with a 'splendid library'. In 1926, Syme moved to North Island, New Zealand where he briefly attended Wanganui Collegiate School until he left in 1927, aged 16, to spend some years on a cargo boat operating across the Pacific. He had a facility for language, and developed a knowledge of French, Italian, Arabic, Maori and Polynesian. This was probably a factor in him becoming enlisted in the British Army Intelligence Corps during the war. After the war he returned to England to devote himself to writing, and his books for Peter Lunn mark the beginning of this career. Gottlieb employed him between 1946 and 1948 as an assistant editor for Lunn and Westhouse. He finally returned to the South Seas in the mid-1950s to live in Rarotonga in the Cook Islands, where in 1960 he married a lady who was both a Polynesian princess and women's tennis champion of Rarotonga. During this period he set up a pineapple canning business on Mangaia (another of the Cook Islands) and wrote two semi-autobiographical books: *The Isles of the Frigate Bird* (Michael Joseph, 1972) and *The Lagoon is Lonely Now* (Millwood Press, Wellington, 1979). He died in 1989.

Syme was a hugely prolific author and wrote over 80 books, mainly for children, many of them set in the South Seas with nautical or historical themes. A large number of these books were in collaboration with **William Stobbs**, who illustrated his second book, *That Must Be Julian*, for Peter Lunn. Syme stated that once he had published a book, his only remaining interest was in the royalties. Syme should not be confused with the contemporary English classical scholar Ronald Syme. (See also **Peter Lethbridge**).

> *Full Fathom Five* (November 1946, PL55)
> *That Must Be Julian* (July 1947, PL104)
> *Julian Strikes Lucky* (unpublished)

PAUL TABORI (*ps* PAUL TABOR, CHRISTOPHER STEVENS)

Paul Tabori, journalist, author and psychic investigator, was born Pál Tábori into a Jewish family in Budapest in 1908. He was the eldest son of Kornél (Cornelius) and Elsa Tábori, and brother of György (George). Cornelius was a prominent crime-reporter and journalist with an interest in the paranormal, which later led Paul to edit and translate into English his father's fifty-year record of encounters with the paranormal as *My Occult Diary* (Rider and Co, 1951). Paul was brought up and educated in Hungary, gained a PhD in 1930, and held various journalistic positions as well as publishing a number of books. During World War II, he, with his mother and brother, fled to Britain to escape Nazi persecution. Sadly, his father did not escape and later died in Auschwitz. A highly regarded 1995 film *My Mother's Courage*, directed by Michael Verhoeven, tells this story through the eyes of Elsa (played by Pauline Collins), and is based on George's memoir of his mother. Both Paul and George worked for the BBC during the war broadcasting to occupied Europe. Both went on to distinguished careers as authors and writers of screenplays, and during the 1960s Paul held various honorary positions at universities in America. Over his life he wrote on a variety of topics, most notably politics, the rise of Nazism (including the allegorical children's picture book *The Lion and the Vulture*), film (including a biography of Alexander Korda for whom he worked in the 1940s), occult phenomena, and sexuality and eroticism. Towards the end of his life, he published two volumes on the rather surprising topic of erotic Victorian and Edwardian fairy tales. He died in London in 1974.

> *The Lion and the Vulture* (June 1944, PL15)
> *International Patrol* (March 1947, PL62)

RUTHVEN [CAMPBELL] TODD (*ps* R. T. CAMPBELL)

Ruthven (pronounced 'Riven') Todd was a poet, novelist and artist, born in Edinburgh in 1914, and educated at Fettes College. His father was an architect, while his mother's time was largely absorbed with bringing up ten children, of whom Ruthven was the eldest. Somehow, she also found time to cultivate an elaborate rock garden, and keep bees. Todd states that his early ambition was to be 'like Dr Dolittle' but this later developed into a desire to become an artist, and he studied for a time at the Edinburgh School of Art. It proved difficult to find work, and he moved to the Isle of Mull, working as a shepherd and farm labourer until finally leaving Scotland to seek work in London. He began to publish books of poetry and fiction, describing the latter as 'pot-boiling'. He was prolific, and over his life wrote or illustrated over 50 books. Although his verses for *First Animal Book* were his only work for Peter Lunn, John Westhouse published eight detective novels under the name R. T. Campbell, featuring his series detective Professor John Stubbs. In the view of Barzun and Taylor[11], Todd was 'a good poet, but not cut out for detective fiction'. Soon after the war, during which he was a conscientious objector, Todd moved to take up a post at the University of Iowa, and he later ran a small publishing house called the Weekend Press. In 1958, he moved to Majorca where he died in 1978.

Among his books for children, he is perhaps best known in America for his 1950s series about 'Space Cat', who travelled cheerfully around the Solar System in a space suit. Todd was also known as a commentator on the poetry of William Blake. He had been a close friend of Dylan Thomas, and was asked by Thomas's estate to write a biography of him, although this project never came to fruition. An interesting bibliographical note is that Syracuse University Archives has an unfinished holograph of a novel by Todd entitled *When the Bad Bleed*, which is described as 'Detective Novel Number 2' by 'Richard Brothers' (presumably a pseudonym of Todd himself). However, I can find no trace of any book previously published under that name. His son, Christopher Todd, compiled *Ruthven Todd (1914-1978): a preliminary finding-list* (unpublished, 1980) of which the British Library has a copy. This contains a list of Todd's prodigious output of reviews, short-story contributions to magazines, and the like, and refers also to four thriller titles which were to have been published by John Westhouse, but seem never to have appeared.

First Animal Book (August 1946, PL51)

GERALD VERNER (*?aka* DONALD WILLIAM STEWARD, *ps* DONALD STUART, DERWENT STEELE, NIGEL VANE)

Gerald Verner's origins are obscured by fog, and it may be that this fog was of Verner's own making. Jack Adrian suggests[12] that he may have been born Donald William Steward in Lambeth around 1896, that he subsequently spent some time in prison and later preferred to cover his tracks. (Adrian does not cite his evidence for these suggestions.) According to a *Daily Telegraph* obituary, he started writing thrillers in the 1920s when living as a down-and-out on the Thames Embankment. During his life he wrote over 130 crime and thriller novels, many of which were adapted for the radio, stage and cinema, although many were re-workings of his own earlier material (as well as, according to Adrian, the material of other authors). Nearly all his books were published by Wright and Brown, although one crime novel *Thirsty Evil*, was published by John Westhouse in 1945. A few of his novels were published under the name Donald Stuart. He also wrote for magazines such as the *Sexton Blake Library* and *Detective Weekly*. Many standard sources state that 'Gerald Verner' was a pseudonym of Donald Stuart, but in fact it is clear that, whatever his name at birth may have been, he became for all practical (and legal) purposes Gerald Verner. This is the view taken by Bill Bradford. In his checklist of Verner's publications[13] he states that he is in possession of correspondence from Verner and his wife, signed 'Gerald and Carol'. Bradford's view is supported by the fact that Verner made a legal claim against John Westhouse under the name 'Gerald Verner', and the fact that I have seen an on-line reference to his son Christopher Verner, who worked in the film industry. In any case, if as determined and experienced a researcher as Jack Adrian cannot further clarify his origins, it seems unlikely that further progress will now be made. Verner died in 1980 in Broadstairs, Kent. Adrian summed him up as 'an immensely likeable old scoundrel'.

[11] Barzun, Jacques and Taylor, Wendell Hertig. *A Catalogue of Crime*. New York: Harper & Row, 1971, p. 98.

[12] Henderson, L. (ed). *Twentieth Century Crime and Mystery Writers*. 3rd edition. London: St James Press, 1991, p. 1046.

[13] Bradford, Bill, *Gerald Verner (Donald Stuart) 1987-1980: A Bibliography*. Swanage: Norman Wright, 2000.

The Forgotten Valley (unpublished)

E[DWARD] H[AROLD] VISIAK (*aka* EDWARD HAROLD PHYSICK)   E. H. Visiak was an author and poet, born Edward Harold Physick in London in 1878. He was the son of the sculptor E. J. Physick. He worked in London and Manchester for the Indo-European Telegraph Company, and during World War I he was a conscientious objector. Visiak published his first book of poetry *Buccaneer Ballads* (Elkin Matthews, 1910), and it seems to have been at about this time he adopted the name Visiak, and used it in both public and private life thereafter. *The Haunted Island* was Visiak's first novel, also published in 1910 by Elkin Matthews. It was followed by another sea-faring novel called *Medusa* (Gollancz, 1929), and this is probably his best-known novel. There are mystical overtones to much of Visiak's fictional work, and indeed to his own experiences of life, as revealed in his autobiography of youth *Life's Morning Hour* (John Baker, 1968). He also wrote commentaries on Milton, Coleridge and Conrad and contributed to a biography of the author David Lindsay. He died in a nursing home overlooking the sea, in 1972.

The Haunted Island (May 1946, PL47)

AUDREY WALTON (*aka* E. M. WALTON, EDITH MARGARET HÜNE)   Audrey Walton was a translator who collaborated with **Marjorie Hill** on *Don Quixote de la Mancha*, by translating *Don Quichotte de la Manche* from French into English. She also translated from the Russian Leonid Andreyev's 'Phantoms', which appeared in *Judas Iscariot*, published by Westhouse in 1947.

(as translator)
Don Quixote de la Mancha (March 1947, PL70, with **Marjorie Hill**)

TUDUR WATKINS   Watkins was a Welsh writer who wrote radio plays for the BBC *The Spanish Galleon* was adapted from an earlier serial play for Children's Hour, and Watkins' radio drama 'Tanglemane' (a horse story) was adapted and published in Welsh as *Y Merlyn Du*. These appear to be the only examples of his radio work which appeared as books. The adaptation of radio plays to book form is not always successful, but *The Spanish Galleon* is elegantly written, and is supplemented by **Jack Matthews'** accomplished and atmospheric illustrations. It was deservedly popular, and appeared in Dutch and French editions, and it was also published in the U.S. by Coward-McCann in 1947.

The Spanish Galleon (November 1945, PL29)

RALPH WIGHTMAN   Born in 1901 to one of a long line of Dorset farmers, Ralph Wightman became an author and radio broadcaster with a memorably strong Dorset accent. He was brought up on Bellamy's Farm in Piddletrenthide[14], Dorset, as the youngest of a family comprising his father Thomas (who doubled as farmer and local butcher), his mother Sarah (Drake) and five much older siblings. Ralph was educated at Beaminster Grammar School and then Durham University. Despite his life of writing and broadcasting on farming and country matters, Wightman never actually farmed himself. He became a well-known voice on radio as compère of *Country Magazine*, as a panellist on *Any Questions?*, and during a long series of weekly broadcasts to America during the war. His first book was *Moss Green Days*, published by Westhouse in 1947 and illustrated by **Clifford Webb**, and he also contributed an article 'Green Pastures' to Westhouse's magazine *Holiday Parade*. It may have been Peter Lunn who

[14] For more information about this village, the interested reader is referred to: Adams, Douglas and Lloyd, John. *The Meaning of Liff*. London: Pan Books, 1983, p. 108.

commissioned Webb to illustrate *Days on the Farm*, although in the event it was not to appear until 1952, published by Hutchinson. Wightman published a series of books during the 1950s and 60s on various aspects of the Dorset countryside. He lived in Dorchester for much of his life, and died in 1971.

   Days on the Farm (unpublished)

DAPHNE WINSTONE   *Flame* is quite a rare phenomenon – a book for children written by a child, or as a contemporary review expresses it: 'written by a child of twelve for other horsy children'. The author details at the beginning of it tell us that the book was published exactly as written except for the alteration of 'a few rather unorthodox spellings'. Daphne was born in 1930 as the youngest of four children, and developed an early love of the country and particularly horses – riding an Icelandic pony called Bessie. She also appears to have had a taste for skiing, skating, films and detective stories. When she was twelve, illness kept her indoors for eighteen months, during which time she wrote *Flame*. It was completed in two and a half months, and appears to have been the only book she published.

   Flame (September 1945, PL25)

DAVID WOOD
   Cook the Explorer (September 1947, PL112)

ILLUSTRATOR BIOGRAPHIES

ACANTHUS (*rn* [HAROLD] FRANK HOAR)   Frank Hoar was an architect, cartoonist and academic, born in Burma in 1909 to Harold and Frances Hoar, where Harold held an Army commission. The family returned to settle in Devon, and Frank attended Plymouth College. At 15, he gained a scholarship to study architecture at the University of London where it is recorded that Henry Tonks, then Slade Professor of Fine Art, helped to develop Hoar's budding skills as a cartoonist by encouraging him to draw caricatures of the entire teaching staff. Hoar's greatest single achievement was probably when, in 1935, he and two student colleagues won a competition to design the first terminal building at Gatwick Airport, by submitting a highly innovative circular design for the terminal, linked by subway to the railway station. This was to launch Hoar's successful architectural practice, which he developed in parallel with an academic career at University College, London. In 1940, he married an Irish concert pianist, Rosamund Leonard. During the war, Hoar was active in the Royal Engineers designing bridges in North Africa. His other war-time activity was as a cartoonist for the *Sunday Express* (as 'Hope') and *Punch* (as 'Acanthus'), often with a satirical or propagandist intent. Also evident in many of his later cartoons was a lampooning of some post-war architectural trends of which he disapproved. Hoar died in 1976.

> *Mukrah the Dwarf* (December 1944, PL22)
>
> *Arbuthnot the Goldfish* (unpublished)

BRUCE ANGRAVE: see Author biographies.

FRANK BABER   Details of Baber's life are scant and uncertain. He is reported to have trained at Bolton College of Art, and may therefore be the Frank Baber who was born in 1910 in Bolton. The Peter Lunn books appear to be the first books he illustrated, although he went on to illustrate an edition of *Pinocchio*, and several children's books published by Peter Lowe at intervals until 1982.

> *Danger in Provence* (December 1946, PL52)
>
> *The Ivory Trail* (February 1947, PL94)
>
> *The Champion* (October 1947, PL98)

JOHN BAINBRIDGE   John Bainbridge was an Australian artist and designer who emigrated to Britain. He was born in Mosman, a suburb of Sydney, in 1918 (some sources say 1920), but moved to Melbourne where he studied art. For a period he was Art Director of the National Theatre in Melbourne. He worked as a war artist in the Far East, before moving to London in 1945 to pursue a career as a theatre and costume designer. He also designed posters for cruise and airline companies, Ealing Studios, and London Transport. Bainbridge died in London in 1978, survived by his wife Nan (Knowles).

> *The Dark Blanket* (November 1946, PL64)

ROBERT A[RTHUR] BARTLETT (*aka* ROBIN BARTLETT)   Robert Bartlett was a painter, illustrator and poster designer, born in Brentford in 1900, the son of an architect Arthur Edward Bartlett and Ella Carlin. He was educated at Shrewsbury School. During World War I, he joined the Royal Navy and saw some service as a French interpreter from 1918, afterwards gaining a History degree from Oxford University. He then trained from 1922 at the Slade School of Fine Art, where he met

Eileen Agar (later to become a famous surrealist artist) and they married in 1925 and shared a studio in Chelsea. Only a year later, Eileen began a relationship with expatriate Hungarian writer Joseph Bard, and she and Bartlett separated (they were to divorce in 1929, and Bartlett was to remarry twice). Bartlett then travelled widely abroad, particularly in America where he began to specialise in graphic art for posters, also painting an acclaimed portrait of D. H. Lawrence's widow Frieda. He joined the Intelligence Division of the Royal Navy in 1939 and spent periods with Churchill in his bunker. After the war he did some freelance book illustration, and much poster design for commercial companies until he retired in 1967 to organise Britain's first 'anti-litter' week. He died in 1976. For most of his professional life, Bartlett was known as 'Robin' Bartlett.

> *Ferry to Adventure* (September 1944, PL19)
> *The Bearded Stranger* (March 1947, PL59)

D[ORA] M. BATTY   Dora Batty was a designer and illustrator. She was best known as a designer who worked for textile and pottery manufacturers, often in Art Deco style. She designed a series of children's 'nursery tiles' and plates for the Poole Pottery, and designs for the textile manufacturer Helios, as well as a series of posters for London Transport and MacFisheries. She appears to have done little book illustration. Apart from one book for Peter Lunn, the only other books on which she is credited seem to be a series of three poetry books by William H. Davies in the 1920s. She was head of the textile department at the Central School of Art from 1950 to 1958, and died in 1966.

> *The Giant without a Heart* (May 1944, PL9)

THOMAS BEWICK   A pioneer in the art of wood-engraving, Thomas Bewick was born in 1753, the eldest son of John and Jane Bewick (Wilson). The family lived in Mickley, Northumberland, where John was the tenant of a small colliery. Although Thomas seems to have been an indifferent scholar, he displayed a talent for drawing, and his father apprenticed him when he was 14 to a friend Ralph Beilby, who ran a jewellery and engraving business in Newcastle-upon-Tyne. For a period during his apprenticeship, Bewick learned the art of engraving on metal, but went on to develop a new technique of engraving on the end-grain of hard woods such as boxwood, using specially adapted versions of metal-engraving tools. This method has since become the basis of modern wood-engraving. Bewick had been, since childhood, an enthusiastic admirer of the countryside and animal life, and it seems that around 1781 (by which time he had become a partner in Beilby's business) he conceived the idea of an illustrated book on quadrupeds, prompted in part by his dissatisfaction with existing natural history publications for children. He began preparing the woodblocks on the same day his father died in 1785. (Bewick's relationship with his father seems to have survived this sad event, since on one occasion in 1815 he is reputed to have been found in a churchyard spending several hours addressing his father's disinterred skull.) The project became a joint venture with Beilby, and in 1790 they published the first of several editions of *A General History of Quadrupeds*, from which the illustrations for *First Animal Book* are derived. The work was highly acclaimed, and it went through two more editions in the next two years. Although many of the engravings Bewick prepared were based on his own examination of wildlife, he was a provincial man, and his representations of some of the more exotic animals must have been adapted from other publications. The text which accompanied the engravings was prepared by Beilby, who was hardly an expert in the field, and his efforts were subject to a considerable amount of editing by Bewick. The book for which Bewick was to become even more better known was *A History of British Birds*, published in two volumes in 1797 and 1804, and it is presumably illustrations from these works which Peter Lunn had planned to publish in *First Bird Book*.

Bewick married Isabella Elliot in 1786, and they were to have four children. The second, Robert, joined his father's business, first as an apprentice, and in 1812 as a partner. (The partnership with Beilby had broken up in 1797 after a disagreement over the authorship of the first volume of the bird book.) In 1818, Bewick and Son published *The Fables of Aesop and Others*, an edition of which was also planned by Peter Lunn. By 1812, Bewick had become quite seriously ill, and moved to Gateshead, where he was eventually to die in 1828, two years after Isabella's death. Bewick is now regarded as one of the pioneers of book illustration, and was lauded by such figures as Wordsworth, Audubon and Ruskin. **Robin Jacques** considered him to be 'central to the best in the English graphic tradition'[15]. His name lives on in 'Bewick's Swan' and 'Bewick's Wren'.

> *First Animal Book* (August 1946, PL51)
> *Fables of Aesop and Others* (unpublished)
> *First Bird Book* (unpublished)

PHYLLIS [MARY] BRAY   Illustrator, mural painter and jewellery collector, Phyllis Bray was born in 1911 in Norwood, South London. She was the daughter of William de Bray, who was once attaché to Maria Fyodorovna, mother of Tsar Nicholas II. Phyllis was attracted to art as a child and particularly to colour – a fascination which lasted throughout her life, and is very well in evidence in her sumptuous illustrations for *The Story of Titania and Oberon*. She was the unusually young winner of a scholarship to the Slade School of Fine Art, where she studied under Henry Tonks. Here she met and married the Yorkshire artist John Cooper who founded the East London Group of painters of which Phyllis herself became a member. In 1934 they had a daughter Phillipa who was also to become an established artist. The marriage ended in divorce in 1936, and Phyllis later married Eric Phillips. Although Bray always maintained a strong connection with London's East End, and in particular painted a series of murals for the People's Palace in Mile End, she also worked more widely in Britain as a muralist, often in collaboration with the German-Jewish émigré artist Hans Feibusch. She illustrated only a small number of books. Her collection of Medieval and Renaissance jewellery was sold for over half a million pounds in 1989, two years before her death.

> *The Story of Titania and Oberon* (September 1945, PL33)

H[ENRY] M[ATTHEW] BROCK   Henry ('Harry') Brock was one of the six children of Edmund and Mary Brock, and was born in Cambridge in 1875. His three older brothers were also artists, although only the oldest, Charles (C. E. Brock) became as well-known as Harry. Their father was a reader and translator for Cambridge University Press. The artistic talent in the family is presumed to have come mainly through the mother's side, Mary being one of the Pegrams, a family of sculptors and artists based in London. Harry was educated at the Cambridge School of Art, and had his first illustrations published when he was 18. The Brocks as a family seem to have been close-knit and rather retiring, working together in an old-fashioned studio in Cambridge. Both Charles and Harry were enormously successful, and Harry became sought-after as an illustrator of boys' public school stories, particularly for scenes of sports matches, with which many books of that genre were liberally peppered. Harry was a keen tennis player himself, and maintained an interest throughout his life in University rugby and cricket fixtures. His work was asked for throughout the earlier part of the twentieth century by school story writers such as Desmond Coke and Hylton Cleaver, and many of his illustrations first appeared serialized in magazines like *The Captain* and *Chums*. The Brock family were great admirers of

[15] Jacques, Robin. *Illustrators at Work*. Corvallis: Studio Books, 1963, p. 9.

Gilbert and Sullivan, and Harry designed a series of cigarette cards of characters from the operas for Players, sets of which are now scarce. He married his cousin Doris Joan Pegram in 1912 and they had three children. Throughout his productive years from 1891 to 1950 (when his eyesight began to fail) Harry was known as an enormously hard worker, often drawing from morning until late evening, and taking completed work by bicycle to catch the 8.30 morning train to London. He died in Cambridge in 1960. An obituary in *The Times* observed rather blandly that he was 'a pleasant and highly successful illustrator and draughtsman'.

Hans Andersen's Fairy Tales (third edition, 1947, PL105)
The Children's Omnibus (n.d.[?1948], PL115)
Alice's Adventures in Wonderland (n.d.[?1948], PL116)
The Rose and the Ring (n.d.[?1948], PL117)
The New Children's Omnibus (unpublished)
The Story of Harchem [?] (unpublished)

[DORA] MARGARET BRYAN Margaret Bryan was an artist (primarily a wood-engraver) who was born (1903), worked and died (1985), in Nottingham.

A Children's Almanac (February 1947, PL74)
Summer Gypsies (April 1947, PL87)
Roundabout House (unpublished)

ANN [DEVEREAUX] BUCKMASTER Ann Buckmaster was born in Lewisham in 1924, daughter of Arthur D. Buckmaster and Theodora (Hambidge), and educated at Bromley High School. She studied art at Beckenham School of Art and Bromley College of Art. At the time of her commissions for Peter Lunn, she was married to the artist Anthony Gilbert, and was living in Bromley. She seems to have done little other book illustration, although she did do some work for magazines, including the *Strand, Vanity Fair* and *Radio Times*. At the time of writing, she lives in Oxfordshire.

Stories from Ancient Greece (March 1947, PL92)
Homer's Odyssey (June 1947, PL110)
The Aeneid and Illiad (unpublished)

TOM [THOMAS C.] ECKERSLEY Tom Eckersley was one of the foremost graphic designers of his generation. He was born in 1914 in Lowton, Lancashire, the son of John Eckersley, a Methodist lay-preacher. His health in childhood was frail, and he was brought up in a house where his father's deep religious faith held sway, particularly on a Sunday when reading and worship were the only permissible activities. Much of Tom's leisure time was spent reading and drawing. After schooling at Lords College in Bolton, his mother encouraged him to enrol at Salford School of Art. Here he and fellow-student Eric Lombers developed a passion for avant-garde poster design, and they moved to London in 1934 to set up a freelance partnership Eckersley Lombers, designing posters. During the period leading up to the war, they attracted many influential clients including London Transport and the BBC The partnership did not survive the war, however, during which Eckersley worked as a cartographer in the RAF, as well as producing many propaganda posters. Examples of his work have now found their way to a number of major museums and galleries. He also designed murals, including one for the Heathrow Underground station. Both before and after the war, he combined freelance work with teaching, and this culminated in his appointment in 1958 as head of graphic design at the London College of Printing, where he remained until 1976. Here he met Mary Kessell, a painter and official war artist, who became his second wife in 1966, until her death in 1977. Eckersley received many awards and honorifics during his career, including an OBE in 1948. He died in London in 1997.

Eckersley was primarily a graphic designer; he did very little book illustration. His illustrations for his first wife Daisy's story *Cat O' Nine Lives* do look rather like miniature posters, but they are nevertheless quite haunting, and seem to me to be among the most successful of those commissioned by Peter Lunn. The book is dedicated to two of Daisy and Tom's three sons, all of whom were later to become graphic designers.

> *Cat O' Nine Lives* (July 1946, PL48)

LIONEL EDWARDS: See Author biographies.

RICHARD FLOETHE Richard Floethe was an American graphic artist, watercolour painter and book illustrator born in Essen, Germany, in 1901. He received art and design training in Munich and at the Weimar Bauhaus, before travelling widely in Europe and finally settling in New York in 1928. There he became a very successful graphic designer who employed a wide range of techniques, particularly woodcut and silk-screen printing. Between 1936 and 1939 he was head of the New York City poster division of the Federal Art Project – part of Roosevelt's Work Projects Administration, set up in 1935 to counter the effects of the Depression by finding ways of getting unemployed Americans back to work. The Federal Art Project, during its existence, employed 5,000 artists and produced around half a million posters, murals, sculptures and paintings. In 1937, Floethe married Louise Lee, a children's author, and he was to illustrate many of her books. In all, he illustrated over 100 books, mainly for children, including *Pinocchio*, *Baron Munchausen* and some American editions of Noel Streatfeild's books. Towards the end of his life, he created many landscape paintings and silk-screen prints of the west coast of Florida where he was then living. He died in 1988.

> *The Avion my Uncle Flew* (December 1946, PL65)

WILL FORREST

> *The Island Sanctuary* (December 1945, PL27)
> *Eeny Meeny Miney Mo* (April 1946, PL37)

ENRIQUE GARRÁN A Spanish 'avant-garde' artist. Advertising for *The Blue Egg* stated that it was the first children's book he had illustrated.

> *The Blue Egg* (December 1944, PL20)

WALTER GOETZ Walter Goetz, artist and cartoonist, was born in Cologne in 1911, the son of Alfred Götz, a German-Jewish silk merchant, and a French mother. He spent his early childhood in Berlin, before being sent by his parents at age 12 to Bedales school in England, where he met Elton Mayo, later to become his second wife (he first married artist Jill Greenwood). Although offered a place at Cambridge University, lack of funds forced him to return to Berlin in 1929 to study painting. The rise of National Socialism prompted a return to England in 1931, where he was granted British nationality three years later. By this time he was drawing cartoons for the *Daily Express* (under the name

'Walter') and magazines such as *Lilliput* and *Punch*. The fact that Goetz was fluent in English, German and French led to his working during the war for the Political Warfare Executive at Woburn Abbey, where he was responsible initially for preparing propaganda leaflet drops over Germany, and later editing the magazine *Cadran* for distribution in France after its liberation. Goetz's voice was the first to be heard at the launch of the BBC's German Service. After the war, Goetz supplemented cartoon work with opera costume design and book illustration, before moving to Paris as a landscape painter and art dealer. He finally returned to England in 1980, and died in London in 1995.

> *International Patrol* (March 1947, PL62)

PHILIP [HENRY C.] GOUGH
Artist and stage designer Philip Gough was born in 1908 in Warrington, and spent his childhood in Cheshire. On leaving school, he studied at art schools in Liverpool, Chelsea and Penzance. His training at Liverpool was as a stage designer, and he subsequently did the designs for productions of *Midsummer Night's Dream* at the Liverpool Repertory Theatre in 1928 and for *Toad of Toad Hall* in the following year. Gough records that 'following the failure of the family fortunes' he worked in London, first in commercial art studios and then designing for London theatres. After the war he settled for the remainder of his life in Chelsea, and devoted more and more of his time to book illustration, although his output was never huge. Much of his earlier work was for children's books (mostly classics), but he increasingly favoured adult books, particularly ones set in historical times. This change of emphasis was probably prompted by his developing interest in late Georgian architecture and furniture. Gough died in 1986, in Kensington.

> *Hans Andersen's Fairy Tales* (second edition, January 1947, PL56)
> *Snowdrops* (April 1947, PL68)
> *Pinocchio* (September 1947, PL91)
> *God of Brazil* (November 1947, PL100)
> *The Silver Florin* (November 1947, PL101)
> *Winged Horses* (unpublished)

FRANCIS [HENRY] GOWER
Francis Gower was a portrait painter, teacher and illustrator born in London in 1905. He trained in art and art history in London during the 1920s and later found work with advertising agencies. During the war he worked in psychiatric hospitals and this gave him the opportunity to compile albums of sketches, some of which he later worked up into oil paintings. During the 1940s, Gower provided line drawings for a number of children's books, including some by Alison Uttley, Charles Hodge and Elizabeth Kyle. In later years he taught and lectured at art schools in the North London area. He died in Watford in 1995.

> *The Lost Mountain* (July 1946, PL43)
> *The Glastonbury Adventure* (October 1946, PL76)
> *The Kingdom of a Thousand Isles* (January 1947, PL77)
> *Black Rock Island* (May 1947, PL83)

[RALPH GORE] ANTONY GROVES-RAINES
Antony Groves-Raines was born in 1913 in Killinchy, County Down, son of the local squire Lieutenant-Colonel Ralph Gore Devereaux Groves-Raines. He was sent as a boarder to Tonbridge School, and went on to Cambridge University, originally intending to pursue a career in the diplomatic service, but turning instead to art. He was probably best-known for

his humorous illustrations for Guinness Brewery, which included a series of 24 advertising pamphlets sent to doctors between 1933 and 1966 at Christmas, in an attempt to persuade them that Guinness was indeed good for them (and their patients). A number of these were parodies featuring characters from *Alice in Wonderland*. Groves-Raines did not do a great deal of book illustration, but amongst those he did for children were editions of *Fairy Tales* by Hans Andersen, and *Tales from the Arabian Nights*, both published in the Heirloom Library series in the 1950s. He was particularly adept at creating convincing three-dimensional illusions, which he achieved by working from assemblies of real objects, held in position by plasticine. Latterly, he lived near Richmond, and died in 1993. His name often appears spelt 'Anthony' in catalogues, and sometimes on the books themselves (including *The Golden String*).

The Golden String (July 1947, PL82)

H[AROLD] W[ILLIAM] HAILSTONE Harold Hailstone was an artist and cartoonist born in Croydon in 1897, the son of William (a dentist) and Nellie Hailstone. He was brought up as one of a large family in Hadlow, Kent, and was educated at Tonbridge, before training as a pilot during World War I (he was later to illustrate a few Biggles stories in *Eagle* annuals). After the war he studied art at Goldsmith's College in London, and went abroad to work in America and Canada in the late 1920s. Returning to England, he did illustrations and cartoons for a number of magazines and newspapers, including *Punch*, *Illustrated London News* and the *Strand Magazine*. During World War II, he and his younger brother Bernard were official war artists, and Harold recorded scenes during the recapture of the Channel Islands. After the war, he worked as cartoonist for the *Daily Mirror* until his retirement. He died in 1982 in Hadlow.

The Master of Magic (May 1947, PL97)

CHARLES HARGENS [JR.] Charles Hargens was an American artist who specialised in painting scenes of the Old West. He was born in 1894 in the Black Hills of South Dakota, the son of a doctor, and as a child he earned pocket-money from neighbours by sketching local scenes. The surroundings in which he grew up were at that time still redolent of the old days of the Wild West, and although he moved away from the Black Hills quite early in life he frequently revisited them, and his days there were to provide the backdrop for his career as an artist. He attended the Pennsylvania Academy of Fine Arts, and in 1921 gained a scholarship to study in Paris. He and his wife Marjorie moved to Carversville, Pennsylvania in 1940, where they remained thereafter, Charles taking a leading role in the local Scout movement for many years. Hargens was an enormously prolific and sought-after illustrator of scenes of the Old West for books and magazines, and he also did advertising work for Stetson Hats (one of which he wore himself), Coca-Cola and beer companies. He died in Carversville in 1997, aged 103.

The Young Cowboy (June 1946, PL41)

BLAIR [ROWLANDS] HUGHES-STANTON A brilliant practitioner and teacher of wood-engraving, Blair Hughes-Stanton was the son of (Sir) Herbert and Elizabeth Hughes-Stanton, and was born in Kensington in 1902. His father was a well-known painter of oils and watercolours. Blair was educated at St Paul's Preparatory School, and then on the school ship *H.M.S. Conway* as a step towards a career in the Royal Navy, for which he was unfortunately rejected. He went on to study art, and particularly wood-engraving, latterly at the Leon Underwood School of Painting and Sculpture. Here he met fellow-student Gertrude Hermes, a wood-engraver and sculptor whom he was to marry in 1926. The couple lived in Chiswick on whatever income they could scrape together from selling their artistic output and teaching, and became acquaintances of literary figures such as Robert Graves and Naomi

Mitchison. The birth of a daughter and a son, and a need for larger studio space prompted a move to rented premises in Suffolk. In 1930, Blair was offered a job as a wood-engraver at the Gregynog private press in Powys, and the family relocated to Wales. Unfortunately, the marriage was already foundering by this time, and Gertrude and the children returned to London in 1931, while Blair took over as head of the Gregynog Press. The couple divorced two years later, but they remained lifelong friends. A few years later, Hughes-Stanton was married for a second time to the poet Ida Graves (a distant relative of Robert Graves) and together they set up the Gemini Press, Blair providing the technically brilliant wood-engravings for her poem *Epithalamion* (Gemini Press, 1934). This marriage gave rise to a further two children, but also ended in divorce, albeit less amicably (Ida was later to indulge in some rather vitriolic character assassination of her ex-husband in a 1994 interview for *The Independent*.) During the war, Hughes-Stanton was sent to Greece with the Royal Engineers, but was captured and became a prisoner-of-war. While climbing the fence of his POW cage to buy some fruit from a local villager, a sentry shot him in the face, and his jaw had to be wired. This injury affected his ability to focus on engraving work, so that he did little more book illustration after the war and turned mainly to teaching. Indeed, *African Folk Tales* was one of the last books he illustrated. In the 1970s, he was married for a third time to an Australian Annie Ross (one of his ex-students) and they lived in Manningtree, Essex, sharing a house for a time with the artist **John Lewis** and his wife. Blair died in 1981 in Manningtree. In 1999, his house was converted into the North House Gallery, and is run by his daughter Penny.

African Folk Tales (November 1946, PL67)

NANCY INNES   Nancy Innes wrote and illustrated *Ring-a-Ring of Roses: an ABC* for Faber in 1942. During the 1940s she also illustrated a handful of books for young children by other authors.

Every Child's Toy Book (December 1946, PL81)

IONICUS (*rn* JOSHUA CHARLES ARMITAGE)   Joshua ('Jos') Armitage was a cartoonist and illustrator, particularly well-known for the covers he drew for the P. G. Wodehouse paperback series published by Penguin Books. He lived throughout his life in the seaside town of Hoylake, Cheshire, and was born there in 1913, the son of a fisherman. He displayed a talent for drawing from a very young age, and went on to study at Liverpool City School of Art. He then taught at a training centre for the unemployed in Liverpool until the outbreak of war, during which he was a Royal Navy gunnery instructor. At this time he also submitted his first cartoon to *Punch* which showed two music critics in front of a concert hall. The Ionic columns on the hall gave rise to the pen-name 'Ionicus' which Armitage used during a long association with the magazine. He became a freelance artist from 1950, and developed enduring associations with a number of magazines and book publishers, most notably Chatto & Windus and Penguin Books. Armitage died in 1998. Although he had prepared illustrations for Gerald Verner's *The Forgotten Valley*, the book was never published.

The Forgotten Valley (unpublished)

ROBIN JACQUES   Robin Jacques was an illustrator of books (primarily for children) and magazines who developed a highly distinctive pointillist style of pen-and-ink drawing, and his work has come to be greatly admired. This is all the more remarkable since he never had any formal art training. His earliest children's book illustrations were those published by Peter Lunn. Jacques credits 'a young publisher of children's books for whom I began to work' (clearly a reference to Gottlieb) for launching his career in book illustration. He had a close working relationship with **John Keir Cross**, with whom he collaborated on a number of books for Lunn and Westhouse. Keir Cross had a high regard for his work, and recalls in an article he wrote about Jacques[16] that he was 'referred to as "The Master" in 'the editorial offices of a publishing house I know of'. To begin with, at least, Jacques' output of book illustrations was not huge, and this is to an extent explained by the meticulous stippling of fine detail which he carried out at full scale; more commonly, illustrations of this sort would be prepared at roughly twice size, and subsequently scaled down for publication. (Jacques himself once described his technique as 'tortuous'.) The low throughput of work meant that he had to supplement his income with other graphic work for advertisers and simpler styles of illustrations for magazines such as *The Strand*, *Punch* and *Radio Times*.

Jacques was born in Sandgate, Kent, in 1920, the son of Robin Jaques, an RAF pilot, and Mary Jaques (Thorn), a theatre actress and singer. Robin's sister Josephine (later to become Hattie Jacques, the actress) was born in 1922; both added the 'c' to their surnames later in life. When their father died on a solo flight in 1923, the family went to live with Mary's parents in Chelsea, where her father Joseph Thorn owned a prosperous jeweller's and pawnbroker's business. Mary found work (and probably amorous involvement) as a live-in housekeeper for a wealthy widower in Gunnersbury, which meant that she saw the children only about once a week and that they were effectively brought up by their grandparents. Robin was sent off to a Masonic boarding school in Hertfordshire, which he hated, and left at 16, already intent on a career as an artist. His mother was unable to finance studies at art college, so Jacques found various temporary jobs and taught himself to draw during his spare time by copying anatomical drawings and drawing exhibits in the Victoria and Albert Museum. In 1941, he did war service with the Royal Artillery and Engineers, but was invalided out in 1945, and it was at this point that he began to work for Gottlieb. When Lunn and Westhouse went into receivership in 1948, Macdonald Hastings, who had recently re-launched the *Strand* magazine, offered Jacques the post of art editor, and he remained in this role until the magazine's final demise in 1950. Around this time he separated from his wife Patricia Bamford, whom he had married in 1943. In 1960 he married a South African model Azetta ven der Merwe, and after a short period working in South Africa, the couple moved to a town on the French Riviera. In 1968, Azetta died, and Jacques returned to London. A third marriage to Alexandra Mann was dissolved within a year. In the 1970s he held various part-time posts teaching illustration at art colleges in London and Canterbury. Jacques died in 1995.

The illustrations for which Jacques is now probably best remembered accompany the collections of fairy stories by Ruth Manning-Sanders published in over twenty volumes by Methuen in the 1960s and 70s. He was also responsible for what were surely the finest ever illustrations of Rudyard Kipling's *Kim* (Limited Edition Club, New York, 1962).

> *The Angry Planet* (first edition, October 1945, PL28)
> *The Owl and the Pussycat* (May 1946, PL39)
> *The Angry Planet* (second edition, July 1946, PL38)
> *Alhambra Tales* (November 1946, PL54)
> *Selected Tales from the Arabian Nights* (November 1946, PL57)
> *Fairy Tales with a Twist* (December 1946, PL85)
> *Don Quixote de la Mancha* (March 1947, PL70)
> *Voyage to Chivalry* (April 1947, PL66)
> *Great Gold Rushes* (December 1947, PL113)
> *The World's Strange Islands* (unpublished)

[16] Cross, John Keir. 'The Drawings of Robin Jacques.' *Alphabet and Image*, 1948, 7, pp. 33-45.

ARNRID [BANNIZA] JOHNSTON   Arnrid Johnston was one of the five children of Arthur Sannox Johnston and Lily Ann Thorburn, and was born in 1895 in Uddevalla, Sweden. She was the great-granddaughter of Alexander Keith Johnston (1804-1871), the famous Edinburgh geographer and engraver, who set up the cartographic firm of W. and A.K. Johnston. Alexander's son (who had the same name) was a geographer and explorer who died aged 35 in Tanzania while leading the Royal Geographical Society's expedition to Lake Nyasa. Arnrid's father seems to have been rather less famous, although he did play cricket for Essex and Middlesex. Arnrid was almost exclusively an illustrator of children's animal books (including a number of Puffin Picture Books), specialising in lithography, although she also designed posters for London Transport for a period before the war. She illustrated an edition of *Fables from Aesop and Others* (Transatlantic, 1944) and had begun to illustrate La Fontaine's *Fables*, but could not complete them because of failing eyesight. She died in London in 1972.

> *The Strange Tale of Sally and Arnold* (August 1944, PL16)
> *Timbu the Monkey* (October 1944, PL17)

Nora Kay: see Author biographies.

BOB [F.] KUHN   Bob Kuhn was an American artist, particularly admired for his skill at depicting wildlife. He was born in 1920 in Buffalo, New York, where as a child he was a frequent visitor to the local zoo; he later recalled having a yearning to make drawings of the big cats. Much of Kuhn's early work was illustrations for outdoor magazines, before he became a more specialised illustrator of wildlife. As well as *How's Inky*, he illustrated another of **Sam Campbell**'s 'Forest Life' series: *A Tippy Canoe and Canada Too* (Bobbs-Merrill, 1946) and a number of books by Felix Salten (Sigmund Salzmann), the creator of 'Bambi'. From the 1970s, in pursuit of first-hand experience of large predators in their natural habitats, Kuhn made many expeditions to Africa and the wilder parts of North America. At this time he also changed artistic direction, and turned to easel paintings of animal life, working mainly in acrylic. Many of these works are now in museums in America. He died in 2007, in Tucson, Arizona.

> *How is Inky?* (1946, PL45)

JOHN [NOEL CLAUDE] LEWIS   Artist, designer, typographer and sailor, John Lewis was born in 1912 in Rhoose in the Vale of Glamorgan, only child of Claude Pritchard Lewis and Margaretta Maria Morris. The family moved to Abergavenny when John (then known as Noel) was an infant. After service in World War I, his father was offered the post of manager of a bank in Farnham in Surrey and the family relocated again. John attended nearby Charterhouse school, where his talent for drawing began to emerge, despite attempts by the school authorities to cure his severe short sight by destroying his spectacles and putting him on the 'Bates System of Perfect Vision without Spectacles'. (This appears to have involved vigorous eye exercises combined with a high-vitamin diet.) He pursued art training at Goldsmith's College before launching his career as a freelance illustrator in 1935. The war was soon to intervene and Lewis spent time in Canada and Italy working on military camouflage. In 1940 he married Griselda Rideout, who was later to publish some books on English ceramics, one in collaboration with John. After the war, Lewis was influenced by friends to explore typography and book design as a career, and he was given an introduction to the prestigious printing and book-binding firm of W. S. Cowell of Ipswich (who printed a number of Peter Lunn books). It seems that Lewis taught the firm as much as they taught him, and he was soon to become their art director, the first outcome being the publication of *A Handbook of Printing Types* (Cowell, 1947). This was the year, of course, in which Lewis's illustrations for *Here Lies Gold* appeared, a commission to which he was presumably attracted by his own nautical interests. In 1949, he and Griselda co-authored a children's nautical adventure story called *The Three Spaniards* (Chambers, 1949) under the pseudonym J. G. Venner. Lewis moved widely in artistic circles, and developed connections with Henry Moore, Matisse and Picasso, among others, as well as teaching at the Royal College of Art throughout the 1950s. In 1975, he and Griselda settled in the coastal town of Manningtree in Essex, where John was able to pursue his by now well developed love of boats and sailing. Lewis also introduced and illustrated his wife's book *The Weekend Sailors' Cookbook* (Studio Vista, 1967). He died in Woodbridge in 1996.

Lewis is credited with coining the term 'printed ephemera'. His ground-breaking publication *Printed Ephemera* (Cowell, 1962), based in part on the collection of Woodbridge antiquarian and fellow-sailor George Arnott, may be said to have launched this area of collecting. According to Lewis's obituary in *The Independent*, the section he wrote on sail makers' needle-packets was 'a model of its kind'.

> *Here Lies Gold* (March 1947, PL93)

JACK MATTHEWS (*rn* JACK MATTHEW)   Jack Matthew was born in Oldham, Lancashire in 1911. He studied at the Oldham School of Art, and later at Goldsmith's College in London, under Rowland Hilder. The majority of the many books he illustrated from the 1930s to the 1960s were children's adventure stories, often with nautical themes. A handful of books between 1945 and 1948 (including those published by Lunn) were under the name 'Jack Matthews', but since he used the name 'Matthew' before, during and after this period, these may have been no more than editorial mistakes. There is no doubt that there is only one illustrator concerned and indeed the synopsis on the dustjacket of *The Spanish Galleon* refers to him as Jack Matthew.

> *The Spanish Galleon* (November 1945, PL29)
> *The Haunted Island* (May 1946, PL47)

C. H. OATES (*?rn* CHRISTINE TATE OATES)   I have been unable to find any other reference to C. H. Oates as an illustrator. It is possible that the artist in question was an oil and water-colour painter Christine Tate Oates. She was born in Bradford in 1913, educated locally, and studied at the Royal College of Art, before teaching art at a number of schools and finally settling in Truro, Cornwall. To further confuse the situation, in 1948 a claim was made against Peter Lunn by a Violet Enid Ratcliff, then living in Roberstbridge, East Sussex, for the costs of the illustrations for *Pasha*. Violet Ratcliff was born in 1899 and died in 1987 in East Sussex. It may be that this claim was for illustrations which were commissioned from Ratcliff but never used.

> *Pasha* (September 1947, PL107)

JOHN R. PARSONS   John Parsons was a member of the Society of Industrial Artists, and did illustrations for a variety of magazines and humorous books including a book of proverbs chosen by himself, called *Innocence Is No Protection* (Sylvan Press, 1949). He was art director of *Vogue* magazine for many years and illustrated the edition of *Vogue's Cookery Book* revised by Evelyn Forbes (Condé Nast Publications, [1948]).

> *Jack Robinson* (December 1945, PL26)

David [Ellis M. M.] Pratt   David Pratt was an artist specialising in wildlife and nature subjects, born in 1911 in Kobe, Japan. He lived in St Austell, Cornwall and died in 1988.

> *The Wandering Otter* (March 1947, PL90)

Nora and Alfons Purtscher: see Author Biographies.

Brian [F.] Robb   Brian Robb was an illustrator, cartoonist and painter of oils and watercolours, born in 1913 in Scarborough and educated at Malvern College. On leaving school, he studied at the Chelsea School of Art and the Slade School of Fine Art. His earliest freelance work was drawing cartoons for magazines such as *Punch* and *The Strand*, and many of his later book illustrations incorporate comic or caricaturist elements. (The Munchausen stories he illustrated for Peter Lunn seem ideally suited to his style.) In the 1930s he did some poster designs for Shell, Guinness and London Transport, before joining the Middle East campaign during the war. A book of war cartoons, many of them originally appearing in the magazines *Crusader* and *Parade*, were published as *My Middle East Campaigns* (Collins, 1944). After the war he lectured at Chelsea College of Art (where Quentin Blake was one of his protégés) until 1962 and then became Head of Illustration at the Royal College of Art until his retirement in 1978. He died the following year. As well as the two books he illustrated for Peter Lunn, he also supplied illustrations for *The Golden Asse* and *Judas Iscariot* published by John Westhouse.

> *The Ginger Gang* (second edition, May 1946, PL34)
> *12 Adventures of the Celebrated Baron Munchausen* (June 1947, PL96)

Leonard [Henry] Rosoman   Leonard Rosoman, illustrator, painter and designer, was born in Hampstead, London, in 1913. After attending school in Peterborough, he went on to study at art schools, first in Durham and then London. Just before the war, he illustrated his first children's book. This minor (and now nearly forgotten) classic of children's fiction was *My Friend Mr Leakey* (Cresset Press, 1937) written by the famous geneticist J. B. S. Haldane, and later issued as a Puffin Story Book. When war broke out, Rosoman joined the Auxiliary Fire Service. During the Blitz his duties led him into dramatic situations, some of which he committed to canvas and are now in the Imperial War Museum. These activities also drew the attention of the Admiralty and in 1943 he joined the Pacific Fleet as an Official War Artist. After the war, Rosoman taught illustration and mural painting at a variety of institutions in Edinburgh and London. In 1963 he married the costume designer Jocelyn Rickards, who already had already had a number of involvements with high-profile lovers including Graham Greene and John Osbourne, but this ended in divorce six years later. Rosoman's reputation as a painter and illustrator continued to grow though the sixties and seventies, and he exhibited widely in Britain and America. He painted a mural for the ceiling of the chapel in Lambeth Palace in 1988. He was awarded an OBE in 1981, and at the time of writing still lives in London.

> *Crooked Lane* (August 1946, PL44)
> *The Ghost of Gordon Gregory* (November 1946, PL60)

Eric Saunders
> *Full Fathom Five* (November 1946, PL55)
> *Arctic Adventures* (April 1947, PL88)
> *Cook the Explorer* (September 1947, PL112, with **John Worsley**)

LAURENCE SCARFE   Artist, graphic designer, mural painter and writer, Laurence Scarfe was born in Idle (a suburb of Bradford) in 1914. He studied art at Shipley Art School and at the Royal College of Art, where he specialised in mural painting. In 1943, Scarfe started to contribute illustrations to Leonard Russell's annual compilation *The Saturday Book*, then in its third year, and he became its art editor. After the war he and a group of other artists, including Paul Hogarth and Ronald Searle, were invited by eastern European communist governments to record and promote their post-war reconstruction efforts. At this time Scarfe was teaching at the Central School of Arts and Crafts and, from 1971, at Brighton Polytechnic. Much of his best-known work during the post-war period was mural art for public spaces, ocean liners and the Festival of Britain. He also wrote a few text books for students on topics such as typography and children's book illustration. He died in London in 1993.

> *The Parade on the Cliff* (April 1945, PL23)
> *Old Dave's Hut* (December 1945, PL30)
> *China Coast Pirates* (December 1946, PL95)

W. SCHLOSSER   Probably to be identified with a German artist Wolfgang Schlosser who was resident in London by 1939.

> *Fairy Tales* (first edition, 1943, PL1)
> *Robinson Crusoe* (1943, PL5)

MENENA J[OY] SCHWABE   Menena Schwabe was born in 1911 in York. She seems to have done little book illustration apart from *The Sampler Story*, and two books by Geoffrey Handley-Taylor. She died in 1994 in Kings Lynn, Norfolk.

> *The Sampler Story* (March 1945, PL21)

WILLIAM STOBBS: see Author biographies.

BERNARD [PERCIVAL] VENABLES   Writer, artist, piscatorial devotee and conservationist, Bernard Venables was born in 1907 in Catford and grew up in Essex near Romney Marsh, where he learnt to fish in local ponds with an stick and a bent pin - angling exploits which were to set the pattern for his life. After his family moved to South London, Bernard left school at 15 and soon afterwards enrolled at Croydon School of Art to study painting and drawing. Before the war he was employed in commercial studios, and later did freelance poster design for a variety of transport companies. During the war he worked for the Ministry of Information as an illustrator of propagandist literature, at which time he published his first book: *Tanks: Their Place in Modern Warfare* (Country Life, [1942]). After a short period working for the *Daily Express* as cartoonist and journalist, he joined the *Daily Mirror* in 1946. This was when Venables became famous for publishing one of the most successful ever sporting books: *Mr Crabtree Goes Fishing* (Daily Mirror, [1949]), which sold over two million copies, and was frequently reprinted thereafter, most recently in 2000. This was derived from his daily strip cartoon in the *Daily Mirror* where pipe-smoking Mr Crabtree (wearing a tie in all weathers) takes his young son Peter (wearing collar, tie and shorts in all weathers) on angling expeditions and instructs him in the techniques of coarse fishing. (Those who understand these things should note that Venables was a strong advocate of the use of chin-gaffing for pike.) Since he had written the strips when an employee of the Mirror, Venables made not a penny in royalties from this book until it was reprinted in 2000, a year before he died.

Venables became a freelance writer in 1953 and published many books on angling, as well as founding the magazines *Angling Times* and *Creel*. As he grew older, he became more adventurous, and his exploits included landing a 1700 lb shark off the coast of Madeira , fishing expeditions to Africa and the Azores, and a trek to the source of the Zambesi. Much of the travel was undertaken while investigating possibilities for 'fishing tourism' on behalf of the BEA and BOAC airlines. Venables wrote and broadcast about his activities until he was well into his eighties, and was awarded an MBE in 1995. He continued to work seven days a week at his Wiltshire home until he was into his nineties. He died in 2001, aged 94.

> *The Hunting of Zakaroff* (September 1946, PL49)
> *The Phantom* (November 1946, PL61)

KEITH WARD   Keith Ward was a prolific American artist, cartoonist and illustrator who was born in 1906 in Iola, Kansas, but spent most of his working life in California. He studied at art schools in San Francisco, New York and Chicago during the 1920s and 1930s. Although he worked in a remarkable range of styles and media, he became best known for his humorous drawings of animals in a slightly Disney-like style. He is particularly fondly remembered (in America) for creating a family of bovines used in advertising the Borden Company's products. They were headed by Elsie the Cow who was the mascot for their range of dairy products, and her husband Elmer the Bull who promoted 'Elmer's Glue'. He illustrated two of **Walter Farley**'s 'Black Stallion' series: *The Black Stallion* and *The Island Stallion*, and a number of other children's books. Later in life, he turned more to easel painting, particularly portraits and landscapes. He died in 2000.

> *The Black Stallion* (November 1946, PL71)

CLIFFORD [CYRIL] WEBB   Clifford Webb was one of the masters of the arts of wood engraving and lithography, and a founder member of the Society of Wood Engravers. He specialised in animal engravings, and illustrated many children's books written by others, as well as a number published by Warne which he wrote himself. He was born in 1894 into an artisan family in Limehouse, in the docklands of London. His artistic training began as an apprentice to a lithographic designer, before this was interrupted by the outbreak of war in 1914 and his enrolment in the Grenadier Guards. He saw service in France and the Middle East before being badly injured by Turkish machine-gun fire – a wound which allowed him only limited mobility in his right arm for the rest of his life (and he was, unfortunately, right-handed). While recuperating in India he took up oil painting, and after demobilisation he studied at the Westminster School of Art, and went on to teach at Birmingham School of Art. Here he met his future wife Ella Monkton, some of whose children's books he was later to illustrate. Around 1930, he was invited to illustrate the first two of Arthur Ransome's 'Swallows and Amazons' series – *Swallows and Amazons* and *Swallowdale*, and both were published by Jonathan Cape in 1931 (the earlier first edition of *Swallows and Amazons* had been unillustrated). Webb apparently modelled two of the children on his own son and daughter. Although Ransome admired Webb's work, he subsequently re-illustrated both books himself, because he felt that they should look as if they had been drawn by the children who appeared in the stories. Between 1937 and 1954, Webb executed some of his finest wood-engraving commissions for a series of private press editions published by the Golden Cockerel Press. Priced at 10/6d, *The Enchanted Glen* was one of Peter Lunn's most expensive titles. It was originally to have had wood engravings by Clare Leighton, and to have been priced at 8/6d, suggesting that by the 1940s Clifford Webb's services could not be bought cheaply. Webb also illustrated Ralph Wightman's *Moss Green Days*, published by Westhouse in 1947, and his book *Days* *on the Farm* which was to have been published by Peter Lunn, but eventually emerged in an edition published by Hutchinson in 1952. Webb died in 1972.

The Enchanted Glen (February 1947, PL69)

ERNEST WIGGLESWORTH

Bright is the Starlight (February 1947, PL78)

WILLIAM [ALBERT] WOOD

Woodheap Cats (November 1947, PL106)
Animal Anecdotes (unpublished)

JOHN [GODFREY BERNARD] WORSLEY
Versatile artist and illustrator of the enduringly popular 'P.C.49' comic strip, John Worsley was born in Liverpool in 1919, the son of a naval officer. When John was only six months old his father was demobbed, and the family upped sticks to Kenya to take over the running of the family coffee plantation. The price of coffee collapsed in 1928, and the Worsleys were forced to return to England where John was installed at boarding school. He won a scholarship to Brighton College in 1932 and went on to graduate in fine art at Goldsmith's College in London. As a lieutenant in the Royal Navy during the war, he was appointed as one of the youngest official war artists – the only one to be on active service in he Navy, giving him a unique opportunity to record the lives of wartime sailors. Unfortunately, he was also the only war artist to become a prisoner-of-war. While at a POW camp near Bremen he became friends with the journalist Guy Morgan and some of their exploits are recounted in Morgan's autobiographical account *Only Ghosts Can Live* (Crosby, Lockwood and Son, 1945). A particular escapade which later became immortalised in the 1953 film *Albert R.N.* (released in America as *Break to Freedom*) involved the substitution of an escaped prisoner during roll-call by a dummy with a papier-mâché head modelled by Worsley. When Worsley returned to England after the war, he set up a studio in West London, and took commissions such as the Peter Lunn book illustrations and some portraiture work for the Admiralty. He first really came to the attention of the public in the 1950s when he illustrated comic strips for the *Eagle* and *Girl* comics. Most famously, he took over from Strom Gould the illustration of Alan Stranks' creation Archie Berkeley-Willoughby (better known as 'P.C. 49'), and he estimated that when the series finally came to an end in 1957 he had portrayed P.C.49 some 3000 times. In later years Worsley did much freelance work in different styles and media, including many books from the 'Colour Classics' series published by Purnell during the 1970s and 80s. He died in London in 2000.

Detectives in Greasepaint (second edition, May 1946, PL40)
Studio J Investigates (second edition, August 1946, PL46)
Cook the Explorer (September 1947, PL112, with **Eric Saunders**)
The Fighting Lieutenant (unpublished)

4

UNFULFILLED BOOKS

When Peter Lunn went into receivership in October 1948, there were naturally books which the company had commitments to publish, but which could not be completed. We know some of the details of these books both from advance advertising and, more fruitfully, from claims made to the Receiver for work already done by authors, illustrators, printers and the like. The list of 'unfulfilled books' which follows gathers together all those I am aware of, although there were no doubt others. None of the items in this list were simply ideas in someone's mind – all had moved some way along the road to production. It seems appropriate to include them in a bibliography of this type in order to give the fullest possible picture of the publisher's intentions, and for that reason I have also cross-referred to them in the biographical entries. If Peter Lunn had continued in business for even a few more months, most of these books would have appeared on the shelves. A few of them were in fact taken to completion by other publishers, though often without the illustrations originally planned for them. As far as I can establish, however, the majority never saw the light of day. *Arbuthnot the Goldfish* stands out from the others in that it was advertised as early as 1945, and was probably abandoned for some reason unconnected with the bankruptcy.

Each entry in the list contains whatever information I have been able to glean about the book, including what elements of the publishing process I know to have been completed. Sometimes there are references to what is probably the same book under different titles, since the final title of a book was often not settled until quite late in the process. Where some uncertainty exists I have indicated this in the entries. I have not included books such as John Keir Cross's *The Man in Moonlight*, which was originally advertised as a forthcoming publication of Peter Lunn, but in the event appeared under the Westhouse imprint, since such books does not really classify as 'unfulfilled'. The list is ordered alphabetically by title.

The Aeneid and Illiad   Illustrations supplied by Ann Buckmaster. Presumably intended as a companion volume to *Homer's Odyssey*.

Animal Anecdotes (?same as **Animal Characters from Dickens**)   Illustrations supplied by William Wood.

Arbuthnot the Goldfish   Advertised as by Stephen Macfarlane (i.e. John Keir Cross) and illustrated by Acanthus (i.e. Frank Hoar). It was advertised in the July 1945 issue of *Publishers' Circular* as a 24-page picture book priced at 6/-, with the following blurb: 'It is the diary of a goldfish who belongs to the Nibworthy family'.

Children Next Door   Written and illustrated by Helen Binyon. Printed. It was a picture-book for young children with very simple text, and was later published by Aladdin Books, New York, in 1949.

Countryside and Seashore   Preface written by 'Craven Hill' (i.e. the journalist Charles Parsons). Proof-read (70,000 words). Referred to as a 'nature book written by Rev. Wood'. One claim was against Westhouse, so it may have been intended for publication by them.

Cousin from France   Written by Nancy Salkeld (i.e. Nancy Conran).

Days on the Farm   Preface written by Francis Dillon. Author was Ralph Wightman. The book was later published by Hutchinson in 1952, illustrated by Clifford Webb.

English Story Tellers (?same as **Storyteller's Story**)   Proof-read (60,000 words).

Fables of Aesop and Others   Proof-read (35,000 words). There was advance advertising on the dustjacket of *My Island Zoo*. The book was to be priced at 8/6d, and accompanied by Thomas Bewick illustrations.

The Fantastic History of the Celebrated Pierrot   By Alfred Assollant, translated by A.G. Munro. Printed. Illustrations supplied by William Stobbs. Advertised in the July 1947 issue of *Publishers' Circular* at 8/6d with the following blurb: 'A thrilling story based on an old Chinese legend'.

The Fighting Lieutenant   Illustrations supplied by John Worsley, who claimed against Westhouse, but stated it to be a children's book.

First Bird Book (?same as **Every Child's Bird Book**)   Edited, proof-read (18,000 words). There is also a reference to 'Buick [sic] Bird Book', so the book was probably intended to have Thomas Bewick illustrations, and to be a companion volume to *First Animal Book*.

The Forgotten Valley   Written by Gerald Verner, illustrations supplied by 'Ionicus' (i.e. Joshua Armitage). Advance advertising on the dustjacket of *The Adventure at Marston Manor*, with the following blurb: 'The purchase of an old book containing an ancient map is the prelude to unforgettable adventures in a primitive valley in South America. The illustrations by Ionicus lend vivid colour to this fascinating tale.'.

Granton Guineas   Illustrations supplied by William Stobbs.

I Find the Past   Written by Sydney Moorhouse. This was a book about archaeology, and may possibly have been intended as a Westhouse publication. A cut-down version entitled 'Digging up the Past' was published by Westhouse in 1947 as an article in their magazine *Holiday Parade*.

In Africa's Service   Written by I. M. Holmes. Printed (print-run 6100). Illustrations supplied by William Stobbs. Published in 1949 by the Saturn Press, with an introduction by Elizabeth James, but without Stobbs' illustrations. James describes the book as a 'brisk biography'.

A Journey into Time   By John Sylvester. Illustrations supplied by William Stobbs. Advertised at 8/6d in the July 1947 issue of *Publishers' Circular*, with the following blurb: 'A story of time travel in which two children learn the secrets of A.D. 3000'.

Julian Strikes Lucky   By N. R. Syme. Illustrations for a book referred to as "Julian No 2 book" were supplied by William Stobbs, and I assume that this is a reference to the one advertised on the back of the dustjacket of *That Must be Julian* as 'Julian Strikes Lucky', although no illustrator is mentioned. This may be the same book as *Julian's River War* by N. R. Syme, published by Heinemann in 1949, but illustrated by John Harris.

The Magic Belt   Proof-read.

Men of Barbary   Illustrations supplied by William Stobbs. This may have been no more than a working title for *Sister to the Mermaid* by Nicholas Cavanagh.

The Mission of Captain Dann   Proof-read (56,000 words).

Mystery Mine   Illustrations supplied by William Stobbs.

The New Children's Omnibus   Illustrations supplied by H. M. Brock. This may have been a working title for *The Children's Omnibus*.

Pizarro of Peru (? same as **Mad Conquistador**)   By John H. Pernull. Illustrations supplied by William Stobbs. Advertised on the dustjacket of *Arctic Adventures*.

Pizarro's Empire   Illustrations supplied by William Stobbs. Apparently not the same book as *Pizarro of Peru*, since Stobbs claimed separately against Lunn for work done on both books.

Roman Holiday   Proof-read (55,000 words).

Roundabout House   Written by Gladys Hirst. Illustrations supplied by Margaret Bryan.

Silver Chief   Type-set.

Suez and Panama (?same as **Rivers of Man** and **Men with a Mission**)   Written by Charles Eden. Dustjackets printed (in two colours). Advertised as 'Suez and Panama' on the dustjacket of *Great Gold Rushes*. Advertised as 'Rivers of Man' on the dustjacket of *Arctic Adventures*. The printer's claim was against Westhouse, so publication by them may have been intended.

The Story of Harchem [?]   Illustrations supplied by H. M. Brock. The last word of the title is difficult to decipher.

Through the Looking Glass   Proof-read (25,000 words). Author presumably Lewis Carroll.

Winged Horses   Illustrations supplied by Philip Gough.

The World's Strange Islands (same as **Strange Islands**)   By Sydney Moorhouse, illustrated by Robin Jacques. Advertised in the July 1947 issue of *Publishers' Circular* at 8/6d, with the following blurb: 'Many fascinating legends and dramatic history of little-known islands in the Indian Ocean'.

A Zoo in your House   Compiled by Hugh Anderson. Dustjacket designed. Advertised. Published in 1951 by Yates, illustrated by Blair Hughes-Stanton.

MAIN SOURCES CONSULTED

Note: Many of the facts and short quotations which appear in Section 1, and which are not otherwise attributed in footnotes, are taken from one of the two sets of wind-up papers of Lunn and Westhouse in the National Archives. These are loose assemblages of legal papers which have no system of running page numbers, and are therefore very difficult to cross-reference from my text.

Archives

Wind-up papers of John Westhouse (Publishers) Ltd. Kew: The National Archives. (Piece No. J 13/18829).

Wind-up papers of Peter Lunn (Publishers) Ltd. Kew: The National Archives. (Piece No. J 13/18933).

General sources

The Author's and Writer's Who's Who. London: Burke's Peerage. (Editions 1-5, 1934-1963).

Books of the Month. London: Simpkin Marshall. (Volumes for 1943-1948).

Contemporary Authors® On-Line. Farmington Hills: Gale Research.

The English Catalogue of Books. New York: Kraus Reprint Company, 1979.

The Publishers' Circular. Beckenham: Office of The Publishers' Circular. (Volumes for 1943-1948).

Whitaker's Annual Cumulative Booklists. London: J. Whitaker & Sons. (Volumes for 1943-1948 – referred to as "Whitaker").

Who's Who in Art. London: Art Trade Press. (Various editions).

Specific references

Bryant, Mark. *Dictionary of Twentieth Century Cartoonists and Caricaturists.* Farnham: Ashgate, 2000.

Buckman, David. *Dictionary of Artists in Britain since 1945 (2 vols).* Bristol: Art Dictionaries, 2006.

Commire, Ann (ed). *Something About the Author.* Detroit: Gale Research, 1971.

Fuller, Muriel (ed). *More Junior Authors.* New York: H.W. Wilson, 1963.

Horne, Alan. *Dictionary of Twentieth Century British Book Illustrators.* Woodbridge: Antique Collectors' Club, nd [1994].

Kay, Ernest (ed). *Dictionary of International Biography.* 5th edition. Cambridge: International Biographical Centre, 1968.

Kunitz, Stanley J. and Haycraft, Howard (eds). *The Junior Book of Authors.* 2nd edition. New York: H.W. Wilson, 1951.

Smith, Alan. *Peter Lunn (a checklist of Peter Lunn titles).* Privately printed, nd. (referred to as "Smith").

Viguers, R.H. et al (eds). *Illustrators of Children's Books 1946-1956.* Boston: The Horn Book, 1958.

INDEX OF BOOK TITLES
AND PERSONAL NAMES

Titles of books published by Peter Lunn appear in bold italics, with other books in normal italics. Personal names are in standard font, with those authors and illustrators who have entries in Section 3 appearing in bold. The main entry for each Peter Lunn book, and the entry for individuals in Section 3 have page numbers in bold.

Colophon

Printed by Cromwell Press Group, Trowbridge on 130 gsm Baldwin Silk.

Book design, layout and typesetting by Omnis Partners, Cumbernauld.

Typefaces: Trinité 1 (Bram de Does) and Thesis (Lucas de Groot).